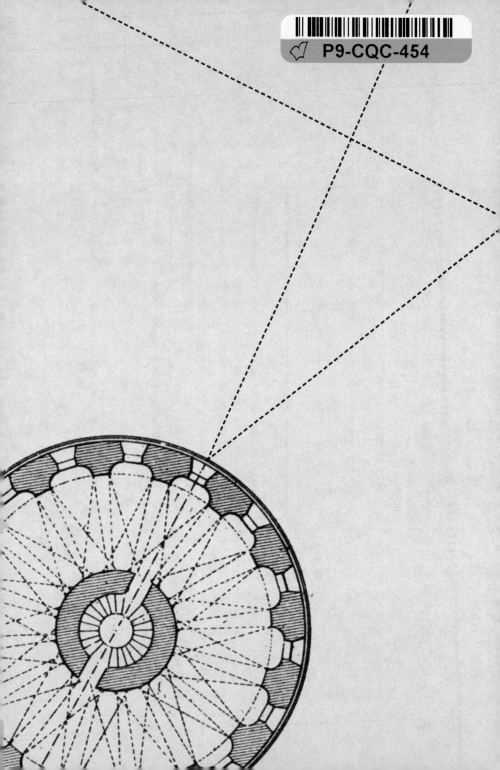

HOW IT HAPPENS

HOW IT HAPPENS
The **Extraordinary Processes** of **Everyday Things**

BARBARA ANN KIPFER, PhD

RANDOM HOUSE REFERENCE

New York
London
Tokyo
Sydney
Auckland

Please address inquiries about electronic licensing of any products for use on a network, in software or on CD-ROM to the Subsidiary Rights Department, Random House Information Group, fax 212-572-6003.

This book is available for special discounts for bulk purchases for sales promotions or premiums. Special editions, including personalized covers, excerpts of existing books, and corporate imprints, can be created in large quantities for special needs. For more information, write to Random House, Inc., Special Markets/Premium Sales, 1745 Broadway, MD 6-2, New York, NY, 10019 or e-mail specialmarkets@randomhouse.com.

Visit the Random House Reference Web site: www.randomwords.com

Printed in the United States of America

Book design by Nora Rosansky

All interior illustrations © Alan Witschonke, excluding pp. 5, 9 © Nora Rosansky, and pp. 92, 153, 162, 191, 208 © BURMAR Technical Corporation

Library of Congress Cataloging-in-Publication Data
  Kipfer, Barbara Ann
    How it happens: the extraordinary processes of everyday things / Barbara Ann Kipfer.—1st ed.
      p.   cm.
    ISBN 0-375-72082-0 (pbk.: alk. paper)
    1. Science—Popular works. I. Title.
  Q162.K53 2005
  500-dc22   2005040453

First Edition
10 9 8 7 6 5 4 3 2

DEDICATION AND THANKS

How It Happens is a collection of cycles, sequences, and processes that I collected in what I saw as a natural follow-up to my Random House book *The Order of Things: How Everything in the World is Organized into Hierarchies, Structures, and Pecking Orders.* I would like to thank my editor, Jena Pincott, for all of her help with bringing this book to publication. I would also like to thank my programmer, Mark Dinan, for his great work in helping me organize and keep track of such a compilation. I had great fun writing this book and that is due to the support of my husband, Paul Magoulas, and the two kids whom I have had the privilege of watching through their growth cycles, Kyle Kipfer and Keir Magoulas.

INTRODUCTION

The world has always been subject to cycles, sequences, and processes—night and day, rising and setting of the sun, phases of the Moon, the cycle of seasons. Poet Alexander Pope said, "Order is heav'n's first law." Much of what is called "intelligence" is our ability to recognize this order in the form of patterns. We recognize cycles (the phases of the Moon), sequences (what happens in a timepiece to make the hands move forward), and processes (how a grape becomes a raisin). The more patterns we know, the better we understand our world.

How It Happens helps people understand the remarkable inner workings of everyday phenomena from grasshoppers hopping to yoga's sun salutation to air circulation in planes to frowning to echoes. This book simultaneously satisfies and inspires our sense of wonder in how the world works. Alfred North Whitehead said, "The process itself is the actuality." *How It Happens* describes more than 500 of these.

This book presents how things happen in our daily life. These are orders in which things are done or occur—actions very interesting to us but whose inner workings are often not evident or are not brought to our attention. The book features lists of "steps" for everyday things that evolve and develop and grow. Each entry emphasizes action and an end result. Interesting processes fill in gaps in our knowledge and make us appreciate the fine workings of nature, technology, business, art, music, science, and the social sciences. Some entries will answer reference needs—questions you've always had. Others that are more whimsical will fall into the trivia category, satisfying our insatiable desire to know neat stuff. I hope you enjoy learning more about *How It Happens*.

Barbara Ann Kipfer

ACNE

There are about 50 different kinds of acne and the condition is generally divided into four grades, depending on severity. Formation does not take long, but curing acne can take months or longer.

1. Sebaceous (oil-secreting) glands of the skin produce excessive secretions of sebum.
2. The sebum oxidizes and forms a blackened plug in the skin pore.
3. Trapped sebum, dead cells, and infection by bacteria inflame the area and can cause a pustule to form.

ACUPUNCTURE

1. Acupuncture points are areas on the body that are designated for their sensitivity.
2. Inserting very fine needles at these points stimulates various sensory receptors.
3. The sensory receptors then stimulate nerves that transmit impulses to the hypothalamic-pituitary system at the base of the brain, which is responsible for releasing neurotransmitters and endorphins throughout the body.
4. Endorphins act as the body's natural pain-killers. Some of the effects of acupuncture on the body include increased circulation, decreased inflammation, and pain relief.

ADOPTION

An adoption usually involves the following steps.

1. A child is placed in the adoptive home.

2. The biological parents formally surrender their rights, but there is a period of time when they can still change their minds.

3. The biological parents make a final surrender of their rights.

4. A waiting period of some months must pass. During this time, the social worker visits the adoptive parents and the child to see how they are doing together.

5. Prior to finalizing the adoption, the adoptive parents must submit several important papers to the court—such as the petition for adoption, adoption agreements, and the financial arrangements for the adoption. One document seals the papers identifying the child's biological parents.

6. A new birth certificate is issued for the child in his or her adoptive parents' names.

7. A private court hearing is held, often in the judge's chambers, and the old birth records are sealed. The adoption is completed.

AEROSOL SPRAY

The contents of an aerosol can include the product itself (hairspray, air freshener, oven cleaner, etc.) and the propellant that carries it. A propellant is something that provides thrust, in this case, something that helps discharge the contents of an aerosol container. The consistency of the aerosol product—mist or foam—depends on the chemical makeup of the product and propellant, the ratio of product to propellant, the pressure of the propellant, and the size and shape of the valve system.

1. The contents are contained under pressure and the outer valve is kept closed both by this internal pressure and a spring.

2. The propellant boils well below room temperature. A layer of gaseous propellant forms over the liquid product as it boils. The gas pressure increases and eventually gets so high that the boiling stops.

3. As the button or nozzle is pushed, the valve opens and the pressure on the liquid propellant is instantly reduced. With less

pressure, it boils. As it boils, particles break free, forming a gas layer at the top of the can. This gas pressure forces the liquid product up the tube and out of the nozzle.

4. The outflow channel is very narrow and causes the product to break up into a fine mistlike spray or become a foam. The liquid propellant may also come out, but it immediately evaporates.

5. The spring re-seals the can when the nozzle is released.

AGES OF MAN

As explained by Shakespeare in
As You Like It.

1. Infant
2. Schoolboy
3. Lover
4. Soldier
5. Justice / Adult
6. Pantaloon / Old Age
7. Second Childhood / Senility

AIR RECIRCULATION IN AIRPLANE

1. Fresh air is fed into the system from the compressors in the engine.

2. The air is mixed with recirculated air, filtered, and sent through the cabin in overhead distribution outlets.

3. The air vents and exhaust air intakes are positioned on every row along the length of the cabin so that air supplied at one seat row leaves at the same row. This decreases the chance that an infection will circulate around the entire aircraft.

4. Some of the cabin air is mixed with fresh air and returned to the cabin. All recirculated air passes through hospital-grade air filters.

5. As outside air enters the airplane, equal amounts are continuously exhausted.

6. Air is not recirculated from galleys or lavatories, keeping passengers safe from kitchen and bathroom odors and contaminants. Air is not recirculated through the cockpit, protecting the pilots.

ALCOHOL AFFECTING BODY

1. After a person swallows a drink containing alcohol, the alcohol is absorbed rapidly into the bloodstream.

2. The alcohol is slowly removed and burned up, changing entirely in the process to carbon dioxide and water, mostly by action of the liver.

3. The effects of alcohol on the body come from its effect on the brain and depend on the amount of alcohol that builds up in the bloodstream. In small amounts, alcohol acts as a stimulant. As with many other poisons, a small amount of alcohol has special effects and may cause some people to become more relaxed and talkative. In a greater amount, it becomes a depressant and may cause people to think and act more slowly, and possibly even lose self-control.

ALKALINE BATTERY

Alkaline cell batteries are some of the most commonly used worldwide in electronic devices such as radios and flash cameras, flashlights, tape recorders, and toys.

1. A cathode of a very pure manganese dioxide–graphite mixture and an anode of a powdered zinc alloy are associated with a potassium hydroxide electrolyte and housed in a steel can.

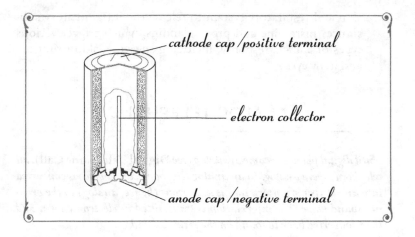

cathode cap/positive terminal

electron collector

anode cap/negative terminal

2. At the anode, zinc turns into zinc oxide.

3. This chemical reaction releases electrons that flow around an external circuit to the cathode.

4. At the cathode, they are collected by manganese dioxide.

5. Inside the cell, negatively-charged hydroxyl ions move from cathode to anode to complete the flow of charge.

6. Electric energy is derived from the chemical action.

ALLERGIES

1. Allergens (pollen, cat dander, dust mites, etc.) can provoke the immune system to produce an antibody called immunoglobulin E. Its molecules coat the surface of cells that are in the skin and the lining of the stomach, lungs, and upper airways.

2. For allergic individuals, exposure to allergens through inhalation or ingestion causes the allergens to bind (cross-link) to the immunoglobulin molecules.

3. Cross-linking causes granules located inside the cells of the

5

skin and respiratory system to release the inflammatory substances histamine and prostaglandins, which trigger various types of allergic response, including sneezing, skin irritation, and itchy eyes.

ANALOG TELEPHONE

Until digital phones became available (see Digital Telephone Call), *all telephones were analog. In an analog telephone call, a voice is converted into an electronic pattern that is analogous (hence, analog) to the original sound wave. The information is transmitted in electronic form and then converted back to sound on the receiving end.*

1. Speaking into a telephone sends sound waves into the microphone in the mouthpiece.
2. The microphone is covered by a membrane that vibrates with the sound waves.
3. As the membrane vibrates, it makes a magnet vibrate within an electrified wire coil. The motion within the coil creates a continuous but varying charge (voltage), which is sent across a copper wire.
4. On the receiving end, the fluctuating voltage moves a magnet, which is attached to the diaphragm in the phone's earpiece speaker.
5. The vibrating membrane in the speaker converts the electrical pattern back into sound waves.

ANESTHETIC

Anesthetics are either general, which put the patient to sleep, or local, which affect only one part of the body. Exactly how these compounds produce a pain-free, unconscious state remains mysterious. This is generally what happens.

1. The anesthetic is supplied in gas form or is injected.

2. The anesthetic may contain a neuroblocker or muscle relaxant or produce sedative effects by triggering the brain's sleep circuits. Generally, the anesthetic interrupts the sensory signals sent by nerve cells to the spinal cord en route to the brain. The nerve cells are trying to send the message of pain.

3. The pain messages are carried by small electrical currents through adjacent nerve cells; the currents are carried by ions. For these currents to flow, the nerve cells must take up sodium and/or potassium ions. Sodium and potassium atoms play an important part in sending these impulses to the brain.

4. The anesthetic blocks the channels that sodium and potassium ions use to send messages of pain to nerve cells.

5. A general anesthetic may cause unconsciousness by suppressing the activity of certain enzymes in the nerve cells—or by changing the properties of the nerve-cell membranes, or even by interacting with water molecules in the brain to form small crystals which affect the path of a signal along a nerve cell.

ANT COLONY

Ant colonies accomplish feats that no individual ant can accomplish. Nests are erected and maintained; chambers and tunnels are excavated; and territories are defended. Each individual ant processes the partial information available to it in order to decide which of the many possible functional roles it should play in the colony. The interactions between ants performing various tasks give rise to emergent phenomena in the ant colony.

1. Ants are often polymorphic, with small individuals working in the nest and medium or medium-large ones working outside; huge-headed individuals become protective soldiers or even use their heads as plugs to stop up the nest entrance to all except for members of the colony.

2. Workers gather food, primarily mosses or bark and roll food into balls. Workers carry food back to the nest. They follow

odor trails to get to the nest. Once an ant becomes a forager, it never switches to other tasks outside the nest.

3. Soldiers guard the workers.

4. Nest maintenance workers abound when debris is piled near their nest opening. When there is a disturbance, such as an intrusion by foreign ants, nest-maintenance workers switch tasks to become patrollers. Once an ant is allocated a task outside the nest, it never returns to chores on the inside.

5. The ants engage in task switching, by which the local decision of each individual ant determines much of the coordinated behavior of the entire colony.

6. Task allocation depends on two kinds of decisions made by individual ants. First, there is the decision about which task to perform, followed by the decision of whether to be active in this task. These decisions are based solely on local information; there is no centralized control keeping track of the big picture.

ANTIBIOTICS

Antibiotics, including penicillin and streptomycin, are chemical substances produced by microorganisms and fungi that are known to inhibit the growth of bacteria and other microorganisms. Bacteria that cause infections go through mass reproduction to cause the symptoms of an infection. Bacteria develop resistance to antibiotics, though, so scientists are constantly developing new ways to stop bacteria from multiplying.

1. The antibiotic interferes with the structure of the bacterial cell walls as the bacteria are being reproduced.

2. The bacterial cell contents leak out and the bacteria die.

Alternatively:

1. The antibiotic poisons the parts of the bacteria that make the proteins they need in order to reproduce.

2. The antibiotic interferes with the genetic codes in the bacteria that allow them to multiply.

ANTIBODY DEFENSE

The scientific study of the body's resistance to disease and the invasion of other organisms is called immunology.

1. A major component of the immune system are B lymphocyte cells known as B cells. They begin as stem cells in bone marrow and develop in the lymph nodes.

2. When a virus or foreign microorganism is introduced, B cells recognize the foreign proteins known as antigens, since they differ from body proteins.

3. Antigens trigger B cells to multiply. Some develop into plasma cells, which secrete antibodies—proteins that attack and destroy only the antigens.

4. Memory B cells are able to recognize an antigen from a previous infection, often preventing the same infection from happening twice, or reducing the severity of subsequent infections.

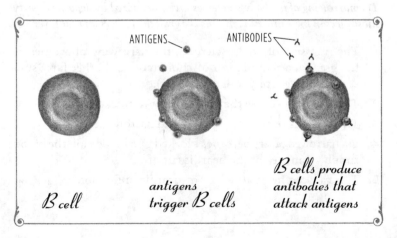

ANTIGENS   ANTIBODIES

B cell   *antigens trigger B cells*   *B cells produce antibodies that attack antigens*

ASPIRIN

1. Pain (such as a headache or muscle ache) results in a release into the bloodstream of prostaglandins, fatty acids involved in physiological functions such as contraction of muscle, inflammation, and body temperature. Some prostaglandins increase the sensitivity of pain receptors.

2. An aspirin pill is digested and goes into the bloodstream.

3. Aspirin inhibits the synthesis and creation of prostaglandins by inhibiting a protein known as cyclooxygenase 2, which creates prostaglandins. Tissue that has been damaged or inflamed in some way makes lots of cyclooxygenase 2. Aspirin sticks to the cyclooxygenase 2 and prevents it from creating prostaglandins or inhibits them so that the receptors connected to the source of the pain are disconnected.

4. Taking aspirin does not eliminate the cause of the pain but, by inhibiting the creation of prostaglandins, decreases the number of pain signals that reach the brain.

ATHEROSCLEROSIS

The narrowing of the body's arteries is characterized by deposits of fatty substances in their inner layer, plus the growth of fibers on that layer.

1. The first sign of atherosclerosis, the narrowing of arteries, is the gradual accumulation of cholesterol and other fatty substances in the artery wall (atheroma).

2. These deposits cause the muscle layer to thicken.

3. The deposits restrict blood flow and narrow the artery.

4. If a narrowed artery becomes blocked by a blood clot, the blood supply to an area of the heart is cut off.

5. This causes a heart attack or myocardial infarction.

ATM

1. When a bank card is inserted into an ATM, the machine reads the data-rich magnetic strip.
2. A PIN (personal identification number), when entered, matches the cardholder to the account.
3. The cardholder enters how much cash he or she needs.
4. The bank's central computer checks to make sure the account has sufficient money and deducts the sum requested.
5. The central computer sends output bits to the local machine which controls a mechanism that selects the correct number of dollar bills from strongboxes or cassettes inside the machine.
6. The mechanism uses an infrared sensing device to determine that the proper denomination has been picked up. If a mistake is detected, the money is diverted to a reject box.
7. The sequence is repeated until the correct number of bills ready at the holding area.
8. The mechanism then delivers the dollar bills to the slot.
9. Motorized rollers feed the dollar bills partially through the slot.
10. The output bits also activate rollers that return your bank card and print out and deliver a transaction slip.
11. The ATM sends a completion message to the bank, and the central computer updates your account.

ATOLL

An atoll is a ring of coral islands formed around a central lagoon.

1. A fringing reef forms as coral grows in the shallow waters along the shoreline of a volcanic island.
2. As the volcano subsides, the island slowly sinks but the coral continues to grow.
3. A lagoon forms and the reef becomes a barrier reef.

4. The volcanic island is submerged, but the reef remains, with the high points topped by small sandy islands.

AUTOFOCUS CAMERA

Most autofocus cameras have a tiny electric motor driving a transmitter that emits a beam of infrared light.

1. The transmitter is linked to the lens, which moves in or out as the beam scans, focusing near to far.

2. The beam reflects back from objects to the camera and a sensor monitors its signals and stops the transmitter when the strongest signal shows that the lens is in focus.

3. This automatically triggers the shutter.

Some cameras have ultrasonic focusing similar to bats' echolocation scanning. A transducer disc sends out high-frequency "chirps."

1. The disc receives the chirps' echoes from the subject and a built-in microcomputer measures the time it takes for a chirp to go out and come back—using this to calculate the distance to the subject.

2. Single-lens reflex (SLR) cameras with autofocus use an electronic phase detection system.

3. Light entering the lens is separated into two images.

4. A sensor measures the distance between the two images, which are a specific distance apart when the lens is in focus.

5. If the distance is incorrect, the sensor causes a motor to move the lens.

AUTOMATIC DOOR

1. When a person approaches an automatic door, a detector sends out a beam of microwaves that strikes him.

2. As the person moves toward the door, the distance between the person and the detector decreases and the frequency of the beam increases because it bounces off the person and returns to the detector.

3. The detector registers the beam's increased frequency and triggers a mechanism to open the door.

4. An invisible safety beam and detector in the doorway pick up one's presence in the doorway and prevent the door from closing until they have safely passed through it.

AUTOMATIC FLIGHT CONTROL

1. Within an aircraft, internal sensors such as gyroscopes and accelerometers collect information on altitude and motion.

2. External commands are issued by the pilot and from navigation systems such as Inertial Guidance and Global Positioning Systems.

3. Feedback signals from position sensors on control surfaces assist the autopilot computers to maintain a smooth output.

4. The autopilot consists of separate roll, pitch, and yaw computers that process data from internal sensors, external commands from the pilot and navigation systems, and feedback signals from control surfaces. These computers produce appropriate output.

5. The autothrust works together with the autopilot. If the autopilot controls altitude by adjusting pitch using the elevators, the autothrust maintains airspeed by adjusting engine thrust.

6. Engine thrust is controlled by the autothrust.

7. An actuator moves control surfaces in response to autopilot commands.

8. Position sensors on control surfaces detect deflection on the control surface.

AUTOMATIC TRANSMISSION PROCESS

1. The accelerator pedal moves a piston, increasing oil pressure in the valve. The automatic transmission can sense the position of the accelerator pedal and responds to the speed of the car.

2. As the pedal is pressed, the throttle valve pressure exceeds the pressure of the governor, a control that maintains a steady speed inside a machine.

3. The shift valve moves back and the low-gear piston engages low gear while the high-gear piston disengages high gear.

4. One end of each shift valve receives oil from the governor and the other end from the throttle valve.

5. When the governor pressure is greater, the shift valve sends oil from the oil pump to the high-gear piston.

6. Oil flows away from the low-gear piston to return to the pump.

7. The oil pump circulates oil through the transmission and engine.

8. The two pistons operate the clutches or brake bands that change gears.

9. Oil at pump pressure from the shift valve moves one of the pistons out to engage a new gear.

10. A spring returns the other piston, sending oil back to the pump at low pressure and disengaging its gear.

11. The pressure at which the oil passes to the shift depends on the speed of the car.

12. The drive shaft that turns the wheels also turns the governor. As the car accelerates, the governor rotates faster.

13. Centrifugal force moves the valves outward, sending oil from the pump to the shift valve.

torque converter,
including flywheel
connected to engine

clutches

governor

output

drive shaft

pistons and brake bands

shift lever and gearbox

AUTOMOBILE PRODUCTION

1. Robot cranes supply rolled sheets of steel to giant stamping machines.
2. The metal is cut to make up the parts of the body.
3. Robot welders join the appropriate sheets to make the body.
4. Robots build the underbody or floorpan.
5. The body sides and roof are welded into place automatically.
6. Doors have been made on another assembly line.
7. Lasers check the car body for distortions or irregularities.
8. The car is cleaned in a degreasing tank, rinsed, and coated with phosphate to make it more receptive to the paint.
9. After several rinses, the base primer coat is applied in several layers.
10. Robot sprayers add final layers of paint.
11. Special wax is then injected into the hollow sections.
12. The mechanics and chassis are assembled (engine, transmission, driveshaft, suspension, brakes) separately.
13. An autocarrier delivers the mechanics and chassis by following a guide wire.
14. The treated body is on a conveyor.
15. The body and chassis are put together.
16. The fuel tank is mounted and the suspension, steering, radiator, and battery added.
17. The electrical wiring is added by humans.
18. Interior features (carpets, seats, fittings) are added by robots.
19. The doors and windows are added.
20. The wheels and tires are put on.
21. The postassembly check takes place.
22. Water, antifreeze, oil, and gasoline are added.
23. The car undergoes a final test and inspection.

AUTOMOBILE IGNITION

In an electronic ignition, the contact breaker is replaced by an electronic switch. Most now use a magnetic device, called a reluctor, that is operated by the distributor shaft to produce timed electric signals, which are amplified and used to control the current to the induction coil.

1. The key is placed in the ignition switch.

2. The key is turned.

3. The key activates the solenoid (a coil of wire that will become a magnet when current passes through it) and then passes current to the induction coil (produces high voltage from a low-voltage source).

4. In the solenoid, the current from the ignition switch flows through a coil and produces a magnetic field.

5. This moves the iron plunger to close the contacts and pass a higher current to the starter motor.

6. A spring returns the plunger as soon as the key is released, breaking the circuit.

7. A very large current flows through the starter motor to produce the force needed to start the flywheel turning. A flywheel is a regulator that stores kinetic energy and smoothes the operation of the engine. (See page 15.)

8. One terminal of the battery is connected to the car body and it serves as the return path for the circuits in the automobile's electrical systems.

9. The contact breaker in the distributor opens and interrupts the supply of low-voltage current to the induction coil.

10. The ignition (induction) coil is really two coils intertwined, with the leads to one going to the spark plug (a device that ignites the gas via an electric spark), and the leads to the other going to the points (contacts through which current flows to the spark plugs). The points close, and a magnetic field builds up. They must stay closed long enough to energize the field.

11. The points open and the magnetic field around the primary

winding collapses, inducing a high voltage in the secondary winding.

12. The distributor routes the successive bursts of high-voltage current to each spark plug in the firing order.

13. The electric spark ignites the fuel-air mixture; the burning of this mixture in the cylinders produces the motive force.

BAKING SODA

Most unwanted odors are either strong acids or strong bases/alkalines. Baking soda is made from soda ash, also known as sodium carbonate, and neutralizes odors chemically. It has a pH of about 8.1, which is slightly basic. The chemical odor removal by baking soda is often called "sweetening" because it is a natural process. The baking soda naturally absorbs the odors and acts to bring acidic and basic odor molecules to a more neutral, odor-free state. It does this chemically.

1. Odors are released into the air.

2. Baking soda, which is slightly basic with a pH of about 8.1, reacts with odors that are either strong acids or strong bases / alkalines. Sour milk, for example, is acidic, while spoiled fish is alkaline.

3. The baking soda neutralizes the odors by using the moisture in the air to start acid-base neutralization.

4. The longer air is in contact with baking soda, the more neutralization takes place. It takes a while for the baking soda to absorb and neutralize the odor molecules.

5. Additionally, baking soda works best in a confined space, such as a refrigerator, the trunk of a car, or a closet. It also is most effective in a somewhat humid atmosphere. Baking soda works for about two months in the refrigerator.

BALDING

The following describes balding in men.

1. Testosterone comes into contact with an enzyme found in the hair follicles.

2. The testosterone is converted to dihydrotestosterone (DHT), a more potent androgen that has the ability to bind to receptors in follicles.

3. This binding, in turn, can trigger a change in the genetic activity of the cells, which initiates the gradual process of hair loss.

4. Some people inherit a tendency for certain hair follicles, in the presence of DHT, to become progressively smaller over time. This causes the growing cycle of the hair follicle to shorten, more hairs to be shed, and the existing hair to become thinner and thinner.

5. Some follicles eventually die, while others shrink to a very small size incapable of sustaining healthy hair.

BALLET POSITIONS

Most ballet moves are based on five classic steps. (See page 20.)

first position

second position

third position

fourth position

fifth position

BAR CODE READER

Barcodes, which serve as identification tags, are found on everything from cereal boxes to library books. They help keep track of an item and quickly retrieve information about it.

1. A bar code is drawn over a scanner/reader. A special code (quiet zone and guard pattern) at both ends of the bar code enables the reader to recognize the beginning and end of the code.

2. The bar code reader has a spinning holographic disk that focuses a laser beam at different points to draw a 3-D grid in the space above it.

3. When the beam is reflected from a bar code, the reader detects a pattern of reflection from the dark and light areas.

4. Dark areas absorb laser light; light areas reflect it.

5. Some light travels back to re-enter the reader. A semisilvered mirror reflects laser light up through the disk but allows returning light to pass straight through it.

6. A photoelectric cell decodes the varying levels of laser light and translates it into a varying electrical signal.

7. The signal is translated into binary (digital) code by the scanner/reader's microprocessor.

8. The microprocessor looks up the binary code in a database to identify the product and the data associated with it.

BASEBALL BAT

1. A Northern white ash tree, at least 60 years old, is cut down.

2. Trees less than 12 inches in diameter are split (cut into long pieces).

3. From the center of the split, a "square" is ripsawed.

4. On a lathe, the square is honed into a round cylinder.

5. On another lathe, the bat is roughly shaped and extra pieces are left on its ends to hold it in place on the lathe.

21

6. The bat is sanded smooth.
7. The bat may then be dipped in lacquer.
8. The bat is branded with the company logo.

BASEBALL BATTING

1. The batter swings.
2. The shoulder turn begins and the batter's eyes are on the ball.
3. The batter may take a short or long step with the front foot.
4. The batter either connects with the ball or misses.
5. When the batter hits a ball just right, he/she has hit it on one of the two or three "sweet spots" of the bat. The sweet spots are the locations on a bat where the force of hitting is completely balanced out by the turning force of the bat. Whenever an object is struck, the sweet spots vibrate in response.
6. These vibrations travel in waves up and down the length of the bat.
7. At the sweet spots, the waves always cancel each other out. If the batter hits the ball on one of the bat's sweet spots, the vibrations from the impact will cancel out, and he or she won't feel any stinging or shaking in their hands.
8. Since little of the bat's energy is lost to vibrations when one of these spots is hit, more can go to the ball.
9. The wrists turn over as the swing continues.
10. The bat is behind the batter at the completion of the follow-through.

BASEBALL CURVE

The curve of a thrown baseball is a demonstration of fluid dynamics.

1. When a pitcher throws a 70 mph curve ball, the ball rotates about 17 times in its 60-foot journey to home plate.

2. As it revolves, its 216 raised stitches drag a thin layer of air around the ball.

3. If the ball spins counterclockwise, the side toward third base travels against the main flow of air, while the side toward first base moves with it. Therefore, the speed of the air relative to the ball surface is different on each side.

4. The air pressure is lower on the first-base side and higher on the third-base side of the ball.

5. Therefore, the ball curves toward first base.

6. Over the course of a pitch, the deflection from a straight line increases with distance from the pitcher. Curve balls do most of their curving in the last quarter of their trip. Considering that it takes less time for the ball to travel those last 15 feet (about 1/6 of a second) than it takes for the batter to swing the bat (about 1/5 of a second), hitters must begin their swings before the ball has started to show much curve. A major league curve ball can veer as much as $17\frac{1}{2}$ inches from a straight line by the time it crosses the plate.

7. The faster the rate of spin, the more the ball's path curves.

BEAVER DAM

1. Beavers select a place in a wooded valley with a small stream.

2. Within minutes, the beavers use their massive, razor-sharp incisor teeth to gnaw through saplings and tree trunks more than 20 inches thick.

3. Saplings felled upstream are floated and sown along specially dug-out channels.

4. The beavers ram a few sticks upright into the stream's bed and drag lengths of felled timber and leafy sticks across these supports.

5. Using rocks, they weigh down the vegetation and bind it with mud from the riverbank.

6. Shaped with a steep upstream side and a more gently sloping

downstream side, the dam is able to withstand the pressure of water in the newly formed lake.

7. The beavers then construct the lodge—a huge, domed edifice of mud, reeds, sticks, and stone about 6 feet high and 40 feet across.

8. Inside, they hollow out the living chamber with a sleeping platform above the water level.

9. To protect themselves from predators, all the entrances are underwater and the only way in is to swim.

10. If the lake threatens to overflow, the beavers drain off water by widening the spillways at each end of the dam.

11. If the lake level drops so low that there is a risk that the lodge entrance will be exposed, they narrow the spillways at each end of the dam.

BEHAVIORAL DEVELOPMENT

These are the stages of behavioral development relied upon by behavioral psychologists.

1. A need arises.

2. Tension results.

3. Activity ensues to resolve tension.

4. Satisfactory resolution is made.

5. A habit is formed.

6. Habit becomes drive.

BICYCLE BRAKE

1. The brake levers are squeezed by the bicyclist's hands.

2. Each hand lever magnifies the grip force several times.

3. The levers pull a cable that connects to a caliper, a part of the

disc-brake assembly that straddles the disc and presses the brake pads against it.

4. The caliper forces brake shoes against the wheel rim, producing sufficient friction to stop or slow the spin of the tires.

5. Release of the levers relaxes the cable.

6. The return spring then moves the brake shoes away from the wheel rim.

BICYCLE GEARS

1. A bicycle with multiple gears has different-sized chainwheels (gears), to which the cranks and pedals are attached, and different-sized sprockets (gears) on the rear wheel. The rear wheel is the freewheel, which has 5–9 gears on it.

2. A freewheel spins freely in one direction and locks in the other. It allows the bicycle to coast when the bicyclist is not pedaling.

3. A chain connects the toothed gears on the chainwheel to the rear wheel hub.

4. Hinged levers at the front and rear of the bicycle, called derailleurs, shift the chain from one sprocket wheel to another.

5. The rear derailleur has two small cogs that both spin freely. The arm and lower cog of the derailleur provide tension to the chain. The cog and arm are connected to a spring so that the cog pulls backwards all the time. The top cog is close to the freewheel.

6. When you adjust the gears with the handle levers, the top cog moves to a different position on the freewheel and drags the chain with it.

7. The chain slips from one gear to the next as the pedals turn.

8. In low gear, the chain connects a small chainwheel to a large rear sprocket. You need less force and the wheel turns slower—helpful when you are riding uphill.

10. In high gear, the chain connects a large chainwheel to a small rear sprocket. You need more force on the pedals, but the rear wheel turns faster.

BIG MAC

Big Macs are assembled in the following order:

1. Bottom bun
2. Special sauce
3. Lettuce
4. Cheese
5. Meat
6. Onions
7. Middle bun
8. Special sauce
9. Lettuce
10. Pickles
11. Meat
12. Onions
13. Top bun

BIOGEOCHEMICAL CYCLE

This is the basic circular path followed by a non-renewable resource (a type of material that can be used only once, like oil and other fossil fuels, and cannot be replaced) through the living and non-living parts of an ecosystem. The following is an example of natural processes that recycle nutrients in various chemical forms from the non-living environment to living organism, and then back to the non-living environment.

1. Rocks are uplifted by tectonic forces and exposed, releasing carbon dioxide into the atmosphere.
2. Plant takes in carbon dioxide and sunlight and grows.
3. Animal eats plant material and uses the carbon to build a shell.
4. After the animal dies, its shell is buried in sediments and formed into marine rocks.

BIRD FLIGHT

A bird's wing is shaped like an airfoil—a convex upper surface and concave lower surface—which naturally generates lift when air flows over it.

1. The wings push upward and almost touch. Feathers fan out to form a large surface area.
2. During the upstroke, the feathers separate to let air through and the wing twists to fan backward to create propulsion.
3. Pectoral muscles pull the wings down. During the downstroke, the wing twists to push down and back, creating forward propulsion and lift.
4. The wings begin to rise again.
5. Feathers flick forward for the next wingbeat.

BIRD EVOLUTION

1. The scales on the reptile became feathers. The scales developed fissures, trapping air, which is useful for insulation. Over time, they got lighter and longer, allowing the possibility of flight.
2. Bones became lighter, thinner, and more hollow—making a lighter body.
3. Forelegs became wings. The finger bones fused and lengthened. The forearms lengthened as the upper arms shortened, leading to wings.

reptile

scale becomes feather, bones become
lighter, forelegs become wings

bird

4. The jaw became the bill. Teeth were lost and bone gave way to horny material, elongating the beak to be used for grasping, preening, and probing.

5. The first of the four toes swung backward, making it useful initially as a weapon and later for perching and grasping.

BIRD HATCHING

1. In the egg, the chick prepares for hatching by turning around so that its beak is pointing toward the egg's blunt end where the air sac is located.

2. With a sudden movement of its head, it pecks at the air sac. The chick is able to breathe air for the first time.

3. Once its lungs are functioning, the chick may call to its mother from inside the egg. This helps the mother prepare for hatching.

4. Hatching begins when the chick finally breaks through the shell. It does this with its egg tooth, a small projection on its beak that breaks the shell and falls off soon after hatching. It also uses a powerful muscle behind the head that powers the egg tooth's blows. Between pecking sessions, the chick stops for long rests. This part of the process can take hours or even days.

5. Having broken open the shell, the chick extends the initial crack sideways. After each bout of pecking, the chick stops and turns itself slightly by pushing with its feet. This continues as it cuts a circle around the base of the egg's blunt end.

6. The chick rests.

7. Having cut a complete circle through the shell, the chick begins to emerge from the egg.

8. The chick hooks its toes over the lip of the shell and starts to push with its feet and shoulders as well as using the powerful neck muscle.

9. With a final push, the chick tumbles out of the shell which has protected it during the 3½ weeks of incubation.

29

10. The chick's feathers dry and fluff up within the next two hours.
11. The chick starts to feed and grow.

BIRD NAVIGATION AND MIGRATION

Birds use a combination of methods for navigating and migrating.

1. Birds follow landmarks, such as rivers, coastlines, and mountain ranges. This is called sighting. Land birds often converge in a specific place to cross the sea.
2. Birds monitor the Earth's magnetic field, apparently with their visual system, and with tiny grains of magnetite in their heads, which form a built-in compass.
3. Birds observe and navigate by the Sun and stars. A bird traveling south can set its course by aiming toward the horizon beneath the Sun. As the day continues, the Sun travels westward, but the bird's brain allows for this movement, thus enabling it to stay on course.

BLACK HOLE

A black hole is a theoretical region of space that is created from the gravitational collapse of a star. This happens when a star has depleted its sources of nuclear energy and no longer expands against the force of its own gravitation.

1. During a supernova explosion, much of a star's mass is projected into space.
2. The core may become a neutron star or, if massive enough, a black hole. The core continues to collapse.
3. The stronger the gravitational pull at the surface of the stellar core, the higher the speed required to escape from it.
4. Light rays are bent by gravity as the core collapses.

5. The density, pressure, and temperature of the core increase as it collapses.

6. The core, now greater than the equivalent of three suns (solar masses), collapses under its own gravity.

7. The core shrinks to become a black hole. In the black hole, even electromagnetic radiation cannot escape because the gravity is so strong.

BLISTER

A blister forms at a place where there is damage—a pinch, burn, irritants, or friction. It forms to protect the flesh from the source of irritation.

1. The walls of tiny blood vessels in the skin fill with serum, the liquid component of blood.

2. Serum fills the space between the source of irritation and the epidermis, the skin's outermost layer, like a balloon.

3. A blood blister, which is different from a serum-filled blister, forms over ruptured capillaries and contains whole blood.

BLOOD CELL FORMATION / HEMATOPOIESIS

Blood cells originate in blood-forming organs, most notably the bone marrow. In the human adult, the bone marrow produces all of the red blood cells and blood platelets as well as 60–70 percent of the white cells. The lymphatic and reticuloendothelial tissues produce the balance of the white cells.

1. Both the red and white blood cells arise through a series of complex, gradual, and successive transformations from primitive stem cells, which have the ability to form any of the precursors of a blood cell.

2. When the blood cell lives in the bone marrow, it is a whole cell with a nucleus.

3. Before the blood cell leaves the bone marrow for the bloodstream, it loses the nucleus. It is no longer a complete cell.

4. Blood cells then work to combine with oxygen in the lungs and exchange the oxygen for carbon dioxide in the tissues. Blood cells have three main functions: transporting of oxygen, acting as immune cells and fighting infection, and assisting in blood clotting.

BLOOD CIRCULATION

In humans, blood transports oxygen and nutrients to the cells and carries away waste products excreted from the cells. In many species, including humans, it also conveys hormones and disease-fighting substances. Blood also transports water-soluble toxic wastes to excretory organs for elimination.

1. The blood is oxygenated in the lungs. The oxygen is necessary for cellular metabolism. Blood disposes of carbon dioxide, which is a waste product of metabolism.

2. It is pumped by the heart to all parts of the body.

3. The blood absorbs nutrients from the gastrointestinal tract and from various storage tissues and carries them to cells throughout the body.

4. The blood circulates through the muscular arteries into smaller vessels called arterioles.

5. The blood ends in capillaries, with walls a single-cell-layer thick, connected to small venules that feed into larger veins.

6. The exchange of materials between the blood and tissues occurs along the walls of the capillaries.

7. The blood is returned to the heart to repeat the process.

BLOOD CLOT

1. A mass of activated platelets in the blood adheres to the site of vessel injury forming a platelet plug that normally stops the flow of blood out of the vessel.

2. Unlike the platelets circulating in the blood and those adhering to minor tissue injuries, these platelets have undergone a biochemical and morphological change characteristic of platelet activation, a process that includes the secretion of the contents of platelet granules into the surrounding blood.

3. Between the platelets develop bundles of fibrin fibers that result in coagulation.

4. These changes occur near damaged collagen, the fibrous protein found in connective tissue that underlies the endothelial cell.

5. The fibrin strands create a mesh at the wound site.

6. The mesh traps red blood cells to form a blood clot.

7. The platelets subsequently degenerate into an amorphous mass, and after several days the fibrin itself is dissolved by an enzyme, plasmin.

8. The fibrin clot is replaced by a permanent framework of scar tissue that includes collagen, and healing is thus complete.

BLOOD PRESSURE READER

There are two numbers in a blood pressure reading: systolic and diastolic. The systolic reading is the measure of the maximum output pressure of the heart. The diastolic reading is the pressure when the heart is relaxed. If the numbers are too high, that means that the heart is having to work too hard. Blood pressure is measured in millimeters of mercury (mm Hg). A typical blood pressure reading for an adult might be 120/80 mm Hg. A sphygmomanometer is the device used to measure blood pressure.

1. The cuff with an inflatable bladder is wrapped around the upper arm over the artery.

2. A rubber bulb, attached by a tube, is pushed to inflate the bladder around the arm.

3. The arterial tension (blood pressure) of a person's circulation is measured when the cuff is pumped to a pressure which occludes or blocks it. The cuff compresses a large artery in the arm, momentarily stopping the blood flow. This gives the systolic measure—the maximum pressure of the blood that occurs during contraction of the ventricles of the heart. Systolic pressure is the pressure of the blood flow when the heart beats (the pressure when the first sound is heard).

4. Air is then released from the cuff until the blood is first heard passing through the opening artery. This gives diastolic pressure—the minimum value of blood pressure that occurs during the relaxation of the arterial-filling phase of the heart muscle. Diastolic pressure is the pressure between heartbeats (the pressure when the last sound is heard).

BLOWHOLE

On many rocky coasts, water erupts like geysers from natural blowholes in the rocks.

1. There is a strong surf against a seaside cave with a hole in its roof.

2. When the surf crashes into the opening, the cave fills with water.

3. The successive waves send fountains of spray spurting through the blowhole.

BLOWING ON HOT FOOD TO COOL IT

1. Blowing on hot food or drink speeds up the process of evaporation. You are blowing the heat off the food.

2. The molecules in hot foods or hot beverages are fast-moving, high-energy molecules. Due to their fast movement, as evaporation proceeds, more of these molecules leave during evaporation than do the cooler molecules that move more slowly. Blowing whisks away the newly evaporated molecules. Faster evaporation produces faster cooling.

3. The food or beverage therefore becomes cooler.

BLUSHING

1. Something a person is thinking about excites him or her and the body warms.

2. There is a lowering of the set point of the heat regulating center in the brain, or more accurately, in the hypothalamus, caused by an overactive sympathetic nervous system.

3. This lowered set point fools the brain into thinking body temperature is too high and must be lowered.

4. Body temperature decreases when the blood vessels near the surface of the skin dilate.

5. When the blood vessels dilate, flooding the skin with blood, they cause the characteristic reddening of the face. In some people, the ears, neck, and chest also blush.

6. The blush is delivered to the skin of the face because the warmth occurs in the brain and that is the skin nearest the brain. It is also true that the blood vessels on the face are quite close to the surface, which helps to make this process more visible.

BOILING

At any temperature a liquid partly vaporizes into the space above it until the pressure exerted by the vapor reaches a characteristic value called the vapor pressure of the liquid at that temperature.

1. Heat is applied to the container holding water.

2. As the temperature of the water increases, the vapor pressure increases.

3. At the boiling point, bubbles of vapor start to form throughout the liquid and rise to the surface. The temperature at which the pressure exerted by the surroundings upon the water is equaled by the pressure exerted by the vapor of the water. This means that at higher altitudes and lower pressures, water boils at a lower temperature.

BONE GROWTH

The epiphyseal plates are found near the ends of the long bones—the femur, tibia, fibula, humerus, ulna, and radius. Bone is formed in the embryo and the general shape is first created by cartilage, which is progressively replaced by bone. This replacement of cartilage by bone is responsible for most growth in length in vertebrates. It begins in the embryo and continues until full skeletal maturity. An injured bone quickly produces new tissue and joins the broken pieces together. At first this new tissue is soft and puttylike; later, it is bony and hard.

1. Cartilage cells divide and increase in the epiphyseal plate within the bone shaft.

2. Cartilage cells form rows/columns. The row farthest removed from the bony shaft is a basal or germinal layer; it is responsible for cell replication and cartilage growth.

3. Cartilage cells enlarge.

4. Calcium is deposited in the matrix between cartilage cells. The columns push older cells toward the middle of the bone shaft.

5. The mature cartilage cells (chondrocytes) farthest from the germinal layer degenerate and die.

6. A thin layer of true bone (primary spongiosa) deposits there. New bone cells (osteoblasts) attach to the calcified matrix.

7. New blood vessels nourish new bone.

BOOKBINDING BY HAND

1. A set of signatures (sheets which when folded become units of the book) are aligned in the correct order.
2. The backs of the signatures are sewn together.
3. Glue is applied to hold the signatures together.
4. The pages are trimmed.
5. A lining is glued to the spine of the book.
6. The cover (case) is glued to the lining.

BOOKBINDING BY MACHINE

1. In a sheet folder, rollers feed a printed sheet into the slot of the folder, which stops it from moving.
2. The rollers force the sheet forward so that it begins to buckle in the center.
3. The lower rollers grip the buckle and pull the sheet through to fold it in half.
4. Alternatively, in a web folder, the signatures are printed consecutively and the folder separates and folds each signature.
5. The web passes over a pointed metal 'nose' and then between rollers that fold the web along the center.
6. A serrated blade pierces the folded web so that the signature is torn loose.
7. A folder blade pushes the center of the signature between a pair of folding rollers.
8. The signature is folded again and the pages are now in the correct order.
9. Signatures are fed into the fan wheel.
10. The fan wheel delivers the signature to a conveyor belt which takes them to be bound into books.

11. The set of signatures is aligned in the correct order.

12. The back of the signatures are glued or sewn together.

13. The pages are trimmed.

14. A lining is glued to the spine of the book.

15. The cover (case) is glued to the lining.

BOOMERANG

Every boomerang has a built-in orbit diameter and throwing it harder or spinning it faster makes no difference. A returning boomerang is basically two wings joined at an angle of between 80 and 120 degrees.

1. When a person throws a boomerang properly, he or she causes it to spin vertically.

2. As a result, the boomerang will generate lift, but it will be to one side rather than upwards because of its curved surface.

3. As the boomerang spins vertically and moves forward, air flows faster over the top arm than the bottom arm. The top arm produces more lift than the bottom arm and the boomerang tries to twist itself.

4. Another tipping force, caused by the center of lift being forward of the center of gravity, is also twisted to make the boomerang "lie down" in flight.

5. Because it is spinning fast, the boomerang acts like a gyroscope and turns to the side in an arc.

6. If the boomerang stays in the air long enough, it will turn a full circle and return to the thrower.

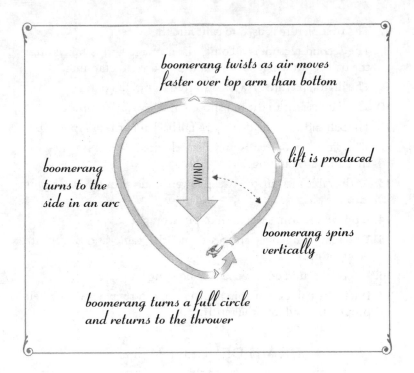

boomerang twists as air moves faster over top arm than bottom

lift is produced

boomerang turns to the side in an arc

WIND

boomerang spins vertically

boomerang turns a full circle and returns to the thrower

BOWLING PIN SETUP

1. The bowler rolls the ball.

2. A small box near the pins contains a photoelectric eye which transmits an infrared beam to a reflector on the opposite side of the lane.

3. When the ball passes, the light is blocked briefly.

4. The ball trigger uses the length of this period of darkness to compute the speed of the ball and it signals the pin spotter to begin cycling.

5. A digital camera with a charge-coupled device is located in front of the pins.

6. The digital camera takes a picture of the pins before and after the ball hits them.

7. The first picture is used to calibrate the system.

8. The second picture is a comparison image and is taken after the ball is thrown. It shows if any pins are left standing.

9. The digital picture data is converted to pin fall data.

10. The data is sent to the pin spotter and scoring computer.

11. The ball and knocked-down pins fall back into the pin spotter pit.

12. The pin table descends and uses clamps to pick up the pins that are still standing.

13. As the table lifts up, the sweep lowers and wipes the fallen pins into the pit.

14. A pin wheel brings them up to pin storage.

15. The remaining pins are reset and the table and sweep are brought up.

16. A special round door senses the bowling ball's weight.

17. It lets the ball exit the pin spotter pit and then a rotating belt propels the ball into the return lane.

BRAIN DEVELOPMENT

1. At three weeks, a tube of neural tissue develops along the back of the embryo. These bulges develop into the three main divisions of the brain—the forebrain, the midbrain, and the hindbrain.

2. At seven weeks, the neural tube flexes and cranial nerves sprout from the hindbrain.

3. Bulges form on the forebrain; one will develop into the cerebrum.

4. At eleven weeks, the hindbrain separates into the cerebellum, the pons, and the medulla.

5. Throughout the remainder of the fetus's development the forebrain develops further and the cerebrum starts to grow back over the hindbrain.

6. At birth, the cerebrum enlarges to become the largest part of the brain.

7. Folding of the cerebral cortex, the external surface of the brain, occurs.

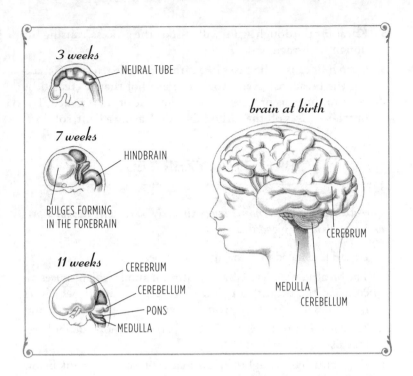

3 weeks — NEURAL TUBE

7 weeks — HINDBRAIN

BULGES FORMING IN THE FOREBRAIN

11 weeks — CEREBRUM — CEREBELLUM — PONS — MEDULLA

brain at birth

CEREBRUM

MEDULLA
CEREBELLUM

BREAD RISING

Yeasts, which causes bread to rise, are one-celled fungal organisms. One ounce of yeast contains 200 billion cells.

1. Yeast is mixed with flour, water, salt, etc. Yeast first produces glucose (a form of sugar) and then breaks down or ferments the glucose into alcohol and carbon dioxide. The proteins in wheat flour form gluten, an elastic substance.

2. The dough is kneaded and the proteins in the flour arrange themselves so that they trap the carbon dioxide produced by the yeast as it ferments the sugars in the flour.

3. The trapped carbon dioxide creates a large number of pores or bubbles in the bread that make it rise.

4. As the dough rises, the yeast cells become separated from the nutrients and the process starts to slow down.

5. Kneading the dough again will re-start the process, causing the dough to rise again.

6. Oven heat causes the gases like carbon dioxide to expand, making the bread rise even more. The alcohol that is created by yeast during this process is released as the bread is baked. The heat also drives off the carbon dioxide, leaving a light, soft loaf.

BREATHALYZER TEST

A breathalyzer test determines approximately how much alcohol a person has in his or her bloodstream.

1. Breath is exhaled into the analyzer tube.

2. The breathalyzer device has a platinum anode which causes alcohol in the breath to oxidize into acetic acid—in which its molecules lose some electrons and create the electric current.

3. The alcohol produces an electrical current; more alcohol creates a stronger current.

4. If the breathalyzer lights up green, the person has drunk below the legal limit. A red light indicates they are above the limit.

BREATHING / RESPIRATORY SYSTEM

The movement of air into and out of the lungs is generated by differences in pressure inside and outside of the body.

1. The vocal cords at the entrance to the larynx are relaxed and open. A space is created between them (glottis).

2. Air is drawn in through the nose, passing from the pharynx through the glottis into the trachea.

3. The diaphragm contracts and fattens, increasing the volume and decreasing the pressure inside the thorax (the chest cavity), sucking air into the lungs.

4. The ribs pull together and rise upward and outward when the external intercostal muscles contract. In forced inhalation, the neck muscles also contract.

5. The diaphragm and external intercostal muscles relax and the internal intercostal and abdominal muscles contract. The ribs move down and in. The volume is reduced and the pressure inside the thorax increased, forcing air out of the lungs.

6. Air passes from the trachea into the pharynx during exhalation. Air passes out through the nose.

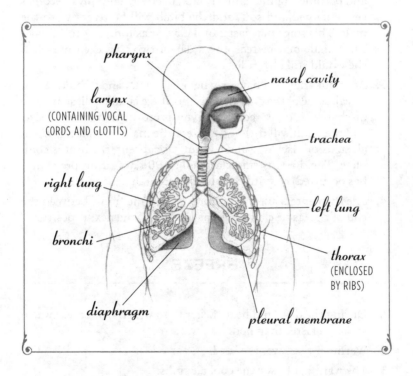

BREEDING CYCLE

In most mammals, the sexual receptivity of the female varies depending upon the stage of the breeding cycle. The description below is the breeding cycle of a dog.

1. The heat cycle of the female lasts from 18 to 21 days. The first stage is called proestrus. It begins with mild swelling of the vulva and a bloody discharge. This lasts for about 9 days. During this phase the bitch may attract males, but she will reject all advances.

2. The next phase is the estrus. Usually the discharge decreases and becomes lighter, almost pink, in color. The vulva becomes very enlarged and soft, and the bitch will be receptive to the male. This stage may last 3 or 4 days or as long as 7 to 11 days. The female may be receptive a day or two past the time when she would still be fertile.

3. At about the 14th day, or whenever estrus ends, the final, or luteal, stage of the cycle begins; this stage is called diestrus. The discharge becomes redder, the vulva returns to its normal size, and the bitch will no longer accept the male for mating. When all signs of discharge and swelling are absent, the heat is complete. The diestrus stage lasts 60 to 90 days (if no pregnancy has occurred) or until the bitch gives birth.

4. She then enters anestrus, which is the time frame between the end of the last cycle and the beginning of the next proestrus.

BREEZE

1. During the day, land heats faster than water. Land areas warm and cool faster than bodies of water.

2. Warm air rises over the land.

3. The warm air flows; the cool air sinks.

4. Cool air is drawn in or flows in to replace the warm air, which creates a sea breeze. The cooler, denser air flows from water to land during the day (and from land to water at night).

5. At night, land cools more quickly than water.

6. Warm air flows and rises over the sea.

7. It cools and sinks and is drawn in to the land, creating a land breeze.

BROKEN BONE HEALING

See **Bone Growth** *for further description of how bones grow.*

1. The self-healing process is more effective if the bone's broken ends are brought back into their natural alignment ("reducing a fracture").

2. Healing of a fracture begins almost immediately. Leaking blood from the broken bone ends forms a clot.

3. After a few days, fibroblasts and osteoblasts, cells that contribute to the formation of connective tissue, make an open network of spongy bone in the gap.

4. A week or two later, the spongy bone gradually fills and becomes harder. Blood vessels have regrown and healed.

5. After two to three months, the bulge at the break shrinks (bone remodeling).

BRUISE CHANGING COLOR

1. Blood is released from damaged blood vessels and capillaries, and damaged cells also release fluid. The area may become swollen with excess fluid.

2. The red blood cells leak out and collect in the tissue underneath the skin. It may look blue, purple, or black to start out— depending on how many red cells are trapped there.

3. The blood cells break down and their contents are absorbed by

the body—changing the color of the bruise to brown and then to yellow before disappearing.

BUBBLE JET / INK-JET PRINTER

1. Software drivers translate an image file in the computer into a pattern of microscopic dots of different colors that blend together to look like a continuous image to the naked eye.

2. That pattern is translated into a sequence of firing instructions for the print head. All inkjet printers have a print head with hundreds of firing chambers (nozzles).

3. A signal from the printer hardware turns on a heating element.

4. To push ink through the nozzle, bubble jet printers heat tiny quantities of ink by passing an electrical charge through a resistor, which quickly reaches 900 degrees Fahrenheit.

5. The heating element vaporizes a tiny layer of ink at the bottom of the chamber for a few millionths of a second, forming a bubble and pushing the ink down the nozzle.

6. The bubble expands and forces a droplet of ink out of the nozzle.

7. The heating element is turned off and cools and the bubble collapses, causing the droplet to separate from the nozzle and creating suction that draws more ink into the chamber from the ink cartridge.

BURPING

1. A person may swallow air, eat gas-producing foods or beverages, or take a medication or nutritional supplement.

2. Gas develops in the stomach. It may pass on to the small intestine, be absorbed into the bloodstream through tiny blood vessels in the stomach wall, or come back up through the esophagus to the mouth.

3. There is a descending contraction wave in the stomach.

4. This wave relaxes momentarily and a little valve opens to let the gas bubble out of the stomach.

5. The gas bubble travels up the esophagus and out the mouth, emitting a low guttural sound.

BUSINESS CYCLE / TRADE CYCLE

A business cycle is defined as a period of economic decline, or a contraction, followed by a longer expansionary period.

1. Peak
2. Contraction
3. Trough
4. Expansion
5. Peak

BUYING AND SELLING A HOUSE

1. Buyer considers purchasing a home. Seller decides to sell property.
2. Each select their real estate agent.
3. Each determines wants and needs.
4. The buyer discusses financial issues.
5. The seller prepares the home for marketing.
6. The real estate agent markets the home.
7. The buyer views and researches target homes.
8. The buyer makes an offer to buy.
9. The seller accepts, rejects, or counters the offer.
10. The offer is accepted.

11. The loan application is made.

12. Inspections take place.

13. The title search is done.

14. An appraisal is made.

15. The loan is approved.

16. The closing papers are signed.

17. The documents are recorded.

18. The funds are transferred to the seller.

19. The seller moves out.

20. The buyer moves in.

CAFFEINE

Adenosine is the chemical in your brain that makes you sleepy. Adenosine binds to adenosine receptors on nerve cells in the brain. This slows nerve-cell activity and causes drowsiness. Caffeine works by blocking adenosine.

1. Caffeine enters your system through a beverage, chocolate, or over-the-counter remedy.

2. The nerve cells in the brain recognize caffeine as adenosine. Caffeine then binds to the adenosine receptors. The nerve cells can no longer detect adenosine because caffeine is taking up all the receptors that adenosine binds to.

3. Caffeine works in the opposite way that adenosine does, by increasing the neuron firing in the brain. The nerve cells also speed up because the adenosine is blocked.

4. The pituitary gland senses this is an emergency situation and releases hormones that tell the adrenal glands to make adrenaline (epinephrine).

5. The pupils dilate, breathing tubes open up, heart beats faster, blood vessels constrict on the surface, blood pressure rises, blood flow to the stomach slows, and muscles tighten.

6. The liver releases sugar into the bloodstream for extra energy.

CANONIZATION

Canonization is the process of selecting an individual for sainthood.

1. A local bishop examines the candidate's life and writings for evidence of "saintly" virtue. The bishop then sends the information on to the Vatican.

2. A panel consisting of theologians and cardinals of the Congregation for Cause of Saints then evaluates the candidate's life and work.

3. If the panel approves of the candidate, then the pope proclaims that he or she is venerable, meaning model of Catholic virtues.

4. The next step is beatification, which allows the candidate to be honored by a particular group or region. In order for this to happen, there must be evidence that the person is responsible for a posthumous miracle. Martyrs, individuals who have died for their religious cause, can be beatified without evidence of a miracle.

5. In order for the candidate to become a saint, there must be proof of a second posthumous miracle. If there is, then he or she may be canonized.

CANYON

1. A swiftly flowing river meanders across a plain. The faster the river flows, the greater the load of rocks and other debris it can carry.

2. The removal of rocks and debris means that bedrock is eaten away. A canyon begins to form.

3. Gradual uplift or tilting of the land surface is often involved through other geological processes. As the surface changes, the river is transformed into a torrent that rapidly deepens the channel.

4. Side streams flowing into the main canyon may isolate buttes that rise from the canyon floor.

5. Layers of erosion-resistant rocks often project as ledges from the walls. The current may undercut projecting fins of rock, producing natural arches.

6. Continued erosion deepens the canyon and shapes its scenery.

CARAMELIZATION

Caramelizing means heat-induced browning of sugar or a food that contains sugars but no proteins. Foods such as fruit and onions are commonly caramelized.

1. When sugar is heated to about 365 degrees Fahrenheit, it dehydrates and melts into a colorless liquid.

2. Further heating turns it yellow, then light brown, then darker browns.

3. If the sugar or starch heated is in the presence of proteins or amino acids, then Maillard reactions take place, which are chemical reactions between an amino acid and a sugar when there is added heat. Part of the sugar molecule reacts with the nitrogen of the protein molecule.

4. A series of complex reactions leads to brown polymers and highly flavored (though as-yet unidentified) chemicals.

5. Heating makes some of the starch break down into free sugars, which then truly caramelize.

CARBON CYCLE

All living things contain the element carbon. There is even carbon dioxide in the atmosphere. This describes how carbon circulates through all life forms and in the environment.

1. During the day during photosynthesis, green plants and microorganisms absorb carbon from the air in the form of carbon

dioxide gas. They convert carbon dioxide into substances such as carbohydrates, which provide energy for them.

2. At night, green plants give out carbon dioxide as a waste product of respiration. Oxygen is taken in by plants for respiration.

3. Animals take in carbon when they eat plants or other animals.

4. Animals breathe in oxygen for respiration. Animals breathe out carbon dioxide as a waste product of respiration.

5. Animal dung contains carbon and it is released into the atmosphere.

6. In the sea, carbon dioxide dissolves in water bodies. Some carbon dioxide evaporates back into the air, but some is taken in by the shells of sea creatures. After sea creatures die, the carbon is locked in sediments for millions of years.

7. Plants and animals die and their bodies decay, releasing CO_2.

8. Fungi and bacteria give off some carbon dioxide during respiration when they break down plant and animal remains.

9. Carbon from plants is also stored in fossil fuels such as coal, natural gas, and petroleum before returning to the environment after combustion.

10. Carbon dioxide returns to the atmosphere.

CARNIVOROUS PLANT

Carnivorous plants are especially adapted for capturing insects and other tiny animals by means of ingenious pitfalls and traps and then subjecting them to the decomposing action of digestive enzymes, bacteria, or both.

1. The conspicuous trapping mechanism of a carnivorous plant, which is always a leaf modification, draws special attention of insects. For example, the Venus flytrap has two lobes, each fringed with interlocking spikes.

2. Inside the spikes are scent glands that attract insects, etc. On each lobe, there are three trigger hairs.

3. When an insect lands on a lobe, it may touch a trigger hair.

4. If it then touches another trigger hair or the same hair again within a fairly short time, the lobes close within a quarter of a second.

5. The interlocking spikes then push inwards, crushing the insect between them.

6. The insect's body is broken down by acid and absorbed by the plant.

7. Carnivorous plants digest their prey through a process of chemical breakdown analogous to digestion in animals. The end products, particularly nitrogenous compounds and salts, are absorbed by the plants.

CAR WASH

1. The correlator device on the conveyor track is a series of rollers that allow a wheel of the car to slide sideways until it is aligned with the conveyor.

2. The car is put into neutral gear.

3. Smaller rollers pop up behind the wheel, once it is on the conveyor. They push the wheel forward, causing the car to roll through the car wash.

4. The car passes an infrared beam and sensor eye, which signals the digital control system that runs the automated part of the car wash. The amount of time that the beam is interrupted is measured to determine the length of the vehicle for smooth flow through the car wash system.

5. The car is given a presoak, often with a mitter curtain that moves cloth strips back and forth along the horizontal surfaces of the car, loosening the dirt.

6. The tire applicators spray the tires with a solution to remove brake dust and brighten the black rubber.

7. A foam applicator applies deep-cleaning detergent. The foam is a mixture of chemical cleaner, water, and air.

8. The car moves on to the scrubbers, which are run by hydraulic

motors. Hundreds of cloth strips rotate rapidly on perpendicular cylinders and clean the vertical surfaces of the car.

9. Some car washes have wraparound scrubbers for the front and rear of the vehicle.

10. The car is rinsed with clean water from the rinse arch. Rinse arches may also be placed after other cleaning stations.

11. Some car washes end with a wax arch, which applies a water-resistant coating. This special formula works on chrome, glass, painted metal and plastic, and rubber surfaces. The wax arch may use foam or nozzles for liquid wax.

12. After a liquid wax, there is another rinse arch.

13. After a foam wax, there is another set of scrubbers, mitter curtain, and rinse arch.

14. The car moves through the dryer, forced through nozzles and then through a silencer.

15. Some car washes have people who hand-dry the car at the end.

CATERPILLAR TO BUTTERFLY

The entire metamorphosis from caterpillar to butterfly takes days, months or even years, depending on the species.

1. The caterpillar selects a suitable site to turn into a pupa. Its hind claspers grip the plant stem.

2. It turns head down and produces silk from the spinneret below its head and weaves silk into a small pad which it attaches to the plant.

3. It turns around again and spins while moving its head from side to side, making a girdle around its body with the silk.

4. The caterpillar is now attached to the stem by its hind claspers and the silk girdle. Under its skin, the chrysalis is starting to form.

5. The caterpillar writhes vigorously and its skin starts to split along its back. The new chrysalis skin beneath starts to show.

6. Gradually the old skin is removed by the caterpillar's vigorous movements. The chrysalis skin starts to harden when exposed to air.

7. The creature, now known as a pupa, works its tail hooks into the silk pad that it spun earlier as a caterpillar.

8. The chrysalis looks like part of a leaf on the plant, providing camouflage for the pupa.

9. The pupa stage is often called the resting stage. Inside its hard skin, though, the creature is undergoing a major transformation controlled by hormones.

10. Once the insect has completed its metamorphosis and is ready to emerge, it begins to pump body fluids into its head and thorax. This helps to split the chrysalis along certain weak points so that the adult insect can begin to force its way out.

11. After several weeks, the skin of the pupa splits. Once the skin of the chrysalis is broken, expansion can proceed more rapidly.

12. The insect can now take in more air.

13. The adult butterfly or moth starts to emerge. The antennae, head, and palps (smaller mouthparts) are visible.

14. Having pushed out of the chrysalis, the butterfly's body now hangs free. The exoskeleton is soft and will expand more.

15. It ejects stored wastes from the abdomen.

16. Blood pumps into the wing veins to expand them.

17. The wings spread and dry. They must harden properly before the butterfly attempts to fly.

18. After some preliminary opening and closing of its wings, it takes to the air—usually to a plant or other food source for its first meal.

CAVE

1. Over thousands of years, rainwater leaching through the soil takes on enough carbon dioxide to form a mild solution of carbonic acid.

2. Penetrating networks of natural cracks and fissures in massive beds of limestones, the acidic water eats away at the rock, dissolving its minerals, and carrying them off in solution.

3. Tiny crevices and cracks form and slowly widen and grow to create deep holes and large tunnels as well as underground rivers and streams.

4. The weakened rock may also cave in. The collapse of "ceilings" sometimes forms huge vaulted chambers.

5. A stream can plunge down a deep (sink) hole to feed an underground river.

6. When the water level in the limestone eventually drops, vast air-filled caverns and passageways remain.

7. The mineral-laden water continues to seep downward. Water dripping from the ceilings begins to form stalactites and other cave formations.

8. Water splashing on the ground builds up into stalagmites.

CAVITY FILLING

1. The procedure usually beings with an injection of local anesthetic, such as novocaine or xylocaine.

2. The dentist then removes the decay by using a high-speed drill. This creates an open space for the filling.

3. A liner is often applied to the tooth to reduce sensitivity, and in cases of deep cavities, a base is often used to insulate the tooth from temperature changes in the mouth.

4. A filling of either silver (amalgam), resin, porcelain, or gold is then layered on top of the liner or base to complete the process.

CD-ROM READER

1. A light beam from a low-powered laser reads the disc from the underside and interprets microscopic pits and flat areas on the playing track that spirals out from the center of the disc. The pits and flats represent sound waves.

2. As the laser beam scans the rotating disc, the various pits and flats affect the beam's reflection, which falls on a light-sensing device (photodiode).

3. The photodiode converts the information that falls on it into electrical signals.

4. These signals are decoded electronically into variable electric current.

5. The current is then amplified and fed to the loudspeakers, which reproduce the sound waves that led to the creation of the pits and flats.

CD-ROM RECORDER

Recordable and rewritable CDs can be used to store computer data and programs and to record music in digital form. CD-R discs can be used only once. CD-RW discs can be re-used as the dark marks can be erased and new bits stored.

1. The sound waves or data are converted into electrical signals by a microphone.
2. The voltage of those signals is measured and coded electronically into binary digits.
3. The compact disc is coated with a light-sensitive resin.
4. The coded signals are fed to the laser as electrical pulses.
5. It emits them as light flashes that cause a pattern of pits and flats on the coating.
6. Each disk is given a thin aluminium coating to make it highly reflective, then lacquered for protection.

When a CD-ROM is recorded or written on by a computer, bits are stored differently on the blank discs.

1. Instead of burning pits, the laser darkens the surface and creates a spiral track containing a sequence of dark marks.
2. The detector in the read-out system reads the marks in the same way as pits.

CELLULAR DEFENSE

Rapid response by the body's defenses may prevent the spread of infection. The building blocks of the immune sysem are white blood cells, specifically the B and T lymphocytes.

1. T lymphocytes (T cells) develop inside the thymus gland.
2. "Killer" T cells react to the remains of specific destroyed anti-

gens and attack them, as well as any infected cells, with powerful proteins called lymphokines.

3. "Helper" T cells activate B cells and T cells.

4. "Suppressor" T cells inhibit the response of other cells to the invading antigens.

5. "Memory" T cells hang around for years and respond to any new attempts at invasion by the same antigen. They mobilize very quickly.

CENTRAL AIR CONDITIONER

1. The condensing unit outside of the building pumps cooled, liquid refrigerant through tubes connected to the evaporator (a device that converts vapor and expels moisture) in the home or building.

2. Inside, a blower sends warm air from the home or building over the evaporator.

3. As the coolant changes from liquid to a gas, it absorbs heat and cools the air.

4. A tube returns the coolant to the unit outside, while the blower forces the cooled air through supply ducts and into the home or building.

A room air conditioner installed in a window works differently.

1. A compressor circulates a refrigerant from an evaporator through a condenser and expansion valve and back to the evaporator.

2. The evaporator is positioned over a fan that extracts hot and humid air from the room. It takes the heat from the air and condenses its moisture into water droplets.

3. A fan removes the heat from the condenser outside of the room.

4. The cool dry air is returned to the room.

CENTRAL HEATER

There are three main types of central heating systems: hot water, forced air, and hydronic. This explanation is for hot-water heating, the most commonly found.

1. A boiler heats water and circulates it using either a one- or two-pipe system, or a "series loop." The boiler is set at the lowest point in the system.
2. A circulator is used to pump the water through the pipes.
3. The hot water rises through the pipes by convection, as well as by pump pressure.
4. Air circulates up from the floor through the tubing and then flows out the top and into the room via a radiator. (There are three types of radiators: vertical tubes, baseboard, and convector.)
5. Some convector systems use a fan to force the heat out of the convector.
6. The cooled water is then moved down through the pipes and returned to the boiler to be reheated.

CEREAL POPPING

Puffed or crisped rice makes a characteristic popping sound when milk is added.

1. Cereal grains contain starch and they are processed to many times their normal size to make air pockets within the starch. The structure of the cereal grains is similar to a very fine glass crystal.
2. Adding the cold milk changes the temperature in the cereal grains, causing "heat stress."
3. The snap, crackle, and pop are caused by the uneven absorption of milk by the air pockets in the cereal grains.

CHAMELEON CHANGING COLOR

The chameleon is normally pale green with yellow stripes. It is a popular misconception that the chameleon changes its color to match that of the background.

1. Color change is determined by such environmental factors as light and temperature as well as by emotions such as fright and those associated with victory or defeat in battle with another chameleon.

2. The mechanism involves dispersion or concentration of pigment in cells containing pigment granules (melanophore cells) that are under the control of the autonomic nervous system. Many can assume green, yellow, cream, or dark brown, frequently with lighter or darker spots on the ground color.

3. Eventually, the skin becomes dark brown.

CHANGING A DIAPER

1. Wash your hands.
2. Gather necessary items—diaper, baby wipes, etc. Make sure the diaper pail or trash can is nearby.
3. Unfasten the diaper on the baby.
4. Fold the used diaper and set it aside or toss it in the pail or trash can.
5. Position the new diaper under the baby by holding the feet in one hand and lifting the baby.
6. Wipe the baby clean with a baby wipe before lowering the baby onto the clean diaper.
7. As quickly as possible, pull the diaper up over the private parts and hold near the belly button.
8. Bring each side in and secure.
9. Kiss the baby.
10. Wash your hands.

CHECKS AND BALANCES
OF U.S. GOVERNMENT

1. Congress can pass federal legislation.
2. President can veto federal bills.
3. Supreme Court can declare new laws unconstitutional.
4. President can appoint federal judges.
5. Senate can refuse to confirm presidential appointments.
6. Congress can impeach federal judges.
7. President can make foreign treaties.
8. Congress can override a presidential veto.
9. Supreme Court interprets the law.
10. Congress can propose constitutional amendments to overturn judicial decisions.
11. Congress can declare executive acts unconstitutional.

CHEWING

1. The muscles controlling the jaw movements are voluntarily controlled.
2. The act of chewing, however, may become a conditioned reflex stimulated by the presence of food in the mouth.
3. The crushing force exerted by the adult molar teeth is between 75 and 200 pounds per square inch (psi), while that of the incisors is 30 to 70 pounds per square inch.
4. The mouth gathers the foodstuff.
5. The tongue is retracted during jaw closing.
6. An up-and-down movement (in humans) of the lower jaw breaks up the food.

7. Saliva in the mouth is mixed with the food, hydrating it and permeating it with salivary enzymes.

8. Food is also lubricated by the mucus in saliva, which makes the food easier to swallow.

9. Food is usually the size of a few cubic millimeters before it is swallowed, but the size is somewhat dependent on the nature of the food and on personal habits.

CHEWING THE CUD

Cows and bulls are often described as ruminants or cud chewers because of the way they digest food. They have large, four-chambered stomachs. Food takes more than three days to pass through the entire digestive system, a complex method that lets the cow extract all the nutrients from food.

1. The cow eats grass and other plants. These are swallowed, then softened and partly digested in the rumen, the first chamber of the stomach.

2. The cow regurgitates (or brings up) the coarse, fibrous parts of the food as small masses called cud.

3. The cow chews the cud to break down its cellulose content, then swallows it again, and it goes into the reticulum, the second chamber.

4. The food then passes into the omasum, the third chamber, where it is further digested with the aid of various essential microorganisms.

5. The food goes on to the abomasum, the fourth chamber, where digestion takes place.

CHURCH BELL–MAKING

1. The dimensions of the bell are worked out.
2. A mold is made, consisting of a core of brick, covered with a coating of loam or sand shaped to the inside of the bell, around which the cope is constructed.
3. The cope, also made of loam or sand, is shaped to the outside of the bell and fits over the core in such a way that a space is left between them.
4. Molten bronze or bell metal is poured into the space at a temperature of 2000 degrees Fahrenheit.
5. The cooling of the metal is carefully controlled to prevent the bell from cracking.
6. After the bell has cooled, the mold is broken.
7. The rough casting of the bell is sandblasted and polished.
8. The bell-founder tunes the completed bell by revolving it and grinding away bits of metal from the inside.

CIRCULATION IN FISH

This is an example of single circulation, in which the blood passes through the heart once on each complete circuit.

1. The gills take in water and food.
2. The materials are passed into the circulatory system.
3. The materials then move on to the liver, gut, kidneys, and tail.
4. After each of these organs takes what it needs, the remaining materials go to the heart.
5. The heart takes what it needs, then excretes through the gills.
6. The whole circulatory system is a one-way arrangement, with the heart pumping only deoxygenated blood from the body forward to the gills to be oxygenated and redistributed to the body.

CIRCULATION IN MAMMALS

This is an example of double circulation, in which the blood passes through the heart twice on each complete circuit, maintaining the system's blood pressure. (See Heart *on page 153.)*

1. Oxygen enters the system through the lungs. The lungs oxygenate the blood.

2. The oxygenated blood moves to the heart.

3. Blood leaving the heart travels from the conus arteriosus into the ventral aorta.

4. This branches to send six pairs of arteries between the gill slits.

5. The arterial branches join the dorsal aorta above the alimentary canal. Anterior to the gill slits, the ventral aorta branches again, forming two external carotid arteries that supply the ventral part of the head.

6. Two internal carotids, which are the anterior extensions of the dorsal aorta, supply the brain in the dorsal part of the head.

7. Deoxygenated blood collects in capillaries and then drains into larger and larger veins, which take it from various parts of the body to the heart.

8. The anterior and posterior cardinal veins, each with left and right components, take blood to the heart from the front and rear of the body, respectively.

9. There is a common cardinal vein on each side, often called the duct of Cuvier, which carries blood ventrally into the sinus venosus.

10. Various other veins join the cardinal veins from all over the body.

11. The ventral jugular veins drain the lower part of the head and take blood directly into the common cardinal veins.

CIRE PERDUE / LOST-WAX PROCESS

To cast a clay model in bronze:

1. A mold is made from the model and the inside of this negative mold is brushed with melted wax to the desired thickness of the final bronze.

2. After removal of the mold, the resultant wax shell is filled with a heat-resistant mixture.

3. Wax tubes, which provide ducts for pouring bronze during casting, are fitted to the outside of the wax shell, which may be modeled or adjusted by the artist.

4. Metal pins are hammered through the shell into the core to secure it.

5. The prepared wax shell is completely covered in layers of heat-resistant plaster and the whole is inverted and placed in an oven.

6. During heating, the plaster dries and the wax runs out through the ducts created by the wax tubes.

7. The plaster mold is then packed in sand, and molten bronze is poured through the ducts, filling the space left by the wax.

8. When cool, the outer plaster and core are removed and finishing touches may be put on the bronze.

CITY WATER

City water supplies generally come from rivers.

1. The water is channeled into screening and pumping stations.

2. Coarse screens filter out heavier debris.

3. Pumps raise the water to storage reservoirs.

4. Because water in the reservoirs is still, solids sink to the bottom.

5. At the same time, oxygen from the air neutralizes other chemical and organic impurities.

6. A system of sluices (gate-controlled conduits that carry a rapid flow of water) takes water from the storage reservoirs to a treatment plant.

7. Usually, water is filtered twice through sand beds which are cleaned daily. In the first bed, the water sinks through coarse sand, which traps larger impurities. The process is repeated through finer sand.

8. The water is chemically treated with chlorine in a closed tank to kill bacteria.

9. It is then de-chlorinated to remove the chemical taste.

10. Water is then pumped under pressure into trunk mains—large underground or overground pipes—which carry it to the users' taps.

11. Treated water pumped into the mains may be used immediately, or diverted for temporary storage into reservoirs or water towers.

CIVIL COURT LAWSUIT STAGES

1. The plaintiff (the person suing) files a complaint describing his or her case and asking for a specified amount of damages.

2. The defendant (the person being sued) files an answer. This is a report describing his or her version of events. He or she may file a counterclaim or parallel lawsuit requesting damages.

3. A settlement can be made any time after the complaint and answer have been filed.

4. If the plaintiff and the defendant cannot settle the case themselves, the process of discovery begins. This is preparation for going to trial. During discovery, each side must reveal to the other the facts that it will use during the trial.

5. If the case is still in dispute after discovery, it proceeds to trial and a judge or jury renders a decision.

6. The plaintiff is awarded money, as decided by the judge or jury.

CLONED ANIMAL

This was the process to make Dolly the sheep, the first cloned mammal, in 1997 in Scotland.

1. A nucleus from a mammary gland cell of a sheep is transplanted into the egg cell removed from a ewe. The egg cell had been stripped of its original nucleus.
2. The nucleus and egg combination is stimulated with electricity to fuse them and to stimulate cell division.
3. The new cell then divides.
4. This new cell in placed into the uterus of a ewe to develop.
5. The baby sheep is born months later.

CLONED PLANT

1. Root cells or leaf cuttings are taken from plants.
2. Root cells or leaf cuttings are put in a nutrient-rich culture.
3. In culture, the specialized cells become unspecialized (dedifferentiated) into calluses.
4. The calluses can then be stimulated with the appropriate plant hormones to grow into new plants that are identical to the original plant.
5. In culture, the end of the cutting forms a mass of non-specialized cells called calluses.
6. These are planted in soil and the callus will grow, divide, and form various specialized cells (roots, stems, etc.), eventually forming a new plant.

CLOTH FROM THREAD

1. Weaving on traditional or automatic looms involves lengthwise (warp) and crosswise (weft) thread.

2. Weft yarns on a bobbin shuttle swiftly back and forth between lowered and raised warp threads while a comblike device (reed) spaces the warp yarns evenly.

3. A cylinder at one end of the frame keeps the warp thread taut while one at the other end holds finished cloth.

4. Looms also have a number of harnesses—framelike devices that operators use to weave a variety of colors, patterns, and threads into the fabric.

CLOUD

Condensation is the basis of cloud formation. A cloud is any visible mass of water droplets, ice crystals, or a mixture of both that is suspended in the air, usually at a considerable height.

1. All air contains water vapor. Warm air can hold more water vapor than cold air. Clouds are formed when relatively moist air rises.

2. As a mass of air ascends, the lower pressures prevailing at higher levels allow it to expand.

3. In expanding, the air cools adiabatically (without heat exchange with the surrounding air) until its temperature falls below the dew point, upon which the air becomes supersaturated.

4. When there are particles in the air for the water vapor to adhere to, the vapor converts into water droplets. These particles (condensation nuclei) can be dust, pollutants, ice or salt crystals, chemical compounds, etc.

5. When there are no particles in the air for water vapor to adhere to, it either remains gaseous or converts directly to ice crystals

through sublimation. These ice crystals are then condensation nuclei for vapor to condense on.

CLOUD SEEDING

Cloud seeding is a way to encourage tiny cloud droplets, which are not growing or growing slowly, to grow big enough to fall as rain or snow. Cloud seeding is a strategy to produce rain or snow where it wouldn't happen otherwise.

1. Tiny water droplets or ice crystals in clouds do not come together to make rain or snow.

2. Dry ice or silver iodide is put into the clouds by airplanes flying through or above them. Also, generators on the ground or in airplanes flying below the clouds can release silver iodide that updrafts carry into the cloud.

3. This causes ice crystals to form and grow from the surrounding water vapor and liquid water.

4. The ice crystals grow big enough to start falling. In warm weather, they melt to fall as rain.

COAL

1. About 300 million years ago, as plants died, they were buried in swamps but did not rot away completely.

2. These dying plants and trees fell into the water and their remains became covered in mud.

3. The plants slowly dried out under the mud, forming layers of peat.

4. Gradually, the layers of peat were buried and became compressed and heated to form lignite, or brown coal.

5. Lignite (a brownish-black coal intermediate between peat and bituminous coal) is dug from shallow pits called strip mines.

6. Intense heat and pressure turned deeper layers of peat into a soft black coal, called bituminous coal, and anthracite.

7. Coal is a fossil fuel because it is made from fossilized plants.

COIN TESTER

A coin tester determines if a coin is real or counterfeit.

1. A coin is put into a vending machine.

2. As the coin enters the slot, an electric current passes through the coin to measure its metal content and size. Only the proper coins conduct the right amount of electricity.

3. Fake coins fail and are passed to a reject mechanism.

Alternatively:

1. The coin passes between the poles of a magnet.

2. Eddy currents induced in the coin by the magnet produce an opposing magnetic field, slowing the coin. The change of speed depends on the coin's size.

3. The coin then passes through light-emitting diodes (LEDs) and light sensors that measure its speed and diameter. Each value has its own particular speed and diameter, which identify the coin.

4. Fake coins fail and are passed to a reject mechanism.

COLD AIR MASS

Cold air masses generally grow in areas where air is slowly descending from high altitudes (as above 30,000 feet).

1. Descending air is compressed, which warms it.

2. The ground loses infrared energy (heat) faster than the air. The frigid ground chills the air near it by conduction. Since air does not conduct heat as well as the ground does, heat from the slightly warmer air above does not reach the ground.

3. As the air cools, it becomes more dense (heavier) and spreads out, forming a huge dome of cold air.

4. As the ground continues to lose heat, the air next to it grows colder and colder.

5. As this air cools, its moisture turns into ice crystals that make light snow or fog, which dries out the air.

6. Eventually, the wind patterns that allowed the cold air to sit in place and get colder change.

7. The wind patterns move either the whole mass of cold or parts of it.

COLOR CHANGE IN ANIMALS

Some animals change color with the season, like the Arctic fox and Arctic hare, other hares, weasels, and ptarmigans.

1. A bird or mammal has to produce a whole new coat of fur or feathers in order to change color. This is also called seasonal molting. Either changing amounts of daylight or shifts in temperature trigger a hormonal reaction in the animal that causes it to produce different biochromes.

2. When they molt in the summertime, the blue foxes turn a dark chocolate, while the white-phase foxes turn grayish with lighter underparts.

3. Before winter, the animal's coat begins to thicken and its hair gets lighter, starting at the tips and gradually working its way down to the base.

4. Once the change is complete, the Arctic fox is almost totally white, blending in perfectly with its wintery white environment.

COLOR FILM DEVELOPMENT

1. Color-negative film has several layers, three of which contain silver-halide crystals that are sensitive to light of different wavelengths.

2. When exposed to light of a wavelength to which they are sensitive, the crystals are chemically altered.

3. The pattern of alteration leaves a latent image on the film.

4. During development, reactions occur between the altered crystals and chemicals called couplers in the film layers, leading to the production of dye.

5. The film is then bleached and the dyes are fixed in place to produce a color negative.

6. Dark areas occur on the negative where all three layers (yellow, magenta, cyan) have been exposed.

7. White light is shone through the negative onto color print paper (with three emulsion layers sensitive to different wavelengths of light) by a machine called an enlarger. It forms a large image.

8. Transparent areas on the negative let through all the wavelengths, exposing the emulsion in all three layers of paper.

9. Colored areas in the negative filter out some of the wavelengths, leaving exposed patches in one or more of the paper's layers.

10. Yellow dye is produced where short wavelengths have been absorbed, magenta dye is produced where medium wavelengths have been absorbed, and cyan dye is produced where long wavelengths have been absorbed.

11. The combination of dyes in the layers produce the colors in the final print.

COMPUTERIZED AXIAL TOMOGRAPHY / CAT SCAN

Computer Axial Tomography (CAT scan) is the process of using a computer to generate a 3-D image of the body one slice at a time from x-ray images.

1. As a person lies inside a CAT scanner, it rotates around him or her, sending narrow beams of x-rays through the body and into a radiation detector as a pattern of electrical impulses.

2. A computer analyzes information from the detector to produce a "slice" through the organs in that part of the body. Data from many such sweeps are integrated by a computer, which uses the radiation absorption figures to assess the density of tissues at thousands of points.

3. A computer produces a 3-D image from thousands of slices. The density values appear on a television-like screen as points of varying brightness to produce a detailed cross-sectional image of the internal structure under scrutiny.

COMPUTER SCREEN RECEIVING IMAGE

1. The incoming digital color signal contains three eight-bit numbers representing the color of a pixel.

2. The bits pass through a graphics card.

3. The graphics card has a digital-analog converter that changes each number to an analog signal of varying voltage. The analog color signals go to the dots in each pixel.

4. Light from a source at the back of the computer screen passes through polarizers and liquid crystal elements. These lighten or darken, depending on the voltage of the signals fed to them.

5. The light passes through red, green, and blue color filters to form red, green, and blue dots.

6. The red, green, and blue dots light up in varying degrees of brightness and merge to form a color image.

CONDENSATION

Condensation is the deposition of a liquid or a solid from its vapor, generally upon a surface that is cooler than the adjacent gas.

1. A substance condenses when the pressure exerted by its vapor exceeds the vapor pressure of the liquid or solid phase of the substance at the temperature of the surface where condensation occurs.
2. Warm air containing water vapor hits something cool or cold.
3. The cold/cool object or substance removes energy from molecules, turning them into liquid.
4. Heat is released when a vapor condenses. Unless this heat is removed, the surface temperature will increase until it is equal to that of the surrounding vapor.

CONDUCTION

Conduction is what happens when atoms and molecules pass thermal energy by direct contact; i.e., it is the transfer of heat or electric current from one substance to another by direct contact. It occurs more readily in solids than in liquids and gases because of the more dense molecular structure.

1. Atoms of a conductor are joined in orderly arrays that enhance energy's ability to travel; e.g., metal.
2. The rate of exchange of energy between the adjacent molecules and electrons in the conducting medium determines the conductivity.
3. The conductor touches something that is of a different temperature.

4. The energy of the conductor generates either cold or heat and transfers it to the item it is touching.

CONIFER LIFE CYCLE

Conifer trees, cone-bearing evergreen trees and shrubs, have separate male and female cones.

1. In wet weather, the cones stay tightly shut and the seeds inside are protected by a waterproof layer of waxy resin.
2. The male cones produce pollen from sacs on the lower surface of each scale.
3. Female cones contain the female sex cells (ovules), which usually lie on the upper surface of each scale. The seeds may take up to three years before they are ripe.
4. When ripe and the weather is warm and dry, a male cone's resin softens and the scales crack open to release clouds of pollen. Air bladders help the pollen float through the air.
5. The wind carries the pollen to the open female cones.
6. After the pollen is shed, the male cone falls to the ground.
7. Many conifer seeds have papery brown wings that help to carry them away from the parent tree.
8. The seeds develop in the female cone, which may remain on the tree for several years.

CONSERVATION

Some people add a fourth: Restore what has been destroyed or damaged in nature.

1. Reduce the amount of goods you consume.
2. Reuse items instead of throwing them out.
3. Recycle items that cannot be reused.

CONVECTION

Convection is the transfer of heat by the circulation or movement of the heated parts of a liquid or gas. Convection ovens, for example, apply this method to cook food.

1. The density of a fluid decreases as it is heated.

2. Its constituent molecules spread farther and farther apart, making the fluid more buoyant.

3. Warm air then rises because it expands and becomes less dense, gradually losing some of its heat to its surroundings.

4. The cooler air grows more dense, then begins to descend.

5. A continuous current of rising and falling air, a convection current, is set up.

CORAL REEF FORMATION

1. Some corals grow in warm shallow water around an island. The calcium carbonate skeletons of dead corals serve as a framework upon which layers of successively younger animals attach themselves.

2. When corals reproduce, free-swimming larvae hatch from fertilized eggs.

3. They settle on a suitable surface, secrete their limestone cups, and then produce replicas (buds) that remain attached.

4. Bright sunlight makes them grow. Reefs grow upward as generations of coral produce limestone, die, and become the base for a new generation.

5. As movements in the Earth's surface make the island sink or water levels rise, the coral reef builds up.

6. Eventually, the island disappears, leaving a ring of coral reefs called an atoll.

COTTON CANDY

1. In a special cotton-candy-making machine, sugar is heated and melts into a liquid.
2. The cotton candy machine forces the sugary liquid through tiny holes and spins clockwise. As it does this, the sugar cools and forms tiny threads.
3. A bowl in the center of the machine catches the threads, where they are collected and served on a stick.

COUGHING

See page 43 for an illustration of the respiratory tract.

1. Inhaled particles or internal particles such as irritants or mucus from an illness stimulate nerve cell receptors in the larynx, trachea, and bronchi.
2. Nerve signals are transmitted to the brain stem.
3. The brain stem relays a response to trigger the coughing reflex.
4. The epiglottis, a leaf-shaped flap of cartilage at the top of the larynx, tilts down during inhalation, closing the vocal cords and trapping air in the lungs.
5. The diaphragm rises and muscles in the abdomen contract so that the lungs are increasingly compressed.
6. Because any decrease in the volume of a gas increases its pressure, air in the smaller space of the chest cavity is under greater pressure.
7. When the pressure reaches its highest point, the epiglottis tilts up and the vocal cords move apart.
8. Air is forced up the airway and propelled out as a cough. This also expels irritants and sometimes mucus from the body.

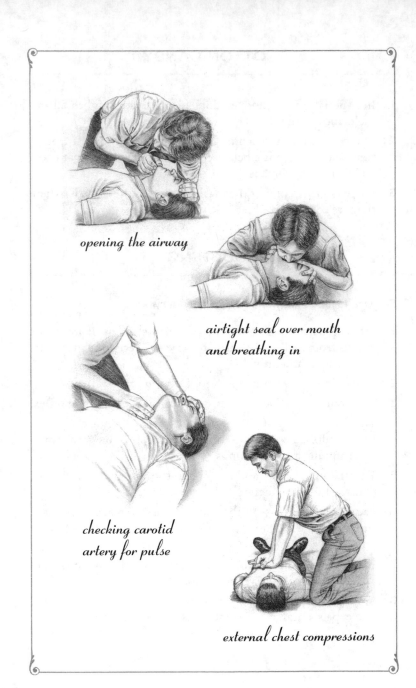

opening the airway

airtight seal over mouth
and breathing in

checking carotid
artery for pulse

external chest compressions

CPR / CARDIOPULMONARY RESUSCITATION

The procedure is modified somewhat for infants and children and under special circumstances.

1. The first step in CPR is to open the airway by placing the individual on his back on a rigid surface, clearing foreign matter from the mouth or airway, and tilting the head back so that the chin is elevated.

2. Clamp the victim's nostrils, making an airtight seal over his mouth and breathe into it about 12 times per minute, allowing for natural exhalation.

3. Check one of the carotid arteries (large blood vessels located on either side of the voice box) for a pulse. Absence of a pulse requires artificial circulation of the blood by means of external chest compressions (at the rate of about 80 per minute for adults). The recommended ratio of chest compressions to breaths administered is 15:2.

4. CPR should continue uninterrupted until normal breathing and circulation are restored or until advanced professional medical assistance can be obtained.

CRAB / CRUSTACEAN LIFE CYCLE

1. A female crab carries a mass of eggs under her body. She guards them carefully.

2. The eggs are ready to hatch.

3. They hatch and produce tiny floating larvae, called zoea.

4. The zoea drift away in the water, living floating in the sea.

5. The zoea slowly change into megalopa larvae, which eventually settle on the seabed to mature.

6. These larvae slowly take on the adult shape and make their way toward shallow water and the shore.

CRATER FORMATION

1. An extraterrestrial impactor hits the earth. There is an explosion upon impact.
2. The front of the impactor collapses. The back of the impactor continues forward.
3. The crater is formed and rocks blast into the atmosphere.
4. Eventually, the crater collapses as the steep sides fall in.

CREAM CENTER IN CHOCOLATE

1. Creamy-centered chocolates contain fondant, which is made by mixing sugar with a quarter of its own weight in water.
2. The fondant is heated slowly until the sugar dissolves.
3. The remaining syrup is boiled until it reaches 240 degrees Fahrenheit. The hot sticky and clear solution is poured out and cooled on a slab to 100 degrees, becoming a mass of tiny sugar crystals.
4. The fondant is reheated to 110 degrees, making it pliable enough to knead in natural or artificial colors and flavorings.
5. The enzyme invertase is also added. It assists chemical changes later in the process.
6. The kneaded fondant is again reheated until it is just liquid and poured into cornflour molds.
7. A shallow flat bed of corn flour passes under a machine which stamps indentations for the shapes, which are then filled with the liquid fondant.
8. As it cools and hardens, the fondant centers pull away from the cornflour slightly and are then turned out onto another conveyor.

9. The fondants go through a bath of melted chocolate, which covers the base, while a curtain of melted chocolate covers the rest of the shape.

10. When the chocolate has hardened, the sweets are heated to 86 degrees Fahrenheit—not hot enough to melt the chocolate, but enough to activate the invertase.

11. Invertase breaks down the sugar in the fondant into glucose and fructose.

12. The glucose and fructose combine with the water in the fondant to liquefy the centers and make them creamy.

CREATION, BIBLICAL

How the world happened, according to Genesis 2:2–3. Compare to Earth's Formation *on page 100, and* Evolutionary Timeline *on page 113.*

1. Light. (Genesis 1:3)

2. Heaven. (Genesis 1:8)

3. The first appearance of dry ground, the seas, and plant life. (Genesis 1:9–13)

4. With the sky now clear, the sun, moon, and stars were dependably visible. (Genesis 1:14–19)

5. Great numbers of birds and sea creatures. God blessed them and said, "Be fruitful and increase in number and fill the water in the seas, and let the birds increase on the earth." (Genesis 1:20–23)

6. Land animals and man. (Genesis 1:24–31)

7. The Sabbath Day. "By the seventh day God had finished the work He had been doing; so on the seventh day He rested from all His work. And God blessed the seventh day and made it holy, because on it He rested (or ceased) from all the work of creating that He had done." (Genesis 2:2–3)

CREDIT / ATM CARD SWIPER

1. A credit card is positioned to go through the reader.
2. All cards have a magnetic strip on the back that holds about 200 bytes of information—usually the card number, the owner's name, PIN, and expiration date.
3. Each data bit is held on the strip as a pair of magnetic domains; a pair of domains pointing in the same direction is a "0" and those pointing in opposite directions are a "1."
4. As the magnetic strip passes through the reader, the domains in the strip induce pulses of electric current in the coil wound around an iron core.
5. The pulses are turned into binary code by a microprocessor.
6. The microprocessor transmits to a central computer.
7. The central computer checks to make sure the card is not stolen, has not expired, has not exceeded a credit limit, etc.
8. The central computer transmits whether it is OK for the transaction to proceed and records the rest of the process for the customer's records.

CRIMINAL COURT LAWSUIT STAGES

1. The person suspected of committing a crime is arrested and brought to the police station for questioning.
2. The suspect is charged during a preliminary hearing. A judge listens to the state's evidence, which is presented by a prosecuting attorney (an employee of the state) before deciding whether to charge the suspect with the crime.
3. At the arraignment hearing, the defendant is formally charged with a crime and given an opportunity to respond to the charges. He or she can respond in one of three ways: plead guilty and be sentenced, plea bargain for reduced charges and

a lesser sentence, or plead innocent—which means a trial where the jury makes the decision.

4. During a trial, the court is called upon to do two things: examine the evidence and apply the appropriate law to bring about a resolution. If found guilty, the court must sentence the person for his or her crime, usually with a jail sentence.

CROSSBOW FIRE

1. The bowstring is held in spanned (loaded) position by rotating catch (nut) set in crossbow tiller.

2. The bolt is laid in groove along the top of stock and aimed by pressing the rear of stock to the cheek.

3. The bolt is then released by pressing up the rear end of the trigger.

CRUISE CONTROL

1. The driver activates cruise control and sets the desired speed.

2. Cruise control puts the throttle valve, a valve that regulates the supply of fuel to the engine, in motion via a cable connected to an actuator, a mechanism that puts something into automatic action. The throttle valve controls the power and speed of the engine by limiting how much air the engine takes in.

3. Two cables are connected to a pivot that moves the throttle valve. One cable comes from the accelerator pedal, and one from the actuator. When the cruise control is engaged, the actuator moves the cable connected to the pivot, which adjusts the throttle. It also pulls on the cable that is connected to the gas pedal, which is why the gas pedal moves up and down when the cruise control is engaged.

4. Many cars use actuators powered by an engine vacuum to open and close the throttle. These systems use a small, electronically-controlled valve to regulate the vacuum.

5. A small computer (microprocessor) connects to the throttle control and several sensors.

6. Sensors measure the automobile's speed and control the carburetor or fuel injectors that admit fuel to the engine cylinders and govern the speed. The carburetor creates the explosive mixture of vaporized fuel and air.

7. The cruise control boosts fuel flow if speed drops when climbing a slope.

8. The cruise control feeds less fuel to the automobile if speed increases when descending a slope.

9. A microprocessor continually checks the speed signal and sends a fuel signal to the carburetor or fuel injectors.

10. The microprocessor can also calculate and display the rate of fuel consumption and can control the engine in order to improve efficiency.

11. If the driver disengages the cruise control by hitting the brake pedal, hitting the resume button commands the car to accelerate back to the most recent speed setting.

CRYING

The physiological processes involved in crying over a speck of dust in the eye are different from crying as a result of emotional upset.

1. If a piece of dust or dirt gets into the eye, little glands produce more tears than the collecting tubes can carry away, and they overflow and drip down from your eyes. This is brought about by an automatic reflex. Bright lights and hot/spicy/peppery foods can cause the same response.

2. When a person is upset or excited, the reflex action is brought about by nerve messages over pathways that go through the brain. Studies have shown that emotional tears are triggered by nerves that pump out chemical messengers near tear glands and by circulating hormones. Neurotransmitters, chemical messengers, clearly trigger tears, as do some pituitary hormones.

3. Tears are always being made by little glands (lachrymal) located above the outside corners of your eyes. They normally just ooze across your eyes at a slow, steady rate, keeping your eyes moist.

4. The eyelids act like windshield wipers to keep them clean.

5. Tears are carried away from the inside corners of your eyes by little tubes (lachrymal ducts) that lead down to the lachrymal sac behind your nose and escape into the nasal cavity.

6. Normal amounts of tears washing down over the front of the eyeball are kept from spilling out onto the cheeks by the oil that the lid glands deposit on the margins of the lids.

CRYSTALLIZATION

This is one method of crystallization; others are cooling molten solids, subliming solids (solid to gas and back), or placing a seed crystal in a supersaturated solution.

1. A seed crystal is placed in a saturated solution.

2. The solvent is allowed to evaporate.

3. The solute coming out of solution attaches itself to the seed crystal, producing a large, perfectly formed crystal.

4. The mother liquor is the solution left after crystallization has taken place in a solution.

CRYSTALLIZATION TO IGNEOUS ROCK

Every mineral "freezes out" and crystallizes at a particular temperature.

1. New lava flows.

2. The surface of the lava cools quickly.

3. Feldspar crystals form.

4. Larger crystals form farther from the surface.

5. Mica crystals form after further cooling.
6. Denser crystals sink down.

DANDELION

1. The dandelion's flower opens in the morning and closes in the afternoon or when it rains.
2. After opening and closing for a number of days, during which time it can be pollinated, the flower finally closes and seed formation begins.
3. The yellow petals wither and the small circle of hairs attached to the top of each fruit (pappus) grows longer. This is the beginning of the parachute.
4. The seed head begins to open, but only in dry weather. The parachutes are squished together at first.
5. As the bracts around the edge of the seed head fold back, the parachutes expand.
6. In windless weather, the fruits stay attached to the seed head and are likely to be eaten by birds.
7. A breeze, however, lifts the parachutes into the air and they can fall closeby or travel long distances. Six miles is the average journey for a dandelion seed.
8. When a fruit lands, the parachute breaks off as it is no longer needed.
9. During the winter, the seeds inside the fruit sink into the soil.
10. In spring, the seeds begin to germinate.

DECAFFEINATION

Two methods are generally used to decaffeinate coffee, direct and indirect contact. In the first method, coffee beans come into direct contact with the decaffeinating agents.

First method:

1. Coffee beans are placed in a rotating drum and softened by steam for 30 minutes.
2. For about 10 hours, the beans are rinsed in a chemical solvent such as methylene chloride.
3. When the chemical has absorbed the caffeine from the beans, both caffeine and chemical are drained out.
4. For about 8–12 hours the beans are steamed to evaporate any remaining solvent. (A minute amount of the chemical, only about 0.1 parts per million, remain in the beans.)

Second method:

1. Green coffee beans are soaked in hot water until the caffeine is drawn from the beans.
2. The drained water containing the caffeine is treated with a chemical (e.g., methylene chloride) which absorbs the caffeine.
3. The mixture is heated until both the chemical and caffeine evaporate.
4. The remaining water is returned to the beans, which helps the beans regain most of their flavor.

DEFECATION

By the time digested food reaches the colon, the nutrients essential for bodily functions have been absorbed. The digestive waste products are changed by the colon into feces that can be excreted / defecated.

1. Segmentation is a series of ringlike contractions that occur at regular intervals, churning and mixing feces, but not moving them.
2. Peristaltic (compressing) waves in the colon push feces into the rectum, triggering the defecation reflex. Muscles behind food contract, while muscles in front relax.

3. Mass movements are strong peristaltic waves that propel feces relatively long distances two or three times a day.

4. Contractions raise the pressure in the rectum until the anal sphincters relax to allow feces to leave the body.

5. Defecation is aided by voluntary contraction of the abdominal muscles.

DEFROSTING

Frost-free refrigerators have a defrost cycle.

1. Defrost is accomplished by either hot gas or electric heating elements.

2. A defrost timer clock is programmed from 3 to 8 defrosts per 24 hours, depending on application.

3. The defrost cycle is time-initiated, temperature-terminated, and adjusts itself to the frost load.

4. The defrost timer has electrical terminals that control which cycle the defrost system is in.

5. The first cycle is cooling, where the compressor is running or is satisfied by the thermostat.

6. The second cycle is the defrost cycle. Every couple of hours, usually 6, 8, 10, or 12 hours, the timer, set by the manufacturer, goes off.

7. When it does, contacts inside the timer turn off the compressor and turn on the defrost heaters for a certain amount of time. The defrost heaters are located in the freezer section and connected to the cold evaporator coils. When electricity coming from the defrost timer activates the defrost heater, it becomes very hot and melts the frost buildup from the evaporator coils. The only function of the defrost heater is to melt the frost on the evaporator.

8. The defrost terminator is a small factory-set thermostat which terminates the defrost cycle when the temperature in the evaporator section reaches a certain level. This defrost terminator is wired in-line with the defrost heaters.

9. When your refrigerator is in the cooling mode, the defrost thermostat closes.

10. When the defrost timer advances to the defrost mode, the defrost terminator is closed, thus allowing the flow of electricity to pass on to the defrost heater(s). The defrost timer is designed to remain in defrost for a predetermined amount of time by the factory.

11. A fan delay is provided at the end of each defrost cycle, preventing restart of the fans until the evaporator coils are cold.

DELIVERY OF BABY

1. In the first stage, the cervix gradually widens.

2. In the second stage, the contractions make the woman feel the strong urge to push.

3. In the third stage, the baby's body rotates as it moves through the birth canal, while the muscles of the pelvic floor are pushed down.

4. The perineum, the area around the vagina and anus, bulges and the vaginal opening widens.

5. As the baby's head emerges, the baby is delivered slowly by the physician or midwife.

6. The baby's head usually emerges facing the anus. The head is then turned sideways as the shoulders move down into the pelvis, restoring the alignment of the baby's body.

7. The physician or midwife runs a finger along the baby's neck to check and see if the umbilical cord is wrapped around it. If it is around the neck, it is slipped off over the head.

8. Fluid is cleared from the baby's nose and mouth and the shoulders are delivered.

9. The baby slides out with the next contraction.

10. After delivery, the umbilical cord is clamped in two places and cut between the clamps.

11. The condition of the baby is evaluated immediately and then the baby is given to the mother to hold.

12. The contractions continue, allowing the placenta to separate from the uterine wall.

13. When this happens, the physician or midwife gently pulls on the umbilical cord and presses on the lower abdomen to ease the placenta out of the vagina.

DETERGENT

The secret of this process is the chemical(s) in detergent that makes water wetter. Water molecules cause surface tension, so water has a type of "skin."

1. The chemical in detergent is a petroleum derivative treated with sulphuric acid and caustic soda.

2. When detergent is added to the water, it weakens the forces between the water molecules and reduces surface tension.

3. Water can now spread more easily and wet things better in the wash. The wetter water is better able to penetrate the fibers of fabric and lift out dirt or grease.

4. The detergent molecules are similar to tadpoles, with heads and tails. The heads are water-loving because water molecules are somewhat electrically positive and detergent is electrically negative. The tails are water-hating.

5. The tails of the detergent molecules attach themselves to the dirt or grease in the fibers, work their way into the fibers and loosen the grime.

6. The dirt and grease particles become coated with a layer of water-loving heads, forming positive electrical charges.

7. These charges repel the ones on other soap-covered dirt particles, keeping the dirt and grease suspended in the water and allowing them to be pulled away from the fabric.

8. The detergent-surrounded particles can no longer adhere to the fabric and they float free.

9. The water bond ends of the detergent molecules then dissolve in the water, allowing only the oily / dirty / greasy particles to be rinsed away.

DEW

1. If the air cools to its dew point—the point at which the air is saturated with water vapor—either dew or frost will form, depending on the air's temperature.

2. If the dew point is above 32 degrees Fahrenheit and the air's temperature cools, its invisible water vapor molecules slow down.

3. As the air cools to its dew point, many water vapor molecules are going slowly enough to clump together into tiny drops of visible water.

4. Water continues to evaporate into invisible vapor, but at the dew point more molecules are condensing into water. Dew drops have formed.

DIGESTION

1. Food is chewed by the teeth and mixed with saliva.

2. The enzyme amylase of the saliva begins the breakdown of starch into sugar.

3. Each soft lump of food (bolus) is swallowed.

4. Each bolus is propelled by contractions down the esophagus into the stomach. It takes about 10 seconds for food to enter the stomach after it has been swallowed.

5. If food contains only a small amount of fat, it leaves the stomach within three hours. Fatty or protein-rich food can stay in the stomach for twice that amount of time.

6. Pepsin is an enzyme made when gastric acid catalyzes inactive pepsinogen. It breaks down proteins into smaller units, polypeptides and peptides.

7. Lipase breaks down a small proportion of the fats into glycerol and fatty acids. It is produced in the stomach and in the pancreas.

8. Hydrochloric acid is produced by the stomach lining and it is used for the action of pepsin and also to kill certain bacteria.

9. Amylase, an enzyme produced in the pancreas, breaks down starch into maltose (a disaccharide sugar).

10. Trypsin and chymotrypsin are pancreatic enzymes that split proteins into polypeptides and peptides.

11. Maltase, sucrase, and lactase enzymes are secreted by glands in the small intestine wall. They convert disaccharide sugars into monosaccharide sugars. The chyme (semidigested food) reaches

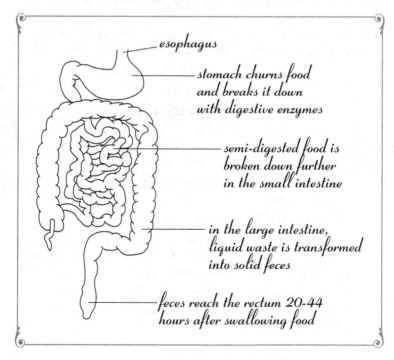

esophagus

stomach churns food
and breaks it down
with digestive enzymes

semi-digested food is
broken down further
in the small intestine

in the large intestine,
liquid waste is transformed
into solid feces

feces reach the rectum 20-44
hours after swallowing food

the halfway point of the small intestine about three hours after it leaves the stomach. Many of its nutrients have been absorbed.

12. Peptidase is an enzyme secreted by glands in the small intestine wall and it splits large peptides into smaller peptides and then into individual amino acids. About eight hours after being swallowed, watery indigestible waste completes its journey to the end of the small intestine.

13. Undigested food enters the large intestine.

14. By the time it reaches the midpoint of the large intestine, a large part of the waste's water and salt have been removed and reabsorbed in the large intestine lining.

15. The residue, waste pigments, dead cells, and bacteria are pressed into feces and stored for excretion. During the 12–36 hours in the large intestine, liquid waste is transformed into solid feces.

16. Feces reach the rectum, the end of the large intestine, between 20 and 44 hours after swallowing (*See* Defecation).

DIGITAL CAMERA

Digital refers to information converted into an electronic pattern that can be represented in binary code of 0s and 1s.

1. Light passes through the lens, which focuses it on the surface of the charge-coupled device (CCD). A charge-coupled device is a semiconductor chip with a grid of light-sensitive elements, used for converting light images into electrical signals.

2. In the CCD, light energy is converted into electrical signals (pixels).

3. When the shutter opens, light falls on the CCD and electrons are released in the semiconductive silicon layer. The more intense the light, the more electrons are released and the bigger the resulting charge. These charges are eventually converted into a digital signal.

4. Each pixel has a color filter to make the pixels color-sensitive and a filter overlay keeps out infrared light.

5. Charge from each pixel is then moved to a register that reads values and sends them to signal processing.

6. The signals are converted into digital information, which can be used later to reconstruct the captured image.

7. Images are stored on memory chips or other removable media for transferring to a computer. CD-ROMs also store images and data.

DIGITAL COMPRESSION

1. The video signal first has to be "digitized" before it can be "compressed."

2. The analog picture is divided into thousands of picture elements (pixels).

3. Each pixel is given a digital code to identify the color and placement.

4. The analog picture is electronically scanned and divided into small squares called picture elements, or "pixels." A typical picture would be divided into at least 300,000 of these pixels.

5. Each pixel is then given a digital code which identifies its placement on the grid, its color, and light intensity.

6. When the picture has been completely scanned and converted into a digital format, it can then be represented by a long string of ones and zeros. It typically requires a series of at least eight digits (ones and zeros) to represent one pixel. A picture with 300,000 pixels would then require 2,400,000 digital bits, or 2.4 megabits to represent it. This is a lot of data, especially when you consider that television pictures are transmitted at a rate of 60 individual pictures or "frames" per second, which would require 140,000,000 digital bits for one second of video.

7. However, much of the information from frame to frame is the same, so by comparing the pixels in each frame and sending a

simplified "ditto" command for the unchanged pixels, it is possible to reduce the amount of data needed to send a top-quality picture by as much as 90 percent with no loss in quality.

8. What this means is that up to 10 or more channels of compressed video could be sent in the same amount of bandwidth as normally required for only one channel.

DIGITAL FACE RECONSTRUCTION

1. For 3-D laser scanning, the skull is placed on a rotating platform.

2. Using a system of mirrors, a laser beam is reflected off the skull and onto an imaging device.

3. Signals are sent to a powerful graphics computer which calculates the skull's shape from the pattern of reflected laser light.

4. Using the scanning data, a digital-wire frame image of the skull is created that can be manipulated in 3-D. Each wire-frame intersection represents a coordinate captured by the scanner.

5. Tissue depth data is used to transform the digital coordinate matrix of the skull into that of a face.

6. Graphical editing software can be used to add color, texture, lighting, and 3-D features such as hair onto the reconstructed face.

7. The completed reconstruction can be displayed on a Web site or downloaded to a printer or storage medium.

DIGITAL TELEPHONE CALL

Most telephones today are digital. (Compare Analog Telephone Call.)

1. Speaking into a telephone sends sound waves into the microphone in the mouthpiece.

95

2. The microphone is covered by a membrane that vibrates with the sound waves.

3. As the membrane vibrates, it makes a magnet vibrate within an electrified wire coil.

4. The motion within the coil creates a continuous but varying charge (or voltage), which is sent across a copper wire.

5. At the phone company's switching station or local conversion station, the signal is run through a computer chip.

6. The computer chip converts the electrical pattern to digital form so it can be sent over a high-capacity fiber-optic line.

7. The chip measures or samples each wave at multiple points, sampling several thousand times per second.

8. Each measurement is converted into a string of eight ones and/or zeros.

9. Before leaving the phone company's part of the network, the digital signal is converted back into analog form.

10. The speaker in the receiving telephone then converts the analog signal into sound waves.

DISHWASHER

The dishwasher has an intricate system of water jets that reach all parts of the dishes and utensils.

1. Detergent is put in the receptacle in the dishwasher.

2. Cold water enters through a water softener, which treats the water so that the dishes dry without spots.

3. A pump delivers water to the dishwasher.

4. The water fills the base of the dishwasher, where it is heated.

5. Detergent is introduced to the water from the dishwasher's receptacle.

6. Hot water is forced through the high-power jets which break

up the spray into droplets as they meet the air. The jets are in the rotating spray arms in the top and bottom of the machine.

7. The pressure of the water in the machine also makes the water jets spin around.

8. The detergent dissolves grease and dirt (*see* Detergent).

9. The water returns to the base of the dishwasher and is pumped out through a drain, where it is recycled after being filtered.

10. Clean water rinses the dishes and utensils.

11. A heating element warms and dries the dishes and utensils.

DISTILLATION OF SEA WATER

Distillation is the purification or concentration of a substance, getting the essence or volatile properties contained in it, or the separation of one substance from another, by such a process. In this case, distillation is the evaporation and condensation of water to separate it from salt.

1. Water is first heated to above its atmospheric boiling point, but in a vessel that is under pressure so that the water does not boil.

2. In the first chamber, the steam from the water rises through a demister that removes any droplets of salt water.

3. The water condenses on the cool condenser tube and drips into a trough.

4. Now slightly cooler, it then flows into a separate chamber at a lower pressure.

5. Some of it instantly "flashes" (flash-boils) into vapor.

6. The vapor is condensed by contact with tubes carrying the incoming supply of cool sea water.

7. The hot salt water that did not boil in the first chamber moves on to a second, at slightly lower pressure again, where more of it flashes into vapor and is condensed.

8. The vapor condenses into pure water.

9. The process is repeated through 10 or more chambers, each at a lower air pressure.

10. The de-salted water is pumped into storage tanks.

DNA FINGERPRINTING

A DNA molecule consists of two intertwined strands that complement each other chemically. When testing DNA, the two strands are chemically unraveled into two single strands. The presence of specific sequences can be detected by adding complementary fragments of single-stranded DNA that will bind only to the sought-after sequences.

1. At the crime scene, samples are taken of any biological material that may have come from the criminal.

2. DNA is extracted from the sample(s) and cut at selected points, using restriction enzymes.

3. The DNA fragments are placed on a gel and separated using an electric field.

4. The electric field causes the fragments to align according to length. Specific DNA sequences end up at specific locations on the gel.

5. The DNA fragments are transferred to a nylon membrane and made single-stranded.

6. DNA probes are added—radioactively labeled fragments of single-stranded DNA that bind to specific complementary DNA sequences if those sequences are present on the membrane.

7. The sheet is exposed to x-ray film.

8. When the x-ray is developed, it provides a barcode-like pattern of the DNA fragments to which the DNA probes have attached.

9. This is the DNA "fingerprint" and it is compared with those from suspects to see if there is a match.

DRYER CYCLE

1. The dryer's electric motor is programmed to turn the drum one way and then to reverse and spin the other way, shaking and separating the clothes.

2. A mechanical or electronic timer controls how long the cycles will last. The cycle switch and heat setting buttons together control which of the heating elements are on at a given time.

3. The air enters the body of the dryer through the bottom or back of the dryer.

4. Air is sucked past the heating element and into the tumbler. Hot air is drawn through the unit by a blower fan.

5. A shut-off sensor is located close to the heating elements in case airflow is blocked for any reason. If this happens, the sensor shuts off the dryer.

6. As the hot air passes through the clothes, it picks up dust and fibers and the air is directed down to the lint screen, which traps the dust and fibers.

7. A shut-off sensor monitors the lint screen and tumbler. If they get too hot, the sensor shuts off the dryer.

8. Air passes through a duct in the front of the dryer and into the fan.

9. The fan forces air into the duct leading out the back of the dryer, thereby exiting the house or building.

DUNE

Dunes are sand hills created by the wind. They form where wind loses energy and drops the sand suspended within it.

1. Most of the sand carried by the wind moves as a mass of jumping (saltating) grains; coarser particles move slowly along the surface as creep and are kept in motion partly by the bombardment of the saltating grains.

2. Saltating sand bounces more easily off hard surfaces than off soft ones, with the result that more sand can be moved over a pebbly desert surface than over a smooth or soft one.

3. Slight hollows or smoother patches reduce the amount of sand that the wind can carry, and a small sand patch will be initiated. If it is large enough, this patch will attract more sand.

4. The wind adjusts its velocity gradient on reaching the sand patch; winds above a certain speed decrease their near-surface velocity and deposit sand on the patch.

5. As the dune grows, the smooth leeward slope steepens until the wind cannot be deflected down sharply enough to follow it.

6. The wind then separates from the surface, leaving a "dead zone" in the lee into which falls the sand brought up the windward slope.

7. When this depositional slope is steepened to the angle of repose of dry sand (about 32°), this angle is maintained and the added sand slips down the slope or slip face.

8. When this happens, the dune form is in equilibrium, and the dune moves forward as a whole, sand being eroded from the windward side and deposited on the lee.

9. The windward slope is eventually adjusted, so that there is an increase in the near-surface velocity up its face to compensate for the drag imposed by the sandy surface.

10. Wind-shifted sand becomes rippled.

11. Over time, distinctive dune shapes are created (crescenting, linear (seif), star).

EARTH'S FORMATION

1. About 4.6 billion years ago, a cloud of gas and dust contracted to form the Sun.

2. The rest of the cloud then contracted further and broke up into large clumps of particles of ice and rock.

3. The particles stuck to each other and began to form planets.

4. The Earth may have taken about 100 million years to grow into a ball of rock.

5. The new planet became hot as the rock particles crushed into one another. The surface was molten and it glowed red-hot.

6. Radioactivity in the rocks caused more heat and the whole planet melted.

7. Molten iron and nickel then sank to the center of the Earth to form its core.

8. Lighter rocks floated above the iron.

9. About 4.5 billion years ago, the surface cooled to form Earth's crust.

10. Volcanoes erupted and poured out gases, which formed the atmosphere, and water vapor, which condensed to create the Earth's oceans.

11. About 3.5 billion years ago, tiny living things began to grow.

12. About 2.3 billion years ago, some of these living things produced oxygen, which began to build up in the atmosphere.

13. About 200 million years ago, the continents broke apart and slowly moved to their present-day positions.

14. Today, the continents are still moving slowly (continental drift).

EARTH'S ORBITAL CYCLES

The Earth's orbit around the Sun combined with the tilt of its axis of rotation creates the cycles that make our seasons. The direction of the rotational axis stays nearly fixed in space, even as the Earth revolves around the Sun once each year.

1. Orbital eccentricity: a 100,000-year cycle in which the Earth's orbital path extends from almost circular to slightly elliptical, altering the distance between the Earth and the Sun.

2. Tilt: a 42,000-year cycle in which the tilt of the Earth's axis

varies, altering the area directly exposed to the Sun. The tilt of the equator changes during the cycle and the tilt of axis varies from 21.6 to 24.5 degrees. As a result, when the Earth is at a certain place in its orbit, the northern hemisphere is tilted toward the Sun and experiences summer. Six months later, when the Earth is on the opposite side of the Sun, the northern hemisphere is tilted away from the Sun and experiences winter. The seasons are, of course, reversed for the southern hemisphere. The solstices mark the two dates during the year on which the Earth's position in its orbit is such that its axis is most directly tilted either toward or away from the Sun. These are the dates when the days are longest for the hemisphere tilted toward the Sun (where it is summer) and shortest for the opposite hemisphere (where it is winter).

3. Wobble: a 25,800-year cycle in which the rotational axis of the Earth wobbles, causing the dates of the solstices and equinoxes to move.

EARTHQUAKE

1. The plates of the earth's surface are constantly moving and creating faults, breaks in the earth's crust where the blocks of rock on each side are moving in different directions. This is called plate tectonics and the majority of natural earthquakes arise from this. When the strain from these movements becomes too great, the rocks suddenly move.

2. Other causes are volcanic eruptions, meteor impacts, and underground nuclear tests.

3. Sudden intense shifts along already-formed faults are the main source of earthquakes.

4. The energy created by this sudden shift or break is radiated out as seismic waves.

5. The vibration travels through the earth's crust.

6. The actual location of the movement is the "focus," which can be at the surface or deep in the crust. The place on the surface above the focus is the "epicenter."

ECHO

1. A sound wave is created.
2. The sound wave reflects off a surface.
3. The sound wave travels back to your ears.
4. The length of time between the moment you shout and the moment that you hear the echo is determined by the distance between you and the surface that creates the echo.

ECOLOGICAL SUCCESSION

Each new disturbance within a landscape, such as a fire, creates an opportunity for a new species to colonize that region. New species also alter the character of the community, creating an environment that is suitable to even newer species. By this process, known as ecological succession, the structure of the community evolves over time. It takes place rapidly at first and then slows down as stability is approached. This example is for a disused or fallow field.

1. The pioneer or first community of grasses, with insects, field mice, etc., comes in. Pioneer plants grow and reproduce.
2. The growth of plants alters soil and life factors and more species colonize.
3. A successional or intermediate community of shrubs and bushes, with rabbits, thrushes, etc., succeeds that.
4. A climax community of deciduous trees, e.g., oak and beech, with foxes, badgers, warblers, etc., settles in. It is stable and will survive without major change as long as the life, soil, and climatic conditions prevail.

ECONOMIC CYCLE

An economic cycle is a period during which the economy, starting from a point when it is judged to be "on-trend," moves first through a phase when it is above trend, followed by a phase when it is below trend, before returning to an "on-trend" point.

1. EXPANSION—rising output and employment
2. PROSPERITY—increasing inflationary pressure
3. CONTRACTION—reduction in business activity
4. RECESSION—falling output and rising unemployment

EGG WHITE STIFFENING

Although egg whites separate from yolks best at refrigerator temperature, they whip to maximum volume at room temperature.

1. The surface tension of the albumen is lower at room temperature.
2. A foam is a superstructure of bubbles with each bubble made up of a pocket of gas (usually air or carbon dioxide) trapped inside a spherical film of liquid.
3. Because egg white is chiefly water, it is difficult to disperse the pockets of gas.
4. Air can easily be incorporated into the albumen to form a foam. If surface tension is too high, it would be too difficult to disperse the pockets of air.
5. Egg white has enough other substances dissolved into it so that its surface tension is sufficiently low to allow foaming.

EL NIÑO EFFECT

During El Niño, the pressure systems that normally develop over Australia and South America are much weaker or reversed. (See also Breezes.)

1. The southeast trade winds are reversed or weakened.

2. Descending air and high pressure bring warm, dry weather to Australia.

3. Warm water to a depth of about 500 feet flows eastward, accumulating off South America.

4. The warm water blocks the normal upwelling of nutrients along the west coast of the Americas.

5. Low pressure and rising air bring rainfall to South America.

ELECTORAL COLLEGE PROCESS

The Electoral College is a method of indirect popular election of the president of the United States. Each state is apportioned a number of electors equal to the total number of their Congressional delegation. The candidate who wins in a state is awarded all of that state's Electoral College votes, except in Maine and Nebraska where the electoral may be split.

1. Voters in each state cast a vote for a block of electors who are pledged to vote for a particular candidate. The candidate who receives the most votes in a state at the general election will be the candidate for whom the electors later cast their votes.

2. Two votes are taken, one for president and one for vice president. Electors are restricted from voting for two candidates from their state.

3. After Election Day, on the first Monday after the second Wednesday in December, these electors assemble in their state capitals and officially select the next president of the United States.

4. The votes of the electors are then sent to Congress where the

president of the Senate opens the certificates, and counts the votes. This takes place on January 6, unless that date falls on a Sunday. In that case, the votes are counted on the next day. An absolute majority is necessary to prevail in the presidential and the vice presidential elections, that is, half the total plus one electoral votes are required. Of the current number of 538 electors, a candidate must receive at least 270 votes to be elected to the office of president or vice president.

5. Should no presidential candidate receive an absolute majority, the House of Representatives determines who the next president will be. Each state may cast one vote and an absolute majority is needed to win.

6. The Twelfth Amendment specified that the Electoral College have separate ballots for president and vice president. So, similarly, the Senate decides who the next vice president will be if there is no absolute majority after the Electoral College vote.

ELECTRIC BELL

1. When the button is pushed, the contacts are closed.
2. Current flows through the contacts and the spring to an electromagnet.
3. The electromagnet produces a magnetic field.
4. The magnetic field attracts the iron armature, which moves toward the electromagnet against the spring.
5. The hammer strikes the bell.
6. The movement of the armature opens the contacts and the current stops flowing to the electromagnet.
7. The electromagnet loses its magnetism.
8. The spring pulls the armature back.
9. The hammer moves away from the bell.
10. The contacts close again.

ELECTRICITY TO BUILDING

The two primary sources of power are water (hydro) and heat (thermal). Hydroelectric power is derived from generators turned by falling water. Most other electric energy is obtained from generators driven by steam produced by a nuclear reactor or by burning fossil fuels.

1. Electricity is made in power plants, which get their power from hydrothermal or hydroelectric generators.
2. It flows through a switchgear which controls its flow and can cut it off if there are any problems along the miles of wires ahead.
3. It goes to a transformer, which increases the pressure so that it can be sent over long distances.
4. High voltage lines then carry the electricity to an area near where it will be used.
5. The power goes on to a substation, where other transformers reduce the voltage (electrical pressure) so that it can be safely used.
6. It is delivered over wires above- and underground to homes, businesses, etc.

ELECTROLYSIS

Electrolysis is a process by which electric current is passed through a substance to effect a chemical change. It is used to destroy hair roots and tumors, among other uses.

1. An electrolytic cell, a device consisting of positive and negative electrodes, is dipped into a solution containing positively and negatively charged ions.
2. The substance to be transformed (such as a tumor) contains ions (atoms which gain or lose an electron to become charged).
3. Electric current (electrons) enters through the negatively charged electrode (cathode).

4. The current is conducted by the movement of ions in the substance and by chemicals deposited at the points where the current enters or leaves the substance.

5. Positively charged components of the solution travel to the charged electrode, combine with the electrons, and are transformed to neutral elements or molecules.

6. The negatively charged components of the solution travel to the other electrode (anode).

7. The negatively charged components give up their electrons, and are transformed into neutral elements or molecules.

8. During this process the substance to be transformed dissolves by giving up electrons.

9. The chemical change is one in which the substance loses or gains an electron (oxidation or reduction).

To destroy hair roots:

1. A needle is inserted into the hair shaft and then an electrical current is passed through the hair follicle.

2. Although hair itself is dry, below the surface of the skin it is immersed in a watery environment with a high mineral content.

3. The electrical current from the needle causes a chemical reaction and turns the water and salt in the hair follicle into sodium hydroxide.

4. This sodium hydroxide dissolves the hair follicle and the papilla, causing a complete and permanent destruction of hair growth.

ELEMENTS OF SONATA

The successive elements of a sonata also is a pattern typically used in the first movement of a symphony. There may also be an Introduction in slow tempo and a Coda or Tailpiece.

1. EXPOSITION—musical subject matter is stated
2. DEVELOPMENT—musical subject matter is explored or expanded
3. RECAPITULATION—musical subject matter is restated

E-MAIL VIA THE INTERNET

1. The sender types a message and attaches any media files.
2. The sender specifies the e-mail address(es) of the recipient(s).
3. The sender clicks Send.
4. Client software encodes the message to enable transmission over a network.
5. A mail server, located either at an Internet service provider or on the sender's server, routes the message to the correct electronic address over telephone lines, DSL, or cable lines.
6. The Internet carries the encoded message to a server, located at the domain specified in the e-mail address of the recipient.
7. The server converts the message into a form that can be read by the recipient's software and places it in the correct mailbox.
8. The recipient logs onto the server and all new e-mail messages are delivered to the recipient's inbox, along with any attached media files.

ENCRYPTION, PUBLIC KEY

Public key encryption is used to send e-mail safely, especially if the e-mail contains financial information. Many browsers such as Netscape and Internet Explorer use public key encryption. An e-mail browser is using encryption when it reads "https" instead of "http" before the address.

1. A secret message is prepared normally.

2. To encrypt the message, the sender uses the recipient's public key together with encryption software. A public key is a value provided by a designated authority (like a browser) to encrypt the message.

3. The sender addresses the coded message.

4. The sender sends the coded message normally.

5. The message travels to the recipient via the Internet. If anyone intercepts it, it cannot be deciphered, even if the recipient's public key is known.

6. The recipient decrypts the message using a private key known only to him/herself along with encryption/decryption software. The private key is provided by the authority as part of the public key.

7. The recipient can now read the secret message.

8. To send a secret reply, the recipient must find out the sender's public key.

EROSION

This cycle could be interrupted by uplift during any of the three periods and thus returned to the youthful stage; this return is called rejuvenation.

1. Erosion begins with uplift of the land so it is raised above sea level. Hills, valleys, and/or mountains are formed.

2. When it is young, a river cuts deep V-shaped valleys.

3. By maturity, meanders and a wide valley form.

4. In old age, the floodplain widens, meanders get bigger, and oxbow lakes develop.

5. Hills are worn down and a level plain (peneplain) is left. In areas where the rainfall is light, it ends with a pediplain which may be covered with a layer of alluvium.

ESCALATOR

An escalator is a set of steps that has been attached to a moving chain.

1. A high-speed electric motor and the drive machinery are located under the top landing.

2. A step chain links the steps so they can be pulled in a continuous length. At the top and bottom of the chain are wheels with metal or plastic teeth. When the motor is turned on, it turns the wheel at the top of the steps and pulls the steps upward and, when they reach the top, sends them back down again underneath.

3. The steps descend on two pairs of rollers riding on the inner and outer tracks.

4. The steps unfold as they travel up or down on the front of the escalator.

5. The outer roller of each step is engaged by the rotating return wheel, the toothed wheel that rotates the steps through 180 degrees.

6. At the floor, disembarkment is allowed when a metal plate meshes with grooves in the step and creates a level place from which to step off.

7. The ascending steps return to the drive shelf located at the top of the escalator. The steps fold flat and hang upside-down from the tracks as they travel underneath the escalator.

ESTIVATION

Just as animals hibernate in order to stay alive in cold places, animals estivate (aestivate) in hot, dry places. Examples of estivators are bees, earthworms, frogs and toads, hedgehogs, lizards, mud turtles, snails, and snakes.

1. When temperatures rise or soils get too warm or dry, the animal may tunnel deep into the soil before the soil hardens.

2. The animal seals itself into a mucus-covered ball or cocoon and goes into a sleep-like state.
3. It can stay there until rain wakes it up again.

ESTUARY

An estuary is a partly enclosed coastal body of water in which river water is mixed with seawater.

1. The tide brings in sand and pebbles which mix with the silt (tiny pieces of rock and plant material), forming mud.
2. Near the sea, the river flows very slowly and the silt sinks gently to the bottom.
3. When the tide goes out, the mud is left behind in the estuary.
4. Slowly, large mud flats are built up.

ETHICAL BEHAVIOR

Before taking a course of action, one should ask these questions to determine whether it is truly ethical.

1. Is it reasonable?
2. Is it responsible?
3. Is it fair?
4. Will I think well of myself?
5. How would my hero do it?
6. Is it honest?

EVAPORATION

This is the conversion of a substance from the liquid or solid phase into the gaseous or vapor phase. The humidity of the atmosphere must be less than the evaporating surface. The evaporation process requires large amounts of energy. For example, the evaporation of one gram of water at a temperature of 100° Celsius requires 540 calories of heat energy.

1. Heat must be supplied to a solid or liquid to cause evaporation. If the surroundings do not supply enough heat, it may come from the system itself as a reduction in temperature.

2. The atoms or molecules of a liquid or solid are held together by cohesive forces, and these forces must be overcome in separating the atoms or molecules to form the vapor.

3. The average speed of the water molecules gets higher as it is heated.

4. During evaporation, molecules escape from the surface.

5. In some solutions, eventually crystallization occurs, leaving crystals behind.

EVOLUTIONARY TIMELINE

This is a simplified understanding of how life on Earth developed.

1. Around 4 billion years ago, a cloud of gas and dust contracted to form the Sun.

2. The rest of the cloud then contracted further and broke up into large clumps of particles of ice and rock.

3. Gravity compressed the particles together into hot gases and began to form the Earth (*see* Earth's Formation).

4. The outermost crust eventually cooled, with heat and gases escaping through cracks and volcanoes.

5. Rain and steam created oceans and other bodies of water.

6. Evaporation created a breeding ground on the surface.

7. Hydrogen, nitrogen, carbon dioxide, and some other chemicals hung in the atmosphere and dissolved in the water.

8. Amino acids and nucleotides either arrived via space debris or were formed on Earth, aided by lightning and ultraviolet light, or both.

9. Nucleotides began forming RNA chains which can copy one another.

10. Fat molecules spontaneously assembled into bubbles or compartments, sometimes trapping RNA molecules inside.

11. Around 3 billion years ago, cell division occurred under pressure and each compartment divided into two.

12. RNA molecules evolved a code for amino acid sequences and began to assemble crude proteins.

13. DNA took over as the information carrier. RNA became the functional link between DNA and the amino acids.

14. Sugar-converting enzymes made limited amounts of adenosine triphosphate (ATP), which is the energy for cell activities.

15. Some microorganisms "learned" to convert sunlight into sugar (photosynthesis).

16. Other microorganisms "learned" to use the waste product of oxygen from photosynthesis to make a lot of ATP.

17. Close to 2 billion years ago, cells then developed hairlike cilia and whiplike flagella, which allowed them to move and look for food.

18. The first sexual encounter occurred when one cell injected its DNA into another.

19. New gene combinations proliferated.

20. A new larger super cell arose with a nucleus protecting DNA.

21. By 2 billion years ago, small simple oxygen-using cells invaded the super cells and became a part of the cell called mitochondria, the energy producers of ATP.

22. Some super cells ate photosynthesizers, which evolved into chloroplasts, the energy producers for plants.

23. Cells began to stick together, creating multicellular organisms.

24. Around 1 billion years ago, multicellular organisms produced special germ (sex) cells which were capable of mixing and sharing genetic information.

25. Plants and animals developed internal electrochemical signals that enabled the cells to communicate with one another. Animals developed central nervous systems. Coelenterates were the best-known of the earliest animals.

26. Animals evolved with radial and then bilateral symmetry and segmented body parts.

27. Some living things like fish developed skeletons, freeing them from the confinement of shells.

28. Seeds developed and this packaging for DNA permitted living things to migrate to land.

29. Various creatures came into being, such as insects. They lived communally.

30. Eggs enclosed the embryos of some animals, enabling some species to migrate permanently to land. Some of these creatures developed feathers. Others developed higher body temperatures and insulation. Some of these creatures evolved into dinosaurs and birds.

31. Flowering plants developed in symbiosis with animals, exchanging nectar for pollen dispersal.

32. Some warm-blooded animals evolved to have vision, opposable thumbs, upright posture, and enlarged brains.

EXPIRATION CYCLE / OPTION CYCLE

The expiration/option cycles are the sequence of expiration dates for options and funds, like money-market funds, that are traded in terms of less than a year. The traditional three cycles are:

1. January, with available expiration months of January, April, July, October

2. February, with available expiration months of February, May, August, November

3. March, with available expiration months of March, June, September, December

However, equity options often expire on a hybrid cycle which involves a total of four option series: the two nearest-term calendar months and the next two months from the traditional cycle to which that class of options has been assigned. For example, on January 1, a stock in the January cycle will be trading options expiring in these months: January, February, April, and July. After the January expiration, the months outstanding will be February, March, April, and July.

FACE RECOGNITION

Face recognition technology is used to identify individual faces in a crowd.

1. A large number of pictures of faces are collected in a database.

2. A set of eigenfaces (two-dimensional facelike arrangements of light and dark areas) is made by combining all the pictures and looking at what is common and different among groups of individuals.

3. The computer system selects a subset of features in each face that differs most from other faces, e.g., nose, eyebrows, mouth, bone structure.

4. The computer uses elastic patterns to depict movements or changes of expression, without losing the basic face structure.

5. To determine someone's identity, the computer takes an image of that person and determines the points that make that individual differ most from other people.

6. The system then starts creating patterns either randomly or based on the average eigenface.

7. For each selection, it constructs a facial image and compares it with the target face to be identified.

8. New patterns are created until a facial image that matches the target can be constructed.

9. When a match is found, the computer looks in its database for a matching pattern of a real person.
10. The system can automatically detect a person's presence and track the head.

FAIRY RING OR FUNGUS RING FORMATION

Fairy rings are circles of toadstools sometimes seen on lawns.

1. A fungal spore lands on the ground and the mycelium (the underground, food-absorbing part of a fungus) develops into an underground network of feeding threads (hyphae).
2. Toadstools may appear on the surface and die away, but the threads continue to grow underground.
3. The threads gradually use up the nutrients in the soil and then have to spread out.
4. The oldest threads die out and the inner band of mycelium decays, leaving a ring of young ones.
5. The young threads continue to grow outward. When these produce toadstools, the "fairy ring" appears.

FATIGUE

1. Lactic acid builds up in the body over the course of a day. It occurs in the blood when glycogen is broken down in muscle.
2. Other fatigue toxins are created during muscular activity. Waste products such as carbon dioxide and uric acid are present in high concentration.
3. Other causes of fatigue are alcohol intoxication or lack of oxygen (hypoxia).
4. The blood carries these throughout the body so that not only the muscle itself, but the entire body and brain feel tired.

FAXING

1. To transmit a document or picture, the user puts it into the fax machine.

2. The user dials the phone number.

3. The machine takes over and signals when it has made a connection.

4. The document or picture is moved across a light-scanner.

5. Light from the tube is reflected off the document or picture and passed by mirrors through a lens onto a charge-coupled device (CCD).

6. The CCD has thousands of tiny cells that convert light into electric current, with the voltages varying according to the light each cell detects. The image sensors convert the data to electrical pulses.

7. These varying voltages are converted to digital signals that are sent to the modem.

8. The modem combines them with a carrier wave of electric current.

9. The modem tests the quality of the telephone line before feeding it the signals. If OK, it sends the signals.

10. When the signals arrive at the telephone receiver, they are demodulated—separated from the carrier wave.

11. The data is converted into digitized information.

12. The signals are fed to a printer that re-creates the document or picture with horizontal chains of ink dots that build up into lines. The printer may use thermal heat for the print transfer.

13. The image dries immediately and the fax is complete.

FERTILIZATION

Fertilization is the process of a sperm fusing with an ovum (egg), which eventually leads to the development of an embryo.

1. The head of the sperm penetrates the outer layer (corona radiata) of a mature ovum (egg).

2. After one sperm head penetrates the ovum, chemical changes that are triggered by enzymes prevent the entry of any other sperm.

3. The sperm sheds its body and tail, while the head containing the nucleus and genetic material continues to move toward the ovum's nucleus.

4. After penetration occurs, the nuclei of the sperm and ovum, each of which contains 23 chromosomes, fuse to form the fertilized egg, also known as a zygote.

5. With its 64 chromosomes, the zygote starts to divide as it travels down the fallopian tube.

6. After the zygote divides several times, a solid cluster of cells called the morula is formed.

7. About 6 days after fertilization, the morula develops a hollow cavity.

8. Now called a blastocyst, it floats freely within the uterine cavity for about 48 hours.

9. The blastocyst drifts to a location where it becomes embedded in the endometrial tissue.

10. Part of the uterine lining thins and softens to facilitate the process of implantation.

FETAL DEVELOPMENT OF HUMAN

1. The fertilized egg is the combination of the egg cell and sperm cell. It divides into two cells, then four, etc., in a ball-like configuration.

2. As the fertilized egg continues to divide, each of the cells in the ball becomes slightly smaller.

3. Living on its stored reserves of yolk, the ball floats along the oviduct to the womb.

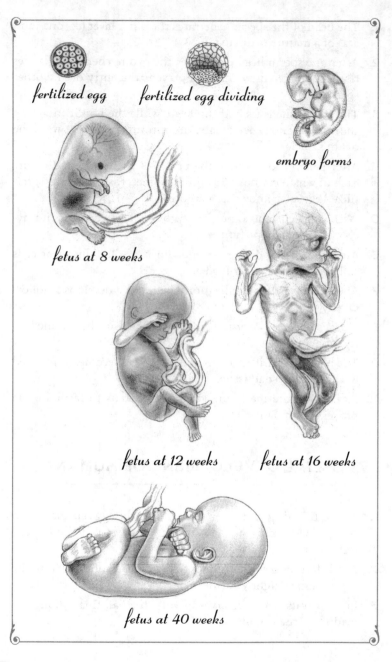

fertilized egg

fertilized egg dividing

embryo forms

fetus at 8 weeks

fetus at 12 weeks

fetus at 16 weeks

fetus at 40 weeks

4. About a week after fertilization, it burrows into the thick womb lining and begins to feed on nourishment provided by the lining.

5. At 2 weeks, the cells multiply into the thousands and start to differentiate into different types—nerve cells, muscle cells, etc.

6. At 4 weeks, the baby's body starts to take shape. The backbone forms a ridge. There is a tiny tail at this stage.

7. After 5 weeks, the eye is recognizable, the ear slitlike. Limbs grow out of the trunk and the tail disappears. The heart draws inside the body. It is an embryo.

8. At 8 weeks, the arms, legs, and major joints of the fetus are forming and it begins to move. The toes and fingers are distinct, but may still be joined by webs of skin. The fetal blood cells circulate within immature blood vessels.

9. At 12 weeks, the head is large, compared with the rest of the body, but it looks like a human being. Major internal organs have developed. Tiny nails grow on the fingers and toes. The external ears, eyelids, and 32 permanent teeth buds have formed.

10. At 16 weeks, the fetus moves more vigorously, though these are still not felt by the mother. External genital organs are visible and delicate, downy hair is on much of the body.

11. Around week 32, the fetus turns head-down and looks much as it will at birth.

12. At 40 weeks, the mature fetus is ready for birth. Its skin is covered by a greasy white substance (vernix) for easing its passage through the birth canal.

FIDDLER CRAB MATING

1. At low tide, a male fiddler crab will stand at the entrance to his sandy burrow.

2. He swings out his large claw to the side in an open position.

3. He rotates it up, then down, then back to the starting position in the lateral display to indicate his interest in a mate.

4. While waving his claw, the fiddler crab also lifts his body up and down.

5. If a female comes within sight, his waving becomes more energetic and the crab frantically bobs up and down.

6. The male also stomps his walking legs and make noises with them in an effort to attract the mate.

7. He then retreats into his burrow, where the female follows him to mate.

8. After mating, the female deposits several hundred fertilized eggs into the sea.

FINGERPRINT IDENTIFICATION

1. A person sweeps his or her finger across a sensor, which is a microchip covered by a heat-sensitive layer containing 14,000 imaging elements.

2. The microchip converts the tiny heat variations it detects into a series of image slices, each showing a fingerprint ridge pattern. About 50–100 slices are generated.

3. Special software reconstructs the slices into a full image.

4. The image may be viewed and stored on a computer.

5. A computer further processes the image using complex algorithms, generating a digital identification code.

FIRE EXTINGUISHER

1. A fire extinguisher contains water and a cartridge of high-pressure gas. Some extinguishers contain an extinguishing gas or liquid (e.g., carbon dioxide) which does not require a gas cartridge.

2. The safety pin is removed so the lever can be pressed.

3. When the lever is pressed, it pushes on an actuating rod.

4. The rod presses a spring-mounted valve down to open up the passage to the nozzle.

5. The bottom of the actuating rod has a sharp pin that pierces the seal on the gas cartridge, releasing gas into the upper part of the cylinder.

6. The gas applies downward pressure on the extinguishing material.

7. The gas pushes the extinguishing material up the discharge tube/siphon and out of the nozzle.

FIRE IN FIREPLACE

1. Open the damper in the fireplace chimney.

2. Gather the supplies—matches, paper, kindling, the wood itself. The wood and kindling should be mostly dry.

3. Set two medium-size logs in the grate with a couple of inches of breathing room between them.

4. Prepare some newspaper loops or logs and put them in between and under the logs.

5. Lay a handful of kindling on top of the logs and newspaper.

6. Place one more medium-size log on top, at an angle.

7. Warm the damper/flue with a match.

8. Light the newspaper sticking out between the two bottom logs, at the ends and in the center.

FIREFLY

Fireflies use special light-emitting organs to communicate, primarily as part of mating.

1. A chemical reaction takes place in which the organic substance

123

luciferin undergoes oxidation when the enzyme luciferase is present. These two are bound up with magnesium and oxygen in the abdomen.

2. ATP supplies the energy for the reaction.

3. The chemical pyrophosphate is released into the abdomen and the bonds holding the other bound-up chemicals are broken and the chemicals are released, creating visible light.

4. Another chemical released seconds later turns off the reaction. The oxidating chemicals produce a high-energy state and then revert to their normal state.

5. The flashing is controlled by the nervous system and the tracheal end organs and takes place in special cells called photocytes.

6. The higher the temperature, the shorter the interval between flashes.

FIRST-AID

The following steps list evaluation procedures and specify treatment, if necessary.

1. Check to see if the victim is conscious.
   a. Ask in a loud but calm voice, "Are you okay?"
   b. Gently shake or tap the victim on the shoulder.
   c. Watch for response. If the victim does not respond, go to Step 2.
   d. If the victim is conscious, ask where he or she feels different than usual or where it hurts. Go to Step 3.
   e. If the victim is conscious but is choking and cannot talk, stop the evaluation and begin treatment for clearing the airway of a conscious victim.

2. Check for breathing and heartbeat.
   a. Look for rise and fall of the victim's chest.

   b. Listen for breathing by placing your ear about one inch from the victim's mouth and nose.

   c. Feel for breathing by placing your hand or cheek about one inch from the victim's mouth and nose.

   d. At the same time, check for a pulse in the victim's neck.

   e. If there is a pulse but no breathing, stop the evaluation and begin treatment to restore the breathing.

   f. If there is no pulse, stop the evaluation and begin CPR.

3. Check for bleeding.

   a. Look for spurts of blood and blood-soaked clothing.

   b. Look for entry and exit wounds.

   c. If bleeding is present, stop the evaluation and begin treatment for stopping the bleeding.

4. Check for the following signs of shock:

   a. Sweaty, but cool skin

   b. Paleness

   c. Restlessness or nervousness

   d. Thirst

   e. Loss of blood

   f. Confusion

   g. Faster than normal breathing rate

   h. Blotchy or bluish skin

   i. Vomiting or nausea

     · If any of these signs are present, discontinue the evaluation and treat for shock.

5. Check for fractures (broken bones).

   a. Check for the following signs of neck or back injury:

     · Pain or tenderness of neck or back area

     · Wounds of neck or back area

     · Paralysis

   b. Ask the victim if he or she can move.

   c. Touch the victim's arms and legs and ask whether he or she can feel it.

   d. If you suspect a neck or back injury, immobilize the victim by doing the following:

- Tell the victim not to move.
- If you suspect a back injury, place padding under the natural arch of the lower back.
- If you suspect a neck injury, place padding under the victim's neck and place objects such as rocks or shoes on both sides of the head.

e. Check the victim's arms or legs for fractures or broken bones. Signs are:
- Swelling
- Discoloration

FISH BREATHING

1. Oxygen and carbon dioxide dissolve in water and most fishes exchange dissolved oxygen and carbon dioxide in water by means of the gills.

2. Water taken in continuously through the mouth passes backward between the gill bars and over the gill filaments, where the exchange of oxygen and carbon dioxide takes place.

3. The blood capillaries in the gill filaments are close to the gill surface in order to take up oxygen from the water.

4. Fishes give up excess carbon dioxide to the water when they breathe out.

5. Some fishes with accessory organs, like a swim bladder, are air breathers and will drown if denied access to the surface, even in well-oxygenated water.

FISH SWIMMING

Cartilaginous fish swim by curving the body from one side to the other, pushing the water sideways and backwards to propel themselves forward.

Bony fish keep their bodies straighter and beat their tailfins from side-to-side to achieve the same result.

1. The fish swings its head to one side, starting an S-shaped wave.
2. The fish's body swivels around a point just behind the head.
3. At the end of each wave, the tail flicks backward against the water.
4. Then the head turns right into the next wave.

FIVE AGES OF MAN

Also known as the Five Rises, this was created by Gerald Heard. Looking at the cultural history of our race and at our own psychological development, Heard came to the conclusion that they developed along similar lines of evolutionary growth. For him, ontogeny (the inner state of our individual being) followed the same evolutionary blueprint as phylogeny (the development of cultural consciousness in our human race).

1. Co-conscious, pre-individual, nonpersonal group constituent, creature of a spoken tradition, infancy
2. Heroic, proto-individual, self-assertive, protesting that tradition, childhood
3. Ascetic, mid-individual, self-accusing, person of self-blame, adolescence
4. Humanic, total individual, self-sufficient, objective individual, first maturity
5. Leptoid, post-individual, leaping off, individual objectively aware of own subjectivity, second maturity

FLINTLOCK LOADING AND FIRING

1. Set the lock to "half-cock" safety position.
2. Pour the correct amount of gunpowder from the powder flask or cartridge down the barrel.

3. Ram the ball, wrapped in its patch or cartridge, down the barrel with the ramrod.

4. Pour a small amount of powder from the powder flask into the priming pan.

5. Close the pan cover.

6. Set lock to "full-cock" position.

7. Fire!

FLOOD

Flooding is a natural event in streams and rivers, and it occurs as often as every other year.

1. The water level in a stream or river usually varies seasonally because of the changes in the atmospheric sources of the water, such as rain or snowmelt.

2. During the high-water season (anywhere from spring through fall, depending on the area), a large rainfall or snowmelt can cause water to rise above flood stage—when the water is level with the stream's or river's banks.

3. The water overflows its natural or artificial banks onto normally dry land.

4. A flash flood is a sudden, unexpected torrent of muddy and turbulent water rushing down a canyon or gulch. It is uncommon, of relatively brief duration (less than 24 hours), usually limited to small watersheds, and generally the result of summer thunderstorms in mountains.

FLUORESCENT LAMP

1. A fluorescent lamp consists of a glass tube filled with a mixture of argon and mercury vapor.

2. A starter and ballast provide extra voltage needed to ionize

(convert into ions, which are electrically charged particles) the gas when the light is turned on and electricity is introduced.

3. The light of a fluorescent lamp comes from the interaction of electrons and argon/mercury vapor atoms.

4. The metal electrodes at each end of the tube are coated with alkaline-earth oxide which gives off electrons easily.

5. Pins pass electric current to the metal electrodes through the ionized gas.

6. This produces ultraviolet radiation that is absorbed by the phosphor coating, a fluorescent powder on the inside of the tube.

7. The ultraviolet radiation energizes the electrons in the phosphor's atoms and fluoresces, which radiates energy as visible white light.

FLY LIFE CYCLE

1. After mating, the female drone fly lays her eggs near a puddle, polluted pond, drain, or other stagnant water.

2. From laying to hatching is about one day. The larvae, known as rat-tailed maggots, live in the water, breathing through the long tail that acts like a snorkel.

3. The maggots feed on rotting, decaying plant and animal matter.

4. The maggots wriggle out of the water to drier soil.

5. They change into pupae.

6. When the adult flies emerge 4–6 weeks later from the pupal cases, they fly off to feed on pollen and nectar from flowers.

FOG FORMATION

Fog is a cloud on the ground. The most common kinds of fog form when humid air is cooled to its dew point, causing water vapor to begin condensing into tiny drops.

ADVECTION FOG

1. Wind pushes warm humid air inland (horizontally) in the winter.

2. As the air blows over cold ground, it cools to the dew point and fog forms.

GROUND FOG / RADIATION FOG

1. On clear nights with winds less than 5 mph, heat radiates away from the ground, cooling the ground and the air next to it. (Strong winds prevent fog by mixing cold air near the ground with warmer air higher up.)

2. Heavier cold air flows into low places.

3. Fog forms as air cools to its dew point.

4. As the sun comes up in the morning, its heat raises the temperature above the dew point.

5. The fog "burns off."

PRECIPITATION FOG

1. Some of the rain falling into cool air evaporates if the rain is warmer than the air.

2. The added vapor increases the dew point to the air's temperature.

3. Vapor condenses into tiny fog droplets.

SEA SMOKE FOG / STEAM FOG

1. Cold air blows over much warmer water.

2. Water evaporates into the cold air, increasing it to the dew point.

3. Vapor condenses into tiny water droplets.

4. This can make "steam" rise from ponds and streams as fog forms a foot or two above the water.

UPSLOPE FOG

1. Wind blows humid air up hills or mountains.

2. As the air rises, it cools to its dew point and fog drifts up the hill or mountain.

VALLEY FOG

1. In valleys, especially in the West during winter, radiation fog can become more than 1500 feet thick.

2. Weak winter sun is not strong enough to evaporate the fog completely. It might warm the ground enough for a layer of fog up to around 500 feet above the ground to evaporate.

3. Such fogs can last for days until a storm comes with strong winds, pushing out the cold air.

FOOD CHAIN

This sequence shows nutrition levels in a simple food chain.

1. Sunlight shines on producers (green plants), which use the sunlight to make food by photosynthesis.

2. Primary consumers (first order consumers) eat producers; herbivores such as rabbits eat cabbages.

3. Secondary consumers (second order consumers) eat primary consumers; carnivores such as thrushes eat herbivores.

4. Tertiary consumers (third order consumers) eat smaller secondary consumers; carnivores eat smaller carnivores. Energy-given material is obtained by the most indirect method—from bodies of secondary consumers, i.e., animals which ate animals which ate producers.

5. Decomposers, such as fungi or bacteria, decompose dead plants, animals, and droppings.

6. The decomposers then release minerals into the soil that may later be absorbed by producers.

FOREST MANAGEMENT

The forest management cycle shows the continuous series of activities required to ensure that the working forest balances economic value with social and environmental values.

1. Planning
2. Harvesting
3. Site preparation
4. Reforestation
5. Stand tending (weeding, thinning or spacing, pruning, fertilization)
6. Protection
7. Research

FOSSILIZATION

1. A creature, such as a shellfish, dies and falls to the sea floor.
2. Its soft body tissue quickly rots away, leaving the hard shell behind.
3. If the shell is buried intact under sediment, it may be dissolved away over millions of years by water trickling through the mud.
4. The sediments compact and minerals dissolve the remains, leaving a shell-shaped hollow known as a mold.
5. Other minerals in the water, such as silica or iron sulfide, fill the mold and harden to form a natural cast. This is called replacement.
6. Other remains are preserved unaltered by the compacting sediment or mineral action.
7. Those remains are destroyed by pressure and heat when sedimentary rock is metamorphosed.

8. The rock is gradually folded and eroded and the fossils are exposed on the surface.

FRECKLES

1. When exposed to ultraviolet (UV) rays, either from the sun or sun-tanning lights, the outer layer of the skin (epidermis) thickens and the skin's pigment-producing cells increase their production of the pigment melanin.

2. Melanin production is the skin's natural way of protecting it against future sun exposure. Uneven distribution of melanin in the skin may cause heavy deposits of the pigment at one spot, which creates a freckle.

3. As the skin is exposed to the sun and melanin is produced and distributed, freckles can appear darker because they are already accumulations of the pigment. This is why freckles appear lighter during the winter and darker during the summer.

FREEZE-DRYING

The freeze-drying process preserves food by rapid freezing, followed by complete dehydration to remove all the moisture.

1. Food is placed in a tightly sealed chamber between hollow plates containing refrigerant liquid. A typical machine consists of a freeze-drying chamber with several shelves attached to heating units, a freezing coil connected to a refrigerator compressor, and a vacuum pump.

2. The refrigerant liquid freezes the food while a high-powered pump creates a vacuum.

3. When the food is frozen hard and the pump has removed nearly all of the air, the cold refrigerant liquid in the hollow plates is replaced by warm gas.

4. Since the pressure is so low, the ice in the food turns directly into water vapor without first turning into water.

5. The water vapor flows out of the freeze-drying chamber, past the freezing coil. The water vapor condenses onto the freezing coil in solid ice form.

6. To keep the nutrients, flavor, and appearance, the food must be frozen as quickly as possible, though the drying process is slow.

7. The vapor is immediately removed by the vacuum pump, but the food takes about 20 hours to completely dehydrate.

8. The food is then packaged to protect it and to seal out all oxygen and moisture.

9. If the package is properly prepared and packaged, it can last for a year or more until it is restored to its original form with water.

FREEZING

1. The lower the temperature, the slower the molecules move and the more they attract one another.

2. At a certain temperature, depending on the liquid, the molecules attract one another so strongly that they move very little and the liquid turns into a solid.

3. The freezing point of a liquid or the melting point of a solid is the temperature at which the solid and liquid phases are in equilibrium.

4. The rate of freezing of the liquid is equal to the rate of melting of the solid and the quantities of solid and liquid remain constant.

FROG CROAK

1. The male frog inhales, closes his nostrils and mouth.

2. He forces the air back and forth between the mouth and lungs.

3. The sound is produced when the air passes over the vocal cords and causes them to vibrate.

4. Many kinds of frogs have vocal sacs that open into the mouth. These sacs become filled with air and enlarge, acting as resonators to give the croaking a peculiar sound.

FROST ACTION / ICE WEDGING

Frost action, also known as ice wedging, is what happens when the road buckles after a cold winter.

1. When water freezes, the molecules realign and expand about nine percent in volume.

2. When frozen water is confined, as under streets, this expansion can create a force of up to 1,400 pounds per square inch.

3. Repeated freezing and thawing throughout the year produces small-scale patterned ground cracks.

4. Repeated freezing and thawing also tends to stir and sort granular sediments, thus forming circles (stone nets) and polygons a few centimeters to six meters in diameter.

5. Permafrost forms an impermeable substratum that keeps the soil moisture available for frost action.

6. Ice lenses form in the soil beneath the pavement. Free water migrates through the soil to a forming ice lens by capillary action (akin to wicking). The size of an ice lens depends upon time, upon the quantity of free water available within the soil and from the water table.

7. When the soil freezes, the free water freezes and expands. Once started, ice lenses continue to grow as long as a source of free water is available.

8. Repeated freezing and thawing cracks the surface slowly and produces upward displacement (heaving) or breaking off of the surface.

FROWNING

1. The frontalis and corrugator supercilii muscles furrow the brow.
2. The nastalis muscle widens the nostrils.
3. The orbicularis oculi muscles narrow the eyes.
4. The platysma and depressors (anguli oris, labii inferioris) pull the mouth and corners of the lips downward and sideways.
5. The mentalis puckers the chin.

FUEL CYCLE OF NUCLEAR MATERIAL

The series of steps involved in supplying fuel for nuclear power reactors.

1. Exploration
2. Mining
3. Milling
4. Uranium conversion
5. Isotopic enrichment
6. Fabrication of fuel elements
7. Interim storage
8. Use in a nuclear reactor
9. Reprocessing to recover the fissionable material remaining in the spent fuel
10. Vitrification (immobilization of waste)
11. Reenrichment of the fuel material
12. Refabrication into new fuel elements
13. Waste disposal

FULFILLMENT IN LIFE

According to Sigmund Freud:

1. Love
2. Work
3. Play

GEOLOGICAL ERAS

1. Pre-Cambrian Era / Neoproterozoic (4.5 billion years ago): Azoic Period, Archaeozoic Period, Proterozoic Period (rise of metazoans, animals having the body composed of cells differentiated into tissues and organs and usually a digestive cavity lined with specialized cells)

2. Paleozoic Era: Cambrian Period (545 million years ago) (first fishes, abundant shell-bearing marine invertebrates, trilobites), Ordovician Period (extinctions, first land plants, expansion of marine shelled invertebrates), Silurian Period (first jawed fishes, first air-breathing arthropods), Devonian Period (extinctions, first insects, first amphibians, first forests, first sharks), Mississippian Period (abundant amphibians and sharks, scale trees, seed ferns), Pennsylvanian Period (great coal forests, conifers, first reptiles), Permian Period (massive extinctions including trilobites; mammal-like reptiles)

3. Mesozoic Era (245 million years ago): Triassic Period (first dinosaurs, first mammals, abundant cycads), Jurassic Period (first birds, abundant dinosaurs and ammonites), Cretaceous Period (massive extinctions, first flowering plants, climax of dinosaurs and ammonites)

4. Cenozoic Era (64 million years ago): Tertiary Period (age of mammals, including Paleocene Epoch, Eocene Epoch, Oligocene Epoch, Miocene Epoch, Pliocene Epoch) and Quaternary Period (modern mammals, including Pleistocene Epoch and Recent Epoch)

GEYSER

It is believed that violent geyser-steam discharges are generated by the flashing of groundwater at some depth below the surface (100 meters/328 feet or more).

1. At the earth's surface close to sea level, fresh water boils at about 100°C (212°F). If the pressure is increased, however, the boiling temperature rises.

2. The neck of a geyser is like a very long vertical pipe or throat.

3. Deep underground, water in a volcanic area is superheated before it reaches the boiling point.

4. When it boils, bubbles of steam rise, expanding and pushing some water out at the surface.

5. As it boils, the water spills out and thus slightly reduces the pressure beneath it and the boiling point is lowered, which in turn allows slightly deeper water to boil. In this way, the boiling level propagates rapidly down the throat, changing in character from a passive boiling at the surface to a violent flashing in the lower parts.

6. The superheated steam and water are pushed out as a powerful jet (flashing).

7. When enough water has seeped back and heated up, the process starts again.

GLACIER FORMATION

1. Newly fallen snow contains masses of air between individual snowflakes.

2. As more snow settles onto a previous fall, the flakes beneath

are compressed and deformed by partial melting and refreezing, into smaller, rounder ice particles.

3. These adhere to each other, initially forming small ice granules and then a material consisting of larger granules (firn).

4. As more snow falls, further compression occurs, causing the firn to weld into solid, dense glacial ice.

5. As glacial ice is formed, there is a gradual decrease in the proportion of air to snow or ice. Depending on the location, the process can take from 5 to 3,000 years.

GLACIER MOVEMENT

1. Ice tends to build up in the accumulation area of a glacier, a simple consequence of the weight and creep properties of ice.

2. A surface slope towards the ablation zone (area of melting or vaporization) is developed.

3. This slope and the weight of the ice induce a shear stress throughout the mass.

4. Glacier ice is under such pressure that the crystals melt slightly and can slide easily.

5. The rate of movement varies according to the slope of the valley, thickness of the glacier, roughness of the valley bottom, and temperature.

6. The differences in the rate of movement within a glacier creates crevasses.

7. Rocks and stones (moraine) fall onto a glacier and are picked up by the ice at the bottom of the glacier.

8. As the glacier moves, the rocks and stones act like sandpaper to widen, deepen, and flatten valley floors.

GLASS

1. Enormous furnaces are used to melt the raw ingredients for making glass.

2. The raw ingredients are silica, lime/frit, and soda, which are combined with cullet (broken/waste glass) and salt cake.

3. Jets of flame pour from the sides of the furnace to melt the ingredients (1,300 degrees C or 2,400 degrees F, but this varies).

4. The melted glass is poured in a stream on the surface of a bath of molten tin.

5. The molten tin makes the glass spread into a flat sheet.

6. As it floats, the glass cools to 1,100 degrees Fahrenheit (because the tin is cooler) and solidifies, smoothing out irregularities in the surface.

7. When cooled, the glass emerges from the bath onto rollers.

8. The glass is cut into sheets and washed with jets of water.

9. Rollers carry off the finished glass sheets.

10. If glass products are being made instead of glass sheets, then after the furnace melting, lumps of hot, soft glass are placed into molds.

11. Air is blown into the molds to make the glass inflate into a bubble, which expands to form the object in the mold.

12. The glass then cools and sets hard.

GLOBAL WARMING

1. Sunlight heats the Earth.

2. Dust from volcanic eruptions affects the global climate.

3. Gases from factories, cars, and forest fires also build up as gases and vapor in the atmosphere.

4. These gases form a layer that traps heat within the atmosphere and reflects it back to earth, rather than allowing it to escape into the outer atmosphere.

5. As the planet warms up, the water in the oceans will expand.

6. The water locked up in glaciers and polar ice caps melts as the climate becomes warmer.

7. This causes sea levels to rise even higher, and many habitats disappear underwater.

8. It also becomes more difficult for living things to adapt to the harmful materials released into the environment as a result of human activities.

GLOW IN THE DARK

1. A phosphor (e.g., zinc sulfide, strontium aluminate) is mixed into plastic and molded.

2. This phosphor is "charged" by holding it close to a light bulb or by simply being in a room that is lit.

3. When you turn out the lights, the phospor emits a soft light, usually green. The persistence factor of the particular phosphor will affect how long it lasts.

GLUE

Glue is a gelatin-like adhesive substance extracted from animal tissue, particularly hides and bones, or from fish, casein (milk solids), or vegetables.

1. Glue contains chemicals. The chemicals are made of molecules that pull on each other with a strong force.

2. Glue fills in the tiny gaps between the surfaces of two objects, so that the molecules of glue pull at the molecules in the two surfaces.

3. The glue bonds by solvent evaporation. The solvent in all-purpose school glue is water.

4. When the water evaporates, the polyvinylacetate latex that has spread into a material's crevices forms a flexible bond.

5. The glue forms weaker hydrogen bonds (or van der Waals bonds) with the surface and is not so firmly attached. The glue's polymer molecules may also extend into the surface, in cracks and fissures, to form a more sturdy attachment. Glue will bind more effectively to a porous, rough surface than to a very smooth, impermeable one.

6. As the glue sets, the chemicals change into new chemicals that pull even more strongly.

7. The objects stick together.

GOLF SWING

A golfer's power is originated and generated by movements of the body. The proper stance and posture enables a golfer to be perfectly balanced and poised throughout the swing.

1. The golfer begins by gripping the club. Both hands work together as one unit.

2. Power is transferred from the player's body to his or her arms and then to the hands.

3. The club is raised above the shoulders and back. On the backswing, the order of movement is: hands, arms, shoulders, hips.

4. The hands start the clubhead back a split second before the arms start back.

5. The arms begin their movement a split second before the shoulders begin to turn.

6. Just before the hands reach hip level, the shoulders, as they turn, automatically start pulling the hips around.

7. As the hips begin to turn, they pull the front leg to the back.

This turning of the hips creates stored-up tension in the muscles between the hips and shoulders.

8. The increased tension unwinds the upper part of the body—the shoulders, arms, and hands in that order.

9. The body and legs move the feet.

10. The shoulders rotate in a continuous incline at the same angle with the ball. The arms and hands (and club) also remain on this same angle of inclination as they swing back.

11. The downswing is initiated by turning the hips. The weight is transferred to the back foot.

12. The plane for the downswing is less steeply inclined than the backswing and its lateral axis points slightly to the outside of the golfer's target.

13. The movement of the hips starts a chain of actions. The contracted muscles of the front hip and thigh start to spin the hip

backswing
of golf club

downswing
of golf club

end of golf swing

around. At the same time, the muscles of the rear hip and thigh start to move the rear hip forward.

14. The cohesive movement of the body, legs, and arms toward the target multiplies the speed and power of the swing. The order of movement on the downswing is hips, shoulders, arms, and hands.

15. The arms and hands are automatically lowered by the movement of the hips.

16. In this chain of action, the shoulders and upper part of the body conduct the multiplying power into the arms.

17. The arms multiply it again and pass it on to the hands.

18. The hands multiply it in turn. The clubhead is tearing through the air at an incredible speed as the golfer hits through the ball. The hands work together and the golfer hits the target as hard with the left hand as with the right hand.

19. The forward wrist begins to supinate at impact. The raised wristbone points to the target.

20. At the point just beyond impact, both arms are straight and the clubhead reaches its maximum speed.

21. The shoulders catch up with the hips at the end of the swing.

GOOSE BUMPS

1. When the body is cold, blood vessels in the skin narrow to conserve heat. This reaction can also occur when you are very afraid or angry.

2. A tiny muscle attached to the base of each hair shortens, pulling the hair upright and lifting the surrounding skin.

3. Small bumps, called goose bumps, appear.

4. This creates a mat of hair, which traps a layer of air next to the skin—helping the body trap heat.

GORGES

A gorge is a deep, narrow valley with cliff walls.

1. Below the surface of the earth, a stream eats away the limestone along a fault line.
2. As the water follows the bedding planes, it opens up caves and caverns.
3. The water enlarges and interlinks a number of caves and caverns, forming a huge cavity.
4. Eventually, the limestone roof caves in, leaving a deep rocky chasm called a gorge.

GPS

The Global Positioning System, used for cell phones, car navigation systems, and other devices, uses 24 satellites which circle the Earth every 12 hours at an altitude of about 12,000 miles.

1. A global positioning system (GPS) receiver determines its position on Earth by calculating its range (distance) from each of at least three satellites, whose exact positions are known. The GPS receiver picks up signals which are being continuously transmitted from satellites.
2. The satellites are powered by solar panels and each contains four highly accurate atomic clocks so that the transmission time of the signals is known precisely.
3. Each satellite broadcasts timing signals, which take time to reach the receiver on earth.
4. The receiver's onboard clock is synchronized with the satellites' atomic clocks, enabling it to calculate the signals' travel times. It generates a constantly changing code.
5. The range of each satellite is calculated, using the time difference between the travel time of its signal and the signal speed (speed of radio waves). The receiver has to lock on to at least

three different satellite signals in order to locate itself in three-dimensional space.

6. Satellite orbits vary slightly over time, so a network of ground stations monitors the orbits and sends updated position information to each satellite along with timing signals.

7. The receiver calculates its distance from Satellite One from a point on the surface of Sphere One. The receiver determines the amount of delay by delaying its own code until it matches the satellite's.

8. The receiver calculates its distance from Satellite Two from a point on the surface of Sphere Two. Since the receiver must also be on the surface of Sphere One, it must be located where the two surfaces intersect.

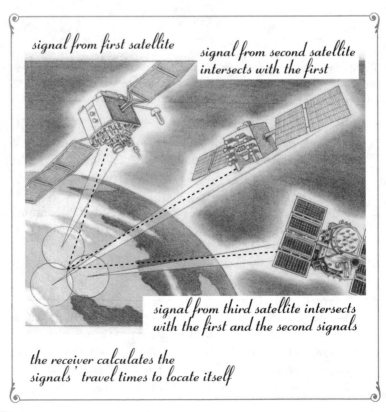

signal from first satellite

signal from second satellite intersects with the first

signal from third satellite intersects with the first and the second signals

the receiver calculates the signals' travel times to locate itself

9. The receiver also calculates its distance from Satellite Three from a point on the surface of Sphere Three. Since the receiver is also on the surfaces of Sphere One and Sphere Two, it must be located where all three surfaces intersect. This technique is known as triangulation.

10. Using triangulation, the three measurements are combined with the satellite position data to locate the receiver. The receiver's position can be fixed with just these three ranges.

11. A fourth range measurement is needed in order to synchronize the receiver and satellite clocks.

GRASSHOPPER LEAP

1. As the insect leaps, its wings open. The front pair is leathery and protects the delicate fanlike wings at the back.

2. The back legs kick out as the grasshopper leaps forward.

3. The wings close as the grasshopper lands.

GRAY HAIR

1. Each hair is connected to a follicle, a small cavity or gland under the surface of the skin.

2. Each follicle creates protein fibers that make up hair. Hair is always growing by being pushed out of the follicle.

3. Hair color comes from pigments (melanin) that are added to the hair follicle as each hair is created. Hair color is determined by genes and each hair cell produces melanin.

4. At some point as one ages, the pigment-producing cells in the hair start to die. It does not happen to every hair at the same time.

5. The hairs that grow from these follicles are actually colorless, but because of the refraction of light, they appear to be white. White hairs mixed with other colors give the look of gray to the hair.

GREENHOUSE EFFECT

The greenhouse effect is the warming of the Earth's surface and lower atmosphere that tends to intensify with an increase in atmospheric carbon dioxide. See also **Global Warming.**

1. The Sun's energy warms the Earth.
2. The Earth radiates away heat as infrared energy.
3. Molecules of carbon dioxide and other "greenhouse gases" intercept some outgoing infrared energy and radiate it back toward Earth.
4. Human activities, especially the burning of fossil fuels, add "greenhouse gases" to the atmosphere.
5. Greenhouse gases send too much heat back, warming the Earth and changing the climate.

GREENHOUSE WARMING

This applies to a glass-enclosed area in which plants grow.

1. Glass lets light rays pass through easily but lets infrared rays (heat) pass less easily.
2. The sun's light can pass easily into the greenhouse, but its heat cannot.
3. Inside the greenhouse, some of the sun's light rays are absorbed by the objects and converted into heat, which cannot get out again easily.
4. The heat is trapped and gradually builds up.

HAIL

Hailstones are no smaller than 2/10 inch in diameter and can grow larger than a softball. Ice pellets are drops of water that freeze as they fall and form sleet. Graupel (soft hail) is ice crystals or snow that falls through supercooled cloud droplets and freeze to them.

1. A frozen raindrop or snow pellet is kept from falling by a thunderstorm's updraft.

2. Supercooled drops in the updraft freeze to the growing hailstone.

3. Many hailstones grow in layers, sometimes by riming (incrustation of ice or snow) and sometimes by supercooled drops spreading out to form glaze.

4. The hailstone falls when it grows too heavy for the updraft to continue holding it up or when the updraft weakens.

HAIR

Hair is continually shed and renewed by the operation of alternating cycles of growth, rest, fallout, and renewed growth.

1. The growth phase (anagen) of human scalp hair lasts 3–6 years.

2. A regressing phase (catagen) is marked by a decrease in cell proliferation, the shortening of hair follicles, and an anchored club hair (hair in resting state) is produced. The growing cells in the follicles stop and they shrink rapidly. This stage is brief and variable.

3. The quiescence phase (telogen) is the resting phase of hair. Each hair will be lost or shed at the end of this cycle. This can last up to five months.

4. As the hair is lost a new cycle of hair growth in that same follicle has already begun.

5. The dermal papilla re-descends into the subcutaneous fat and the whole follicle regrows within 3 months.

HAIRDRYER

1. The hairdryer contains a miniature electric heater or heating coil and a simple motor-driven fan.

2. When turned on, electrical current flows through the dryer.

3. The heating element is made from special resistance wire, which

acts to partially resist the flow of electricity through it—thereby producing heat as the electricity forces its way through.

4. The current makes the motor spin, which drives the fan.

5. The fan blows air down the dryer's barrel, over and through the heating element.

6. The heat from the element warms the air by forced convection and the hot air comes out of the end of the barrel.

7. Moisture-laden air is blown away from your hair, replacing it with fresh dry air. The blowing air speeds up the evaporation from the hair's surface by increasing the temperature of the air around each strand. The increase in temperature makes it easier for water molecules to lose their attraction and move into a gaseous state.

HALOGEN LAMP

1. A halogen lamp bulb is made of heat-resistant quartz. This allows a higher filament temperature, which produces a brighter, whiter light.

2. The tungsten filament becomes very hot when an electric current passes through it.

3. The atoms on the filament evaporate from its surface.

4. Tungsten atoms mix with argon and halogen gases in the tube.

5. In the cooler part of the lamp near the bulb wall, tungsten atoms react chemically with molecules of halogen gas to form tungsten-halide molecules.

6. These tungsten-halide molecules eventually drift back toward the filament.

7. Tungsten-halide is unstable at high temperatures, so those molecules near the hot filament decompose, depositing tungsten back onto the filament, leaving behind molecules of halogen gas.

8. This increases filament life and maintains brightness by preventing tungsten deposits on the bulb.

HEADPHONES

A headphone is basically a miniature loudspeaker. A speaker is the reverse of a microphone; it takes electrical signal and translates it back into the physical vibrations to create sound waves.

1. The pair of earphones contains a thin but rigid cone (diaphragm) fixed to a coil.
2. The electric signal goes to the coil, which is inside a magnetic field created by a circular permanent magnet around or inside the coil.
3. The coil also produces its own magnetic field, which varies in strength as the varying signal passes through it.
4. The two magnetic fields push and pull on each other, causing the coil to vibrate in step with the variations of the signal. A stereo signal constantly reverses the flow of electricity. This alternating current causes the polar orientation of the electromagnet to reverse itself many times a second.
5. When the electrical current flowing through the voice coil changes direction, the coil's polar orientation reverses. This changes the magnetic forces between the voice coil and the permanent magnet, moving the coil and attached diaphragm back and forth.
6. The diaphragm vibrates at the same frequencies as the original sound waves that struck the two or more microphones or other sound sources, causing the surrounding air to vibrate and reproduce the original sound waves.

HEARING

1. Mammals have special outer flaps to channel sounds into the ear.
2. Sound waves entering the ear canal make the eardrum vibrate.

3. The ossicles (three tiny ear bones) pass the vibrations from the eardrum to the inner ear.

4. The inner ear (also called the labyrinth) has a complex system of canals. The organ of hearing is in the snail-like cochlea. Structures in the inner ear translate the vibrations into nerve messages.

5. Waves in the cochlea cause pressure changes in the fluid. Motion of the fluid in the canals registers the slightest movement of the head.

6. The waves stimulate the thousands of sensory hair cells.

7. The hairs translate mechanical movement into electrical sensory impulses.

8. The hairs cause nerve fibers (receptors) to send impulses directly to the brain.

9. Sound waves gradually fade out.

HEART

The heart, although a single organ, can be considered as two pumps that propel blood through two different circuits. The left one sends blood out along the arteries to the whole body. This blood gives up oxygen and returns along veins to the right pump. From here it is sent to the lungs to get more oxygen. A reasonable estimate for the number of heartbeats in a lifetime is about three billion.

1. The right atrium receives venous blood from the head, chest, and arms via the large vein called the superior vena cava and receives blood from the abdomen, pelvic region, and legs via the inferior vena cava.

2. Blood then passes through the tricuspid valve to the right ventricle, which propels it through the pulmonary artery to the lungs.

3. In the lungs, venous blood comes in contact with inhaled air, picks up oxygen, and loses carbon dioxide.

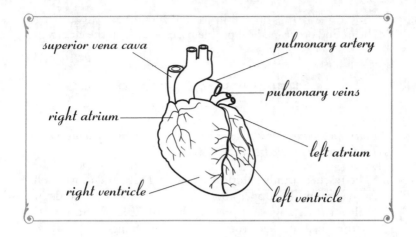

superior vena cava

pulmonary artery

pulmonary veins

right atrium

left atrium

right ventricle

left ventricle

4. Oxygenated blood is returned to the left atrium through the pulmonary veins.

5. It is pumped to all of the body (except the lungs) from the left ventricle.

6. Valves in the heart allow blood to flow in one direction only and help maintain the pressure required to pump the blood.

HEAT AFFECTING THE BODY

1. The hypothalamus, the body's thermostat, determines that the body is too warm.

2. Blood vessels expand and the heart beats faster and fuller to increase blood flow.

3. Blood carries heat from deep inside the body to the skin's surface.

4. Evaporation of sweat from the skin carries away large amounts of heat, thereby cooling the body. High humidity interferes with this process.

5. If fluids lost by sweating are not replaced, the body becomes dehydrated and heat exhaustion may result.

6. Additional stress on the heart and blood vessels can trigger heart and other medical problems, especially in the elderly.

HEIMLICH MANEUVER

The Heimlich maneuver is an emergency procedure to help someone who is choking due to food lodged in the trachea.

1. The rescuer stands behind the choking victim and wraps his arms around his upper abdomen, joining his two hands just below the rib cage and pressing his balled left hand into the victim's belly between the navel and the rib cage.

2. Grasping one fist in the other, the rescuer then makes four sharp upward squeezes or thrusts into the victim's abdomen, thus forcing out of his lungs the air that will expel the foreign object from the throat.

3. An unconscious victim is laid on his back and the thrusts administered from above with the rescuer straddling the victim's thighs.

4. The abdominal thrusts are repeated until the foreign object is expelled.

HIBERNATION

1. Animals that hibernate (sleep all winter) try to put on as much fat as possible during the autumn. This is a special kind of fat, called brown fat. This special fat is found across the back and shoulders of hibernating animals, close to an animal's organs (brain, liver).

2. Just before winter, a special substance in the blood of hibernating animals (HIT, Hibernation Inducement Trigger) is triggered. This is still somewhat of a mystery.

3. The animal goes to sleep.

4. The heart rate and body temperature drop dramatically.

5. In some animals, like the woodchuck, the teeth stop growing.

6. True hibernators do get up every few weeks to nibble on food and, in the case of the woodchuck, use an underground toilet room.

7. Bears are not true hibernators and are easily awakened from their long winter naps. Bears, skunks, raccoons, and opossums breathe a little more slowly and lower their body temperature a few degrees while sleeping, but they wake up to forage between winter snows.

8. Brown fat works fast to deliver quick energy to an animal coming out of hibernation.

9. Cold-blooded animals like snakes, turtles, and frogs cannot warm themselves up, so they need to find a way to protect themselves from the cold. Frogs and turtles bury themselves in the mud below the frostline. They get oxygen from air trapped in the mud. In the spring when the sun warms the mud, they come out. Snakes may go underground or into other sheltered places.

HOLE IN PASTA

1. Pasta is made by hand or with a mixer.

2. The dough is kneaded until it reaches the correct consistency, and then it is pushed or extruded through a die, a metal disc with holes in it. Hollow pasta, such as macaroni or penne, requires a special type of pasta maker that comes with die attachments.

3. The shape of the holes in the die governs the shape of the pasta. For spaghetti, the die has round holes. For macaroni wheels, the die pushes out the pasta, leaving a large hole in the middle, and gaps left by the spokes. As the pasta emerges, the spokes join up to the center.

4. When the extruded pasta reaches the right length, it is cut with sharp blades that rotate beneath the die.

5. The pasta is then sent through large dryers which circulate hot, moist air to slowly dry the pasta. To be dried properly, pasta needs alternating heat and moisture.

HOLES IN SWISS CHEESE

The cow's milk used to make Swiss cheese originated in the Emme River Valley in Switzerland.

1. The curd, formed from rennet, the stomach lining membrane of a calf, is shaped into large wheels about 36 inches in diameter and about 6 inches thick.

2. The wheels are salted in strong brine and wrapped to prevent drying.

3. Complete ripening (3–6 months) is done in humidity- and temperature-controlled rooms where the microbial enzymes slowly change the curd's composition, texture, and flavor.

4. The enzymes Streptococcus thermophilus, Lactobacillus bulgaricus, and Propionibacterium shermanii are added in the ripening process to give Swiss cheese its characteristic flavors. The latter bacterium lives on lactic acid excreted by the first two bacteria, giving off large amounts of propionic acid and carbon dioxide gas.

5. The gas collects in large pockets to form the holes (or "eyes") in the cheese.

HOMING PIGEON

There are two hypotheses regarding this phenomenon.

1. Young pigeons learn an "odor map" by smelling different odors that reach their home in the winds from various directions. The pigeons learn that a certain odor is carried on winds

blowing from the east, for example. If a pigeon were transported eastward, the odor would tell it to fly westward to return home.

2. Another hypothesis is that a bird may be able to extract its home latitude and longitude from the earth's magnetic field, as there is some magnetite in birds' brains.

HOMOGENIZATION OF MILK

Homogenization is the process of reducing substances, such as the fat globules in milk, to extremely small particles and distributing them uniformly throughout a liquid, such as milk.

1. Fat is lighter (less dense) than water, so it floats to the top of a liquid. Unhomogenized milk has cream on top. If fat globules are made small enough, they cannot rise in a liquid but are rather kept suspended in place because water molecules are bombarding them from all directions.

2. Milk is shot out of a pipe and forced through small openings of a sieve under high pressure (2,500 pounds per square inch), thus breaking up the fat globules and making them small enough to stay suspended.

3. When milk is properly homogenized, the cream will not rise to the top.

HONEY

The honey-making process takes about three days. The bee colony's survival in winter depends on an ample supply of honey.

1. A worker bee visits a flower, checks for nectar, and sips nectar if there is some.

2. The bee stores the nectar in a special sac and flies back to the hive.

3. When the bee is in the flower sipping the nectar, pollen dust falls on it.

4. When the bee flies off, it carries the pollen dust, which falls off inside another plant. This helps plants reproduce.

5. In the bee's sac, the sugars found in the nectar undergo a chemical change.

6. At the hive, the bee regurgitates the nectar and passes the thin runny fluid to a house bee, which mixes it with glandular secretions in its mouth and evaporates some of the water.

7. The bee then deposits the nectar in an open cell in the honeycomb.

8. Bees favor hexagons, which have the shortest walls, so less precious wax is needed. Secreting wax from glands in her abdomen, the worker bee lays down a thick ridge for the cell wall.

9. To prevent honey and nectar from dripping out, the worker bee tips the cells up 13 degrees from the base.

10. Other house bees fan the open cells continuously with their wings, evaporating water and completing the transformation of the nectar into honey.

11. Cells filled with finished honey are sealed with an airtight cap of wax until the bees need the food.

HONEYBEE DANCE

In the hive, honeybees use dance as a means of communication. Every wriggle, waggle, spin, and step is loaded with valuable information. The dance that a returning forager performs to give details of a food source is sophisticated in nature.

The round dance is used for food found within 80 feet (25 meters) of the hive .

1. The honeybee walks around in a tight circle, regularly changing direction.

2. Watching closely, her nestmates touch her constantly with their antennae.

3. The number of changes of direction and overall vigor of the dance indicate the quality of the food.

The waggle dance is a figure-eight movement used to indicate a distant food source.

1. The movement is a figure eight that is flattened top to bottom.

2. The longer the straight walk between the two ovals, the more she waggles her abdomen—and the farther away the food is.

3. The dancer turns herself into a compass to send the bees in the right direction. The angle of her straight run from the vertical (she is dancing on a vertical hanging slat) is the same as the angle between the Sun (as seen from the hive's entrance) and the food.

4. Using her internal clock, she is able to compensate for the Sun's movement.

5. The more high-frequency buzzes she makes and the vigor of the dance indicate the quality of the food.

A dance between the round dance and waggle dance is used for food at distances of 27–110 yards (25–100 meters).

HORSE EVOLUTION

The evolution of modern horses from a dog-size ancestor took over 50 million years and did not follow a single straight line but branched off in various directions and included genera that are now extinct. Here are the four main ancestors leading to equus, the modern horse.

1. Hyracotherium's forefeet had four toes supported by a pad. It had spayed toes and was a forest dweller. It was about the size of a dog.

2. Mesohippus had three toes on all feet with a prominent central toe. It had splayed toes and was a forest dweller.

3. Merychippus's feet had three toes but the weight was increasingly carried on the middle toe. This horse lived in grasslands.

4. Pliohippus had single-toed feet but the remnants of other toes persisted in some. This horse was also a grazer.

5. Equus, the modern horse, carries all of its weight on a single-hoofed toe. All of these changes increased the speed with which it could flee if an attack was imminent.

HOT-AIR BALLOON

Hot air balloons are based on a very basic scientific principle: warmer air rises in cooler air. Essentially, hot air is lighter than cool air.

1. A hot air balloon has three essential parts: the burner, which heats the air; the balloon envelope, which holds the air; and the basket, which carries the passengers.

2. To keep the balloon rising, the air needs to be reheated; this is done with a burner positioned under an open balloon envelope.

3. Propane in the burner flows out in liquid form and is ignited by a pilot light.

4. As the flame burns, it heats up the metal in the surrounding tubing. When the tubing becomes hot, it heats the propane flowing through it. This changes the propane from a liquid to a gas (hot air), before it is ignited.

5. The hot air rises into the envelope, which is constructed from long nylon gores, reinforced with sewn-in webbing.

6. The hot air won't escape from the hole at the bottom of the envelope because buoyancy keeps it moving up.

7. As the air in the balloon cools, the pilot can reheat it by firing the burner. If the pilot continually fires the fuel jets, the balloon will continue to rise.

HOUSE WIRING SYSTEM

Electricity is the lifeblood of a home, powering appliances and systems. When supplied by a power company, electric current enters a home through underground or overhead cables. It goes through a meter that measures how much electricity is used and then flows to a service panel that distributes it over a wire network in the house. See also **Electricity to Buildings.**

1. Overhead or underground cables bring electric current into a building.
2. The service panel distributes it throughout the house or building over a network of circuits running inside ceilings and walls.
3. Protected by circuit breakers or fuses, the circuits carry 120 or 240 volts regulated by a pair of 120-volt hot wires that transport power from the source.
4. A neutral third wire returns current to the panel, completing the circuit. A safety ground wire protects the system when over-voltage occurs.
5. A meter connected to the panel measures the flow of electricity in kilowatt-hours.

HUMAN COLOR PERCEPTION

1. White light consists of a mixture of wavelengths.
2. When light strikes the retina at the back of the eye, it stimulates one or more classes of receptor cells called cones. Each class of cone responds to different wavelengths of light (long wavelengths = red, orange, yellow; medium wavelengths = yellow, green, cyan; short wavelengths = blue, violet; mix of long and medium wavelengths = red and green).
3. When light of a particular wavelength stimulates a class of cones, the cones send electric signals to the brain's visual cortex via the optic nerve and the light's color is processed.

1. *Ardipithecus ramidus* is the most primitive hominid found so far, with more chimpanzee-like features than any other human ancestor. It may have walked upright and lived in the forest. Lived 4.4 mya.

2. *Australopithecus anamensis* exhibited some chimp-like characteristics; its jaws were more primitive than those of later hominids. The humerus (an arm bone) was quite human-like and characteristics of its tibia (lower leg bone) indicate it walked on two feet. Lived 4.2–3.9 mya.

3. *Australopithecus afarensis,* the species which includes "Lucy," the 3.2 million-year-old fossil, had small braincases and relatively large teeth and chewing muscles similar to those of chimpanzees. Their teeth and leg and pelvis bones exhibited human-like characteristics. They were 3.5–5 feet tall and walked upright. Lived 3.5–2.9 mya.

4. *Australopithecus africanus* had a slightly larger brain, smaller canine teeth, and larger molars. The wear of the teeth suggests it ate fruits and foliage. Lived 3.0–2.4 mya.

5. *Australopithecus robustus* had a large, heavier, thicker skull, as well as a jaw and large teeth that were well adapted to chewing. Like some present-day apes, this species had a "sagittal crest" (a

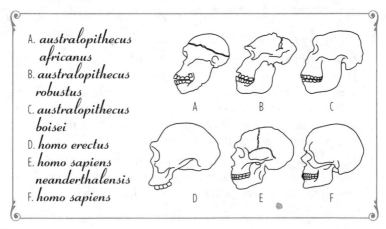

A. *australopithecus africanus*
B. *australopithecus robustus*
C. *australopithecus boisei*
D. *homo erectus*
E. *homo sapiens neanderthalensis*
F. *homo sapiens*

A   B   C

D   E   F

ridge running from front to back on the top of the skull) from which muscles running to the jaw were attached, 2.1–1.6 mya.

6. *Australopithecus boisei* had an even larger skull and teeth. It walked upright. Lived 2.3–1.1 mya.

7. *Homo habilis* ("handy man") was apparently the first species to make and use primitive stone tools. About five feet tall and weighing 100 pounds, it had a larger brain than the largest Autralopithecus brain, but smaller than the Homo erectus brain. Lived 2.4–1.5 mya.

8. *Homo erectus* (first example: "Java Man") had a skeleton very similar to that of modern humans, although thicker and heavier. Homo erectus was probably the first hominid to use fire, 1.8 mya–300,000 years ago.

9. The archaic *Homo sapiens* (also known as *Homo heidelbergensis*) had a brain that was larger than the Homo erectus, and it was enclosed in a skull that was more rounded. Lived 500,000–200,000 years ago.

10. *Homo sapiens neanderthalensis* averaged 5.5 feet in height and had short limbs. Neanderthal's brain was larger than the brain of living humans, although its shape was longer from front to back and not as rounded in the front. Lived 230,000–30,000 years ago. (Recently, many experts have claimed that Neanderthals are "cousins" and not immediate predecessors of modern humans. This is an area of continued study and much controversy.)

11. *Homo sapiens* (modern, also known as *Homo sapiens sapiens*) have been around for the past 120,000 years. Homo sapiens living about 40,000 years ago made elaborate tools out of bone, antler, ivory, stone, and wood, and produced fine artwork in the form of carvings and cave paintings.

HUNGER

The hunger center is responsible for the long-term, metabolic, regulation of food intake over weeks and months. The hunger center maintains normal quantities of nutrient stores and controls physiological hunger.

1. The brain has a hunger center in the hypothalamus section that acts like a brake on the activities of the stomach and intestines. When the bloodstream has sufficient nutritive materials, the hunger center stops the activities of the stomach and intestines.

2. When there is a lack of nutritive materials in the bloodstream, the intestines and stomach become active. This is why your stomach rumbles when you are hungry.

3. When glucose concentration in the blood is lowered, hunger develops, which increases feeding activity until the glucose concentration stimulates the satiety center to eliminate the hunger.

4. When amino acids concentration in the blood decreases, hunger increases, although this effect is not as powerful as the need for glucose.

5. When the quantity of fatty molecules in the body increases, physiological hunger decreases.

6. When exposed to cold weather there is a tendency to eat more as cold temperature interaction in the hypothalamus increases the metabolic rate and provides fat for insulation to correct for the cold state.

7. Appetite, located in the brain stem, is the mechanism that makes one choose the varied diet that the body requires. Appetite includes and is influenced by time of day, smell, and sight of food. Appetite relates to the desire for specific types of food and eating experiences, instead of food in general. Appetite helps select the quality and balance of food as learned by an individual in his or her environment.

8. When you overeat and overstretch the abdominal cavity, nerves in the upper gastrointestinal tract signal to stop eating.

9. The satiety center, which is neurologically connected to the hunger center and the appetite, signals when the hunger is satisfied and extinguishes the need for food. When these "eating factors" controlled in the brain stem have been satisfied, the hunger center in the hypothalamus becomes temporarily inhibited.

10. Since complete inhibition of the hypothalamus does not occur

until both hunger and appetite are satisfied, you may desire food soon after you have eaten if appetite has been satisfied but not hunger. This also explains why people eat when they do not have hunger.

HURRICANE

1. For a hurricane to happen, ocean water must be above 80 degrees Fahrenheit. The water must be about 200 feet deep because the storms stir up the ocean and bring up cold water from below.

2. Winds converge near the surface.

3. The air is unstable and rises.

4. The air is humid and begins being pulled up and the extra water vapor supplies more latent heat energy. This latent heat warms the surrounding air, making it lighter. This air rises.

5. Pre-existing winds come in from nearly the same direction and close to the same speeds at all altitudes.

6. The warm wet air rises and as it cools in the cold air above, it condenses into thunderclouds.

7. Thunderstorms begin growing in a disturbed area over the tropical ocean.

8. As the water turns into raindrops, it releases heat.

9. That heat rises in the cloud and sucks up air off the sea surface, fuelling the winds further.

10. The storm grows as it takes moisture and warmth from the sea.

11. Air sinks 20–40 feet a minute in the storm's center, warming it and suppressing clouds. The winds are mostly calm.

12. Air is also rising under the bands of the thunderstorms that make up the storm.

13. Wind reaching the top of the storm, above 40,000 feet, in the eye wall and in bands of thunderstorms flows out. Water vapor left in the air forms cirrostratus clouds, which cap the storm.

14. Thunderstorms organize into a swirl; this is a tropical depression. It is made of bands of thunderstorms that spiral around the center. These "rain bands" or "spiral bands" are 3–30 miles wide and 50–300 miles long.

15. As the winds grow stronger, they get sucked into the middle of the storm where the warm air is rising fastest and eventually spins around a central "eye."

16. Warm humid air is spiraling inward, speeding up as it approaches the center.

17. Air flowing out from the center of the storm begins curving clockwise.

18. Winds spiraling upward in the eye wall (thick clouds surrounding the clear eye) are the fastest.

19. The winds pick up to more than 39 mph and it is called a tropical storm.

20. When the winds reach 74 mph, the storm is a hurricane.

21. Flooding by the storm surge begins before the eye hits land.

22. The hurricane begins to weaken after hitting land. The storm dies out when it runs out of warm seas from which to draw energy or when high-altitude winds destroy the storm's structure.

ICE CUBES MADE IN FREEZER

1. A switch in the circuitry sends a current to a water valve. A measured volume of water flows into the ice cube mold when the shutoff arm is put in the down position.

2. A thermostatically controlled cooling mechanism that freezes the water is then activated.

3. When the thermostat senses that the water has frozen, a heating element warms the bottom of the mold enough to loosen the ice.

4. The electrical circuit then activates the icemaker's motor. The

motor-driven ejector blade scoops the ice cubes from the mold and pushes them into a collection bin underneath the icemaker.

5. The revolving shaft has a notched plastic cam at its base, and just before the cubes are pushed out of the icemaker, the cam catches hold of the shutoff arm and lifts it up.

6. The ejector blade continues to rotate and pushes the ice cubes up to the shutoff arm, which opens, allowing the ice cubes to drop down into the ice-cube tray. After the cubes are ejected, the shutoff arms falls down again.

7. The refrigerant is compressed and pumped.

8. This sequence continues until the quantity of ice cubes in the tray prevents the shutoff arm from falling down or closing—or stops when the arm is manually put in the "off" position.

9. The process is suspended until ice cubes are removed from the tray.

ICE SKATING

1. Skates move over the ice on a thin layer of water.

2. The weight of the skater is concentrated into the skate blades.

3. This causes pressure under the blades, which makes the ice melt as the skates move over it. The pressure on the ice lowers the freezing point, which is why the ice melts.

4. The ice makes the water re-freeze behind the skates.

IGNEOUS ROCK FORMATION

Igneous rock is produced under conditions of intense heat.

1. Molten rock (magma) collects in underground chambers within the earth's crust.

2. It may solidify in place to form an intrusion made of large, slow-cooling crystals.

3. Alternatively, it may erupt at the surface (as a volcano) to form an extrusive igneous rock with quick-cooling, glassy to fine-grained matrix.

IMAX / 3-D PROJECTION

IMAX movies are shot using film that is 10 times normal size and the system uses two films shot simultaneously by a binocular camera.

1. Two films are projected simultaneously through separate polarizing filters, one of which polarizes light vertically and the other horizontally.

2. The film is shown on giant screens that extend beyond the range of the viewers' peripheral vision.

3. A 3-D effect is produced when the projected images are viewed through glasses that have one vertically- and one horizontally-polarizing lens.

4. The vertically-polarizing lens allows vertically-polarized light through to one eye but blocks out the horizontally-polarized projection.

5. The horizontally-polarizing lens transmits horizontally-polarized light to the other eye but blocks out the vertically polarized projection.

6. Each eye sees an image recorded by only one of the camera lenses.

7. The perspective difference between the two images creates a 3-D effect.

IMMUNE SYSTEM ATTACKING COMMON COLD

1. After being carried by infected droplets, virus particles enter the body and invade the cells that line the throat and nose.

2. These virus particles then replicate to produce new viruses, which continue to multiply rapidly.

3. The blood supply brings lymphocytes (white blood cells) to the infected mucosa.

4. The blood vessels within the nasal mucosa swell and cause secretion of excess fluid, resulting in a runny nose.

5. Some types of lymphocytes make virus-specific proteins (antibodies) that immobilize the virus particles, while other types secrete chemical substances that can destroy infected cells.

6. Phagocytes, a type of white blood cell, can engulf and destroy viruses, immobilized virus particles, and damaged cells.

7. After 1–2 weeks, symptoms of the cold subside.

IMMUNIZATION

Naturally acquired active immunity occurs when the person is exposed to a live pathogen, develops the disease, and becomes immune as a result of the primary immune response. Artificially acquired active immunity can be induced by a vaccine, a substance that contains the antigen. A vaccine stimulates a primary response against the antigen without causing symptoms of the disease. Artificially acquired passive immunity is a short-term immunization by the injection of antibodies, such as gamma globulin, that are not produced by the recipient's cells.

Active immunization:

1. A vaccine with dead or harmless living forms of an organism is injected into a person.

2. The vaccine stimulates the immune system to memorize the organism and produce antibodies.

3. In any subsequent infection with this organism, the antibodies stop the infection.

Passive immunization:

1. Blood with antibodies is taken from humans or animals who have had the infection recently.

2. Blood serum containing antibodies is separated from the blood, processed, and injected.

3. Antibodies either attack a current infection or provide short-term protection.

INFANCY

Infants pass through a predictable pattern of development, although each progresses differently. This is generally what happens.

1. After one month, the infant watches the mother's face, and smiles.

2. At about 5–6 weeks, the infant can grasp a finger, is startled by loud noises, and can lift its head 45 degrees.

3. Around six months, the infant can sit up unsupported, roll over, turn head to look around, digest semisolid food, see a full range of colors and shades, distinguish voices from other sounds, grasp between thumb and index finger, pick up a small object, turn to the sound of a familiar voice, and play with his/her own feet. Also, the first lower baby teeth appear.

4. Around nine months, the infant can poke at objects with index finger, babble, shout to attract attention, crawl, walk by holding on to furniture, stand without help, and eat with fingers. The first upper baby teeth appear.

5. At one year, the infant can walk with one or two hands held, understand simple commands, hold arms and legs out to be dressed, learn single words, and drink from a cup.

INSECT FLIGHT

1. The vein along the leading edge of the insect wings is thicker than the rest of the framework of veins, providing the rigidity needed to cut through the air.

2. Power comes from two sets of large muscles attached to the thorax (the part that bears the wings and legs). One pair pulls vertically on the top and bottom of the thorax; the other pair runs longitudinally.

3. Wing muscles work by changing the shape of the thoracic walls.

4. When the vertical muscles contract, the roof of the thorax is pulled down and the wings flap upwards.

5. Rapid contraction of the longitudinal muscles raises the thorax roof and the wings beat downward.

6. The muscles rapidly relax.

7. Since the thoracic walls are elastic, they spring back to their original position—so only minimal muscle power is needed to work the wings.

INSECT POLLINATION

1. In flowering plants, the ovules are contained within a hollow organ called the pistil and the pollen is deposited on the pistil's receptive surface, the stigma. Since one load of pollen contains enough pollen grains to initiate fertilization of many ovules, most individual bee flowers produce many seeds.

2. Insects are attracted to flowers by their color, smell, and sugary nectar.

3. They are able to taste several different sugars and also can be trained to differentiate between aromatic, sweet, or minty odors. Fragrance may be the decisive factor in establishing the honeybee's habit of staying with one species of flower as long as it is abundantly available.

4. As the bee crawls into the flower, the flower's anther rubs up against the bee.

5. Pollen grains are dusted onto the bee and stick to its abdomen. The pollen grains of most bee flowers are sticky, spiny, or highly sculptured, ensuring their adherence to the bodies of the bees.

6. When the bee visits another flower of the same species, pollen grains are transferred to the flower's sticky stigma.

7. The flower both delivers and receives a load of pollen during a single visit of the pollinator, and the pollinator never travels from one flower to another without a full load of pollen.

INSTANT MESSAGING

1. The user's ICQ client connects to the ICQ server, which uses a proprietary protocol for communication.

2. The user enters the user name and password to log onto the server. In doing this, the user also sends the IP address and port assigned to the ICQ client.

3. The server creates a temporary file with the connection information and the user's list of contacts.

4. The server then checks to see if any of the users on the contact list are currently logged on.

5. If the server finds any contacts logged on, it sends a message back to the ICQ client on the user's computer with the connection information for the contacts. It changes the status of that person to "available" or "online."

6. To contact that person, the user clicks on that person's name, enters a message, and clicks Send.

7. The message is sent directly to the ICQ client on that person's computer. The ICQ server is not involved anymore; the communication is directly between the two ICQ clients.

8. The other person gets the user's instant message and responds.

172

9. The conversation continues and when complete, the users close the message window.

10. When the user closes the connection and exits ICQ, the user's ICQ client sends a message to the ICQ server to terminate the session.

11. The ICQ server sends a message to the ICQ client of each person on the user's contact list indicating that the user has logged off. Their computers register the user as "unavailable" or "offline."

12. The ICQ server deletes the temporary file that contained the connection information for the ICQ client.

INTERNET-BASED PHONE CALL

1. Users dial as usual to make a call.

2. An adapter, which plugs into a high-speed Internet connection on one end and to a phone at the other, converts the analog signal of a phone call into the digital packets of the Internet, carrying the call onto the Internet rather than the usual telephone network.

3. The call travels over the Internet to a hub near the call's destination.

4. The hub converts the call back to an analog signal.

5. It funnels the call into the local telephone network.

6. The local telephone network carries the call to the phone dialed by the user.

IRIS-BASED RECOGNITION

The iris is the colored ring of tissue surrounding the pupil of the eye. Every iris has a unique pattern of features that remains constant throughout life and cannot be faked. The iris is a highly effective personal identifier.

1. A series of images of the eye are captured over several seconds by a device similar to a camcorder.

2. The device contains a lens that projects images onto a charge-coupled device (CCD).

3. Analog image data from the CCD is digitized and sent to a processing unit for analysis.

4. Special software processes the images, first identifying and removing any eyelid data.

5. The software then locates the borders between the iris, pupil, and white of the eye and isolates the data for the iris.

6. The program maps the data to points on the iris, using a coordinate system that takes into account the degree of constriction of the pupil.

7. Brightness data is gathered for each iris point and analyzed.

8. The generated code is a binary number and it is stored in a database.

9. During recognition, a person who needs security clearance has his or her iris scanned by the device.

10. The generated code is now compared with the codes held in the database, looking for a match. A 75%-degree of matching is enough evidence to gain the person's clearance; an exact match is not needed.

ISLAND FORMATION

Islands are formed in several ways.

1. Many pieces of continental crust broke off long ago from continents and drifted out to sea.

2. Some low islands also are formed on continental shelves by coral reefs and by sediment building up slowly over time in shallow tropical waters.

3. Another way is that volcanoes on the sea bed (submarine volcanoes) push up so that rock is exposed in the ocean.

4. Above sea level, island formation continues with thousands of far-spreading thin lava flows that build broadly rounded, dome-shaped mountains. This type of island has no life to start out.

5. Soil develops.

6. Plants grow.

7. Animals come to live on the island by swimming, flying, being blown in a storm, or are brought there by humans.

JET STREAMS

A visible and fast-moving river of air known as a jet stream sometimes forms at about 1,000 feet above the ground after sunset.

1. On a clear evening the atmosphere cools down.

2. If conditions are calm, a stable temperature "inversion" sets up where cool air aloft, which is heavier than warm air, sinks to the ground, and any leftover warm air sits on top of it.

3. The stable air in an inversion acts like a nearly solid object and allows the air above it to flow rapidly past the inversion-like wind blowing over water.

4. Differences in air pressure on either side of the developing low-level jet help to concentrate the flow of air into a corridor or stream less than several hundred miles wide.

5. Winds in the stream can flow at speeds of 60 mph or more. Mountain ranges can further enhance low-level jet stream winds.

6. Nighttime, low-level jet streams are marked by a rapid change in wind speed with height.

7. The light of day kills the low-level jet stream. Once the sun begins to heat the land, the lower atmosphere begins to mix as the warm air rises, breaking the inversion.

8. As this happens, the jet stream rises in some places and sinks in others like a giant roller coaster.

9. Without a smooth surface to glide over, the jet stream encounters friction and slows down. But the same conditions the next night could allow the low-level jet stream to reform with equal strength and similar consequences.

JUMPING BEAN

1. A particular moth (Carpocapa saltitans) is partial to laying its eggs inside the flowers and beans of the Mexican bean plant (spurge).
2. The egg hatches inside the seed pod, producing a larva/caterpillar inside the bean.
3. Sunshine or heat on the bean will agitate the larva, causing it to wiggle.
4. The movement of the caterpillar inside the bean makes it appear to jump.
5. At maturity, the caterpillar will spin a cocoon and turn into a moth, emerging from the bean.

JUMP-STARTING CAR

1. Everything in the car should be turned off—lights, A/C or heat, etc.—anything that uses electricity.
2. If there are cracks in the battery casing or it is leaking, do not try to jump-start it.
3. If there is corrosion on the battery terminals, clean them off first.
4. If it is freezing outside, remove the vent caps carefully to see if the battery fluid is frozen. If that is true, the battery cannot be jump-started until the fluid is unfrozen.
5. The car that is assisting should be as close as possible to the car that needs assistance, but must not touch it.
6. Attach one red cable to the positive red battery head of the car that needs to be jump-started.

7. Attach the other red end to the other car's positive red battery head.

8. Attach one black cable to the other car's negative black battery head.

9. Attach the other end of the black cable to the unpainted frame or a metal part of the engine block. Do not attach it anywhere near or onto the battery. This is the grounding end of the connection.

10. The assisting car is started.

11. The assisting car gently revs its engine.

12. Wait a couple of minutes.

13. Without disconnecting anything, try to start the dead car.

14. If it does not start, wait a few more minutes and then try one or two more times. If it does not start after five minutes, it is probably not going to start.

15. If it does start, keep the engine running and remove the cables in reverse order: the grounding end, the other black end, the red on the other car, the red on your car.

16. Drive for at least 15 minutes to give the battery a chance to recharge and do not turn off the car for at least one-half hour.

KEY TURNING A LOCK

1. Most cylinder locks consist of a series of pins of varying lengths that are stacked into pairs. Each pair of pins is pushed to the base of the lock's cylinder by a spring.

2. When a key is inserted, the series of notches in the key push the pin pairs up so that the point where the two pins come together lines up exactly with the point where the cylinder and the housing meet (this is called the shear line).

3. All of the upper pins will be situated in the cylinder, while all of the lower pins will rest in the housing, thus allowing the key to turn freely.

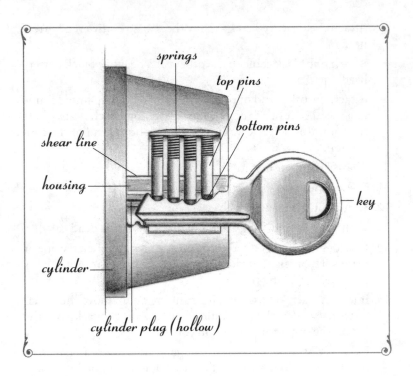

springs

top pins

bottom pins

shear line

housing

key

cylinder

cylinder plug (hollow)

KEYBOARDING

Computer keyboards work in the following way.

1. Keyboards rely on switches that cause a change in the current flowing through the circuits in the keyboard. When the key presses the keyswitch against the circuit, there is usually a small amount of vibration between the surfaces, known as bounce.

2. The key matrix is the grid of circuits underneath the keys.

3. Most keyboards use rubber dome switch technology. Each key sits over a small, flexible rubber dome with a hard carbon center.

4. When the key is pressed, a plunger on the bottom of the key pushes down against the dome.

5. This causes the carbon center to push down also, until it presses against a hard flat surface beneath the key matrix. As long as the key is held, the carbon center completes the circuit for that portion of the matrix.

6. When the key is released, the rubber dome springs back to its original shape, forcing the key back up to its at-rest position.

7. Each circuit is broken at the point below a specific key.

8. When a computer key is pressed, it causes electrical contacts beneath it to close and current to flow.

9. The computer's processor monitors the key matrix for signs of continuity at any point on the grid.

10. When it finds a circuit that is closed, it compares the location of that circuit on the key matrix to the character map in the system's memory. The character map is basically a comparison chart for the processor that tells it what the key at x,y coordinates in the key matrix represents.

11. If more than one key is pressed at the same time, the processor checks to see if that combination of keys has a designation in the character map.

12. As you type, the processor in the keyboard is analyzing the key matrix and determining what characters to send to the computer.

13. Once the keyboard data is identified as either system-specific or application-specific, it is processed accordingly.

14. The processor scans and sends it to the BIOS (input-output) chips.

15. After the coded signal goes to the CPU (computer processing unit), the screen displays the pressed letter or number.

KIDNEY DIALYSIS

A kidney dialysis machine filters waste products from the blood of patients who have kidney disease. In other cases, it removes poisons and drugs from the kidneys. It allows wastes, but not blood cells, to pass through a permeable membrane.

1. Blood flows from a patient's vein through a tube of semipermeable membrane in the machine's tank, which holds a special solution called dialysate.
2. Through selective diffusion, unwanted materials in the blood pass through the membrane.
3. The dialysis machine then pumps them out.
4. Cleansed blood returns to the patient's vein.

KIDNEYS

1. The kidney contains over one million nephrons (tubules that allow excretion). Each nephron contains a glomerulus (rounded tuft of tiny capillaries) and a long thin renal tubule.
2. As blood squeezes through the glomerulus, most of its water, sodium bicarbonate, potassium, glucose, amino acids, and the waste products urea and uric acid are forced into the outer part of each kidney filter (renal corpuscle). A filtered liquid is created.
3. The filtered liquid moves into the next tubule and reabsorption takes place.
4. Most vitamins, glucose, and amino acids are taken back into the blood in the capillaries.
5. Some minerals are also taken back. The hormone aldosterone controls reabsorption of more if needed.
6. Some water is also taken back. The hormone ADH controls reabsorption of more if needed.

7. Some substances (surplus acids, potassium, ammonia, and some drugs) pass from the blood into uriniferous tubules.

8. Resulting urine passes into the collecting duct or collecting tubule.

9. This duct carries urine from several uriniferous tubules into the pelvis of a kidney.

KNEE-JERK REFLEX

Testing the body's reflexes can give a physician useful information about how nerves and muscles work. One simple test is the knee-jerk reflex.

1. A tap just below the kneecap touches stretch sensors that send out nerve signals to stretch the tendon there.

2. The signals pass along the sensory nerves to the spinal cord.

3. These signals go through the motor nerve pathway.

4. At the same time, other signals travel up the spinal cord to the touch centers of the brain.

5. The signals arrive at the muscles in the front of the thigh.

6. The muscles contract and jerk the lower leg upward.

LACTATION

1. Milk production by the mammary glands is stimulated by the hormone prolactin.

2. Several other hormones, including oxytocin, female sex hormones, and the growth hormone, are also involved in milk production.

3. Prolactin levels climb during pregnancy and are kept high during breastfeeding.

4. Oxytocin is also released when a baby starts sucking at its mother's breast.

5. This triggers a reflex that ejects milk through the nipple.

LADYBUG LIFE CYCLE

1. An adult 7-spot ladybug lays eggs in groups on leaves.
2. After 3–7 days, the larvae hatch.
3. The wingless larva preys on other insects, such as aphids. The larval stage lasts 2–4 weeks.
4. The ladybug grows rapidly, molting several times.
5. A month after hatching, the larva forms a dormant pupa that attaches to a leaf.
6. Metamorphosis takes place inside the pupa. Inside, its body tissues are broken down and then completely rebuilt to form an adult insect.
7. A new adult (at first yellow) emerges after a week.
8. Its soft wing cases harden within a few hours.
9. Once its wings have expanded, it can fly and reproduce.

LAKE FORMATION

Lakes are transient features on the earth's surface and generally disappear in a relatively short period of geologic time by a combination of processes (e.g., erosion of an outlet or climatic changes that bring drier conditions). These are the ways in which lakes are made:

1. Many lakes were formed as a result of glacial action 1.8 million to 11,000 years ago during the Pleistocene ice sheets. In some areas, e.g., the Great Lakes, basins were carved into bedrock by the erosive action of the advancing ice mass.
2. Lake basins are also formed by glacial moraine deposits that dam pre-existing stream valleys.
3. Lakes also form in calderas, holes in the earth created by the collapse of volcanic craters.
4. Tectonic activity in the earth's crust forms lake basins in many ways, such as fault-generating rift valleys that often fill with water.

5. Precipitation on saturated land, especially land formed into a depression, can form a lake.

6. A lake may also be formed when a river meets a barrier, resulting in buildup of water into a lake.

7. Where extensive limestone deposits underlie a region, groundwater can dissolve great volumes of the limestone, forming caves that often contain underground lakes and eventually, if the roofs collapse, leave deep lake basins. Underground water can rise to the surface through land shifts, erosion, or springs.

8. Oxbow lakes form in abandoned stream channels in floodplains of meandering rivers.

9. Deposition of sediment along a shoreline can cut off bays, forming coastal lagoons. Saltwater lakes can be created by land cutting off a part of the ocean.

10. Humans often form lakes by building dams across river valleys for flood control, hydroelectric generation, or recreational purposes.

LASER

Laser is short for Light Amplification by Stimulated Emission of Radiation.

1. For a laser beam to be created, chromium atoms have to be excited (have their electrons raised to a higher energy level, i.e., population inversion).

2. A flash tube coiled around a ruby rod (a crystal of aluminum oxide) supplies light energy, which excites the chromium atoms.

3. An excited atom emits light when its electron spontaneously drops from a higher energy level to a lower one. The photon emitted has the same energy as the difference in energy levels.

4. Stimulated emission (the beam) occurs when an excited atom is hit by a photo emitted by another excited atom. During the brief instant that an atom is excited, light of a certain wavelength strikes it, and the atom emits radiation that is in phase (in step) with the wave that stimulated it.

5. This emission amplifies the wave and the laser beam releases light.

6. The light bounces between mirrors at the ends of the rod, stimulating more chromium atoms to emit light.

LAWNMOWER

1. A small engine is connected to a back roller and the blades.
2. The heavy black front roller is linked to the rotating cutting blades by a chain.
3. These blades are angled in the form of a shallow helix, so that each one approaches the base blade with a scissorlike action.
4. Grass is trapped between the roller and the blade, snipped off, and thrown into the grass catcher.

LEAVES CHANGING COLOR AND FALLING OFF

Before leaves drop in the autumn, a number of changes occur.

1. As the daylight shortens and the nights become cooler, deciduous trees "sense" the onset of winter and prepare to shed their leaves.
2. They do this by sealing the leaves off from the vascular system of the tree.
3. Deprived of water and nutrients, chlorophyll (green pigment of photosynthesis) and other useful substances break down and flow back into the tree out of the leaves.
4. Waste products, such as tannins, pass into the leaves.
5. The dying leaves change color as chemical changes take place. Since leaves contain about 2/3 chlorophyll, the other colors cannot be seen. These include xanthophyll (yellow), carotin (orange), anthocyanin (red). As the chlorophyll disintegrates, the other pigments become visible.
6. Cold nights cause the breakdown of sugars and convert them into red and purple pigments.
7. A layer of cork (a compact layer of cells) then forms across the

base of each leaf's petiole (stalk). On the twig, there is a scar that marks the former position of each leaf.

8. The leaves eventually fall off, leaving a scar on the twig.

LEGISLATIVE PROCESS

This process describes how legislation is passed.

1. Legislation is introduced in one of four principal forms: the bill, the joint resolution, the concurrent resolution, and the simple resolution. A bill is the form used for most legislation.

2. It is assigned a number, e.g., H.R. ~.

3. Any member in the House of Representatives may introduce a bill at any time while the House is in session by simply placing it in the "hopper" provided for the purpose at the side of the Clerk's desk in the House Chamber. It must be signed by the sponsor.

4. It is assigned a second number.

5. The bill is referred to the appropriate committee by the Speaker with the assistance of the Parliamentarian (expert in rules and procedures).

6. The bill is then printed in its introduced form.

7. Usually the first step in this process is a public hearing, where the committee members hear witnesses representing various viewpoints on the measure.

8. Each committee makes public the date, place, and subject of any hearing it conducts.

9. A transcript of the testimony taken at a hearing is made available for inspection in the committee office, and frequently the complete transcript is printed and distributed by the committee.

10. After hearings are completed, the bill is considered in a session that is popularly known as the "mark-up" session. Members of the committee study the viewpoints presented in detail.

11. Amendments may be offered to the bill, and the committee members vote to accept or reject these changes. This process

can take place at either the subcommittee level or at the full committee level, or at both.

12. At the conclusion of deliberation, a vote of committee or sub-committee Members is taken to determine what action to take on the measure. It can be reported, with or without amendment, or tabled, which means no further action on it will occur.

13. If the committee has approved extensive amendments, they may decide to report a new bill incorporating all the amendments. This is known as a "clean bill," which will have a new number.

14. If the committee votes to report a bill, the Committee Report is written. This report describes the purpose and scope of the measure and the reasons for recommended approval.

15. Consideration of the measure is done by the full House. In some circumstances, it may be brought to the Floor directly.

16. The consideration of a measure may be governed by a "rule." A rule is itself a simple resolution, which must be passed by the House, that sets out the particulars of debate for a specific bill—how much time will allowed for debate, whether amendments can be offered, and other matters.

17. Debate time for a measure is normally divided between proponents and opponents. Each side yields time to those Members who wish to speak on the bill. When amendments are offered, these are also debated and voted upon.

18. After all debate is concluded and amendments decided upon, the House is ready to vote on final passage. In some cases, a vote to "recommit" the bill to committee is requested. This is usually an effort by opponents to change some portion or table the measure.

19. If the attempt to recommit fails, a vote on final passage is ordered.

20. After a measure passes in the House, it goes to the Senate for consideration. A bill must pass both bodies in the same form before it can be presented to the President for signature into law.

21. If the Senate changes the language of the measure, it must return to the House for concurrence or additional changes. This back-and-forth negotiation may occur on the House floor, with the House accepting or rejecting Senate amendments or complete Senate text.

22. Often a conference committee will be appointed with both House and Senate members. This group will resolve the differences in committee and report the identical measure back to both bodies for a vote. Conference committees also issue reports outlining the final version of the bill.

23. Votes on final passage, as well as all other votes in the House, may be taken by the electronic voting system which registers each individual Member's response. These votes are referred to as Yea/Nay votes or recorded votes, and are available in House Votes by Bill number, roll call vote number, or words describing the reason for the vote. Votes in the House may also be by voice vote, and no record of individual responses is available.

24. After a measure has been passed in identical form by both the House and Senate, it is considered "enrolled." It is sent to the president who may sign the measure into law, veto it and return it to Congress, let it become law without signature, or at the end of a session, pocket-veto it.

LIE DETECTOR

The lie detector is an assembly of three different instruments whose outputs are recorded as separate traces on a graph. One measures variations in breathing, another checks blood pressure, and a third monitors electrical current in the body.

1. The lie detector is an assembly of three different instruments.

2. The pneumogram records breathing patterns. A rubber tube is strapped across the person's chest.

3. Instruments measure fluctuations in the volume of air inside the tube, caused by variations in breathing.

4. The cardiosphygmometer detects variations in blood pressure and pulse rate.

5. The information is picked up by a bladder and cuff over the upper arm, as in blood pressure checks.

6. The galvanometer monitors the flow of electric current through the skin.

7. Electrodes of the galvanometer are taped to the hand.

8. The instruments' outputs are fed separately to the lie detector and recorded as separate traces on a graph.

LIGHT BULB

Only about 10% of the light produced by an incandescent light bulb is in the visible spectrum.

1. Electrical current comes through the light fixture from the electrical outlet.

2. Light bulbs have two metal contacts at their base that connect to the ends of an electrical circuit.

3. Two stiff wires extend from the contacts up into the bulb, and to each end of a thin metal tungsten filament. Tungsten has an abnormally high melting temperature.

4. When current comes from the power supply, current flows from one contact to the other, through the wires and the filament.

5. The electrons are bumping into the atoms of the filament. The energy of these bumps heats the atoms.

6. Current passing through the filament heats the wire to more than 4,000 degrees Fahrenheit, resulting in the emission of visible light. The electrons rise to a high energy level, then back to normal and are releasing their extra energy in the form of light photons.

7. An inert gas (such as argon) fills the bulb to reduce the possibility of the filament's oxidizing. If a tungsten atom evaporates, it will likely collide with an argon atom and bounce back toward the filament, rejoining the solid structure.

LIGHTNING

1. Water and ice particles inside thunderclouds collide and become charged with static electricity.

2. The rubbing in static electricity knocks negatively charged electrons off the atoms so they become positively charged. Smaller positively charged particles move to the top of the cloud.

3. The freed electrons move to other atoms and become negatively charged. Heavier negatively charged particles collect at the bottom of the cloud.

4. The negative charge from the base of the cloud induces a positive charge on the ground beneath.

5. If it is strong enough, the charge in the cloud forces its way through the air to the ground and discharges as lightning.

LIQUID CRYSTAL DISPLAY (LCD)

Liquid crystal displays are used on most electronic screens, including computer monitors, digital watches, and digital clocks.

1. Liquid crystal molecules flow like liquid but line up regularly like crystals.

2. The rod-shaped liquid crystal molecules naturally align side by side.

3. If the liquid crystal is trapped between grooved plates (alignment layers) then the alignment becomes twisted. Depending on the alignment, the liquid crystal molecules twist the polarization of the light from vertical to horizontal.

4. If an electric field is applied across the liquid crystal layer, the molecules align end to end.

5. If an electric field is applied in the direction of light propagation, the liquid crystal directors align with the orienting field.

6. A grid of these placed side by side may be used to display images.

7. If the electric field that is attached to the parts of the grid that lie where the image is to appear is turned on, these points will turn black while the remaining points of the grid stay white. The resulting patchwork of dark and light creates the image on the display.

8. Small and inexpensive LCDs are often reflective. The numbers

appear where small electrodes charge the liquid crystals and make the layers untwist so that light is not transmitting through the polarized film. On a watch, calculator, or computer, numbers or letters are formed this way.

LITHOGRAPHY

Lithography means "writing on stone," as that was how it was first used. It is a method for printing, based on the repulsion of oil and water. The surface on which the image will print is ink-receptive and the blank area is ink-repellent.

1. The printing plate is treated to deposit lacquer (greasy coating) on the image areas.

2. The printing plate is covered with a wetting solution and the lacquer rejects the water. This solution collects on the uncoated areas of the printing plate.

3. An inked roller runs across the printing plate; the lacquer accepts the oil-based ink but the wet surface repels the ink.

4. A rubber-coated blanket cylinder is rolled across the plate, and picking up ink and water from it, forming a reversed copy of the original image.

5. Paper is pressed against the blanket cylinder by an impression cylinder and absorbs the ink.

6. On the paper, the image is reversed again, so that the printed image is identical to that on the printing plate.

LOCK WORKING

Locks are used to raise or lower ships from one water level to another. Canals and harbors have locks.

1. If a ship is going to a lower water level, the lock fills with water and the ship sails in.

2. Lock gates open for the ship to sail in only when the water on each side is level.

3. Opening the paddles or valves in the sides and the gates of the lock allows the water to flow out.

4. Closing the upper gates and letting out the water gradually lowers the ship to the level of the water outside the lower gates.

5. When all the water has drained from the lock, the gates open and the ship can continue on its way.

LUNAR ECLIPSE

The total phase of a lunar eclipse, when the Moon passes through the central part of the Earth's shadow (umbra), lasts for up to one hour.

1. Sunlight hits the Earth.

2. The Earth passes directly between the Sun and the Moon.

3. The partial shadow is the penumbra.

4. The full shadow of the Earth that falls on the Moon is the umbra.

5. The Moon is not totally black but appears reddish brown because sunlight passing through the Earth's atmosphere is re-

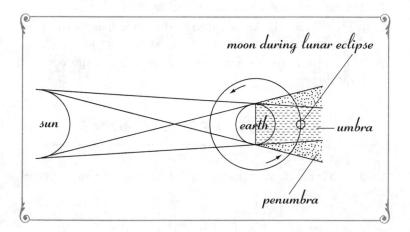

fracted so that some of it strikes the Moon. Most of the blue part of the spectrum is scattered by the atmosphere, leaving red light to reflect off the Moon.

LUNG CANCER

Cigarette smoke is the primary cause of lung cancer.

1. Tobacco smoke is a mix of more than 3,000 different substances.
2. In the lungs, columnar cells topped by cilia (tiny hairs) line healthy bronchi. Under this layer are basal cells, which constantly divide to replace the damaged columnar cells.
3. Mucus made by goblet cells lubricates the bronchi.
4. Each lung contains millions of air spaces. Carcinogenic (cancer-causing) substances from tobacco smoke, such as tar, are able to pass from these spaces directly into the bloodstream.
5. Over the years, columnar cells damaged by smoke will flatten and turn into squamous (platelike) cells which gradually lose their cilia.
6. In trying to replace the damaged squamous cells, the basal cells change and multiply at an increased rate (dysplasia). Some of these become cancer cells.
7. The cancer cells start replacing healthy cells.
8. If the cancer cells break through the underlying membrane, they can metastasize and spread cancer to other sites.
9. The tumor in the bronchi may enlarge or bleed and obstruct breathing.

MAGNETIC TAPE RECORDING

1. Sound is fed from a microphone, radio, compact disc, or other device.

2. With digital audio tape, the electrical signals from the microphone are converted into numerical values represented by binary numbers.

3. For recording, the erase head first cancels existing magnetic patterns on the tape. An electromagnet fed with high-frequency current upsets the existing alignment of the magnetic particles on the tape.

4. Current of varying strength through the recording head exerts changing magnetic attraction.

5. Magnets on the recording tape rearrange metal particles. Each metal particle on the magnetic tape becomes a magnet and these particles form patterns that vary according to the sounds.

6. The tape records on one face only. Two tracks are made for each direction of play on the tape.

7. Recording and playback is done by one electromagnet. The electromagnet's coil carries electrical signals that represent the sound.

8. When the tape is played back, its magnetic pattern sets up an electric current in the electromagnet head.

9. The current is fed to an amplifier and then to loudspeakers that produce pressure waves.

10. The waves vibrate a person's eardrums and sound is heard.

MAGNETISM

A material that attracts certain metals is called a magnet. Iron, for example, contains millions of tiny magnets called magnetic dipoles. Magnetism is a special property found only in a few metals. In a magnet, the dipoles point the same way so that their magnetism combines. (In nonmagnetic objects, all the dipoles point in different directions so that the magnetism cancels out.)

1. Every magnet has two poles. One pole is attracted to the north and the other is attracted to the south.

2. The north pole of one magnet and the south pole of another magnet attract each other.

3. The area around a magnet in which its magnetic force works is called its magnetic field.

4. A magnetic pole repels another pole of the same kind.

5. Materials that retain their magnetism all the time are called permanent magnets.

6. An electric current flowing through a coil produces an electro-magnet.

MAGNIFYING GLASS

1. A magnifying glass is a large convex lens.

2. The lens makes the rays from an object converge as they enter the eye.

3. The brain assumes that light rays arrive at the eye in straight lines—so it perceives the object as being larger.

MALARIA

1. A female Anopheles mosquito bites a person or animal, injecting saliva that contains sporozoites, the infective form of the malaria parasite.

2. Sporozoites enter liver cells and multiply.

3. In the liver, the sporozoites develop into merozoites, another form of the parasite.

4. Merozoites are released from the liver cells into the bloodstream.

5. Merozoites invade red blood cells and multiply in them.

6. Red blood cells rupture and release the merozoites, which invade other red blood cells and cause recurring chills and fever.

7. Some parasites develop into gametocytes, male and female cells that reproduce if ingested by a mosquito.

MATCH

For safety matches, the matchbook or matchbox surface contains a substance that is needed to make the head of the match catch fire. These matches are "safe" because they do not light when struck on other surfaces.

1. A match head contains substances that catch fire with very little heat.

2. The head of the match is moved over the rough surface on the matchbook or matchbox.

3. The friction of the surfaces makes the head of the match get hot.

4. The heat produced by moving the match head over the rough striking surface makes it burst into flame.

MATERIAL LIFE CYCLE

1. Manufacturing of material
2. Distribution and retail
3. Use and re-use
4. Maintenance
5. Recycling
6. Waste management

MEAT TENDERIZER

There is more than one way to tenderize meat.

1. Meats are composed of protein molecules.
2. Cooking meat breaks down its large protein molecules. The connective tissue polymers combine with water and form smaller molecules that are easier to digest.
3. Meat tenderizers are composed of enzymes that chemically break down meat proteins. They are usually made of papain, an enzyme in papaya.

MEIOSIS

Meiosis is the cell division that produces gametes (sex cells) such as sperm and eggs, which are used in sexual reproduction. See also Mitosis.

1. Each of the 23 pairs of chromosomes in the diploid germ cell replicates and lines up with its partner to make a joined pair of duplicate chromatids.
2. Meiosis begins with the contraction of the chromosomes in the nucleus of the diploid cell.
3. Homologous (similar but not identical) paternal and maternal chromosomes pair up along the midline of the cell. Each pair of chromosomes—called a tetrad, or a bivalent—consists of four chromatids. The homologous chromosomes exchange genetic material by the process of crossing over. Crossing-over is like shuffling a deck of cards and it combines genes in a way that will never be exactly repeated.
4. Threads form a structure (spindle) between the poles of the cell.
5. The homologous pairs then separate, each pair being pulled to opposite ends of the cell, which then pinches in half to form two daughter cells. Each daughter cell of this first meiotic division contains a haploid set of chromosomes. The chromosomes at this point still consist of duplicate chromatids.

6. Each new cell, complete with a new nucleus, now has a chromosome from each of the 23 pairs.

7. In the second meiotic division, each haploid daughter cell divides. There is no further reduction in chromosome number during this division, as it involves the separation of each chromatid pair into two chromosomes, which are pulled to the opposite ends of the daughter cells.

8. Each daughter cell then divides in half, thereby producing a total of four different haploid gametes. Each of the four new cells contains a unique set of 23 chromosomes that contain DNA from the original cell's 46 chromosomes.

9. When two gametes unite during fertilization, each contributes its haploid set of chromosomes to the new individual, thereby restoring the diploid number.

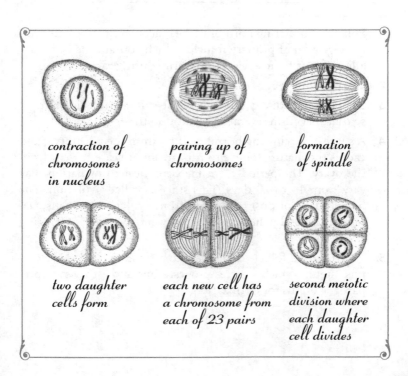

contraction of
chromosomes
in nucleus

pairing up of
chromosomes

formation
of spindle

two daughter
cells form

each new cell has
a chromosome from
each of 23 pairs

second meiotic
division where
each daughter
cell divides

MELTING POINT

1. The atoms in solids vibrate all the time.

2. When solids are heated they vibrate even more.

3. If the solid gets hot enough, the atoms move around so much that they cannot stay together. This is the melting point, the temperature at which a solid becomes a liquid.

4. At the melting point (which is generally considered the same as the freezing point of the corresponding liquid), both solid and liquid states are present.

5. An increase in pressure increases the melting point.

MENSTRUAL CYCLE

1. Follicle-stimulating hormone (FSH) acts on the ovary to stimulate growth of primary follicles which contain the egg. Usually only one follicle reaches maturity during each cycle.

2. The developing egg enlarges.

3. By about the 7th day, the cells of the primary follicle multiply so that they form several layers around the egg.

4. A surge of luteinizing hormone (LH) from the pituitary gland causes the mature follicle to rupture and release the egg from the ovary. The period from menstruation to ovulation may vary from 14 to 20 days. This stage is called ovulation. The luteal phase, or post-ovulation (from ovulation to menstruation), is generally the same length for most women—averaging about 14 days.

5. The ruptured follicle develops into a structure called the corpus luteum, which secretes progesterone and estrogen to prepare the uterus for fertilization.

6. If fertilization does not take place, the corpus luteum breaks down during the second week after ovulation, at around day 28. The uterine lining (endometrium) is shed and there is bleeding. Bleeding—or "menstrual flow"—lasts about three to five days.

7. The endometrium regrows to prepare the uterus for nurturing a fertilized egg. This cycle repeats itself unless or until the woman becomes pregnant.

METABOLISM

Hundreds of coordinated, multistep reactions, fueled by energy obtained from nutrients, ultimately convert readily available materials into the molecules required for growth and maintenance. This is a major simplification of these processes.

1. During digestion, the complex carbohydrates, fats, and proteins in food are broken down into glucose, fatty acids and glycerol, and amino acids, respectively.

2. These nutrients are the raw materials of metabolism.

3. Catabolic processes break down substances and release energy from them.

4. Anabolic processes take in energy and use it to build substances and make the body work.

5. Organic molecules involved in these processes are called metabolites and their interconversions are catalyzed by enzymes.

6. The transformation of one molecule into another and then into another and another in sequence is termed a metabolic pathway.

7. Exercise, food, and environmental temperature influence metabolism.

8. During this energy interchange, some energy escapes, chiefly in the form of heat.

METAL DETECTOR

1. Electric current is sent through a transmitter coil and produces an electromagnetic field. The size of the transmitter coil may vary, which affects the size and shape of the electromagnetic field transmitted.

2. When the electromagnetic field created by the detector encounters a metal object, the field induces electric currents in the object, which generate a smaller magnetic field.

3. That secondary magnetic field and the disturbance it causes is what the metal detector detects.

4. The effect of the buried metal's own magnetic field generates an electric current in a second detection coil.

5. That current is amplified by electronics in the detector.

6. The control box emits a noise to alert the user.

7. Highly conductive metals produce strong currents and others produce weaker currents.

8. Some detectors can discriminate between metal objects and highly magnetic ground minerals (iron).

METHOD ACTING / STANISLAVSKY METHOD

The Method starts from a series of exercises that develop actors' physical freedom on stage so that they can control their muscles, be keenly conscious during their performance, and see and hear on stage as they do in real life. The actor trains his or her concentration and senses so he or she may respond freely to the total stage environment.

1. Through empathic observation of people in many different situations, the actor attempts to develop a wide emotional range so that onstage actions and reactions appear as if they were a part of the real world rather than a make-believe one.

2. Building on this base, the Method then focuses on the connection between a character's inner psychological reality and external physical actions. Every physical action arises from an internal action. The two components form an organic union.

3. The Method requires an actor to ask what he or she as a person would do in a similar situation, helping to define the similarities and differences between the actor and the character. This process helps the actor learn how to make the character three-dimensional and also come to understand his or her actions. Genuine emotion can result from this combination of inner reality and external action.

MICROPHONE TO DIGITAL CODE

1. A microphone is a transducer and converts energy from one form (sound) into another (electricity).

2. The varying electrical voltage made by a microphone is a copy (analog) of the varying air-pressure waves associated with sound.

3. In condenser microphones, a diaphragm moves in response to sound waves, producing a varying electrical signal.

4. In dynamic microphones, a diaphragm's movement controls a coil inside a magnetic field, which produces a varying electrical current in the coil.

5. To convert the continuously varying electrical voltage wave produced by a microphone into digital code, the voltage signal must be sampled.

6. Sampling involves measuring the amplitude of the wave at regular intervals.

7. The code can then be reconverted into an analog signal for playback.

MICROWAVES

1. An electric current is used to generate microwaves in a magnetron.
2. Electrons are emitted by a heated filament, forming a cloud that moves around in a circle due to the magnetic field.
3. As the electrons pass close to vanes in an anode block, they induce rapidly changing positive and negative charges, creating an electromagnetic field oscillating at microwave frequency (2450 MHz) in the cavities between the vanes.
4. The electromagnetic field causes an antenna to emit microwaves at this frequency through a metal wave guide into the oven, where they are scattered by a rotating paddle or spinning fan.
5. Some of the microwaves penetrate the food directly while others are reflected off the walls into the food, ensuring even cooking.
6. Inside the food, water molecules rotate in time with the changing polarity of the electrical field. Each wave of energy causes the water molecules to align and then reverse alignment extremely rapidly.
7. Friction between rotating water molecules generates heat, thereby cooking the food.
8. An electronic timer controls cooking time.

MIRANDA RIGHTS

When a person is arrested, these are the rights the person is told by the police.

1. You have the right to remain silent.
2. Anything you say can and will be used against you in a court of law.
3. You have the right to have an attorney present before any questioning.

4. If you cannot afford an attorney, one will be appointed to represent you before any questioning. Do you understand these rights?

MITOSIS

Mitosis occurs during asexual reproduction and growth. It is the simple copying process that organizes and redistributes DNA during cell division. See Meiosis *for contrast.*

1. The stage that precedes actual cell division is called interphase, which is a resting phase. During this phase, molecules of DNA are loosely organized into a network of extended filaments, which is known as chromatin.

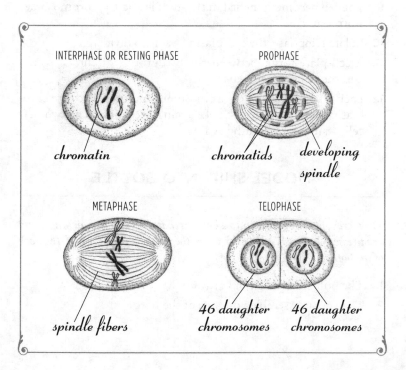

INTERPHASE OR RESTING PHASE

PROPHASE

chromatin

chromatids

developing spindle

METAPHASE

TELOPHASE

spindle fibers

46 daughter chromosomes

46 daughter chromosomes

2. In prophase, DNA strands replicate and coil up, forming spiral filaments (chromatids) that join at the centromere.

3. These filaments condense and form 46 X-shaped pairs of chromosomes.

4. In metaphase, chromosome pairs line up in the middle of the cell.

5. Threadlike fibers create the spindle that connects the centromere of each chromosome pair to the opposite poles of the dividing cell.

6. In anaphase, each centromere splits, dividing the paired chromosomes so that there are 92 single chromosomes.

7. Forty-six of these daughter chromosomes move toward each side of the cell.

8. In telophase, the spindle fibers disappear and a nuclear membrane forms around each group of 46 daughter chromosomes.

9. The cell becomes pinched in the middle and the chromosomes start to uncoil.

10. In late telophase, the cytoplasm begins to divide.

11. A cell plate forms between the two groups of chromosomes and the cell splits in two.

12. Each cell has a set of 46 chromosomes and these revert to chromatin filaments. This is, once again, interphase. The two new cells wait before dividing again.

MODEL SHIP INTO BOTTLE

The secret of putting a ship into a bottle is that the masts are on hinges and are pressed flat against the deck when the ship is passed through the neck of the bottle.

1. The hull is carved from hardwood.

2. The ship is assembled outside of the bottle.

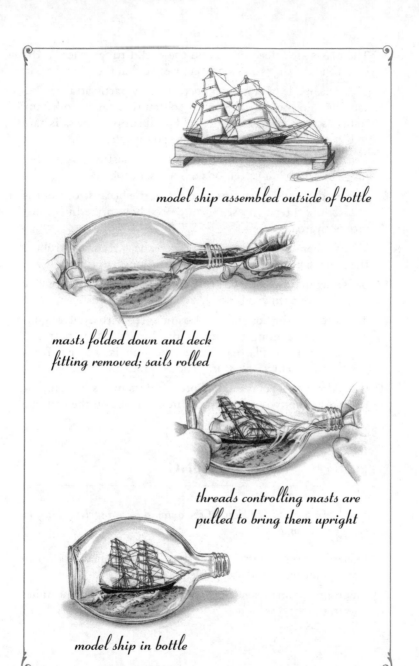

model ship assembled outside of bottle

masts folded down and deck fitting removed; sails rolled

threads controlling masts are pulled to bring them upright

model ship in bottle

3. The masts are folded down and the deck fittings, such as the wheel and the ship's boats, are removed so that the masts lie flat.

4. The sails, made of cloth or paper, are only partly attached before the ship goes into the bottle, so that they can be rolled up. If it is a square-rigger, then the yards that support the sails have to be swiveled parallel to the hull to go into the bottle.

5. Before the ship is put in the bottle, blue Plasticine is pressed into place with long steel rods to represent the sea.

6. The model is slid stern first into the bottle because one of the controlling threads passes through the bowsprit which must face outwards.

7. When the model is nearly in position, the threads controlling the masts are gently pulled to bring the masts upright.

8. Sails are carefully unrolled and fastened with tiny drops of glue on the tip of a thin rod.

9. The thread at the bowsprit is also anchored with a dab of glue. The threads coming out under the hull are kept taut and pressed into the Plasticine after the hull is secured. Extra thread can be cut with a thin-handled modeling knife.

10. Once the model is inside the bottle and its masts upright, the fittings are dotted with glue and put in place on the end of a long wire.

MOLTING

Molting is the periodic shedding of the outer skin, exoskeleton, fur, or feathers of an animal.

1. Lifeless horny structures (outer skin, exoskeleton, fur, or feathers) become worn and incapable of being repaired.

2. Environment and chemical signals are involved and hormones govern the process.

3. In most animals the process is triggered by secretions of the thyroid and pituitary glands.

4. An outer layer or covering of feathers, hair, horns, or skin is shed or cast off.

5. Its replacement is formed.

6. Nearly all birds molt annually in the late summer, losing and replacing their feathers gradually over a period of several weeks.

7. Some birds undergo a second or prenuptial molt in the spring, changing from dull to bright plumage.

8. The development of the young bird is marked by successive molts: first, from the down of the very young to the juvenal plumage, which resembles that of the female in species showing color differences between the sexes; then to the first winter plumage, when the bird is called an immature; and finally to the first nuptial plumage, the adult stage.

9. Arthropods (e.g., insects and crustaceans) must molt their exoskeletons periodically in order to grow; in this process the inner layers of the old cuticle are digested by a molting fluid secreted by the epidermal cells, the animal emerges from the old covering, and the new cuticle hardens.

MOOD RING

The stone in a mood ring is a clear shell filled with liquid crystals that are very sensitive to changes in temperature.

1. The body's temperature is capable of increasing or decreasing as a physical reaction to an emotion. When this happens, the liquid crystals in the mood ring change position and affect the wavelengths of light which they absorb and reflect.

2. As a result, the color of the stone appears to change, with different colors representing different moods or emotions.

MOON PHASES

Following the Waning Crescent is New Moon, beginning a repetition of the complete phase cycle of 29.5 days' average duration. The time in days counted from the time of New Moon is called the Moon's "age." Each complete cycle of phases is called a "lunation."

1. New Moon (daylight side turned away from Earth)
2. Waxing Crescent
3. First Quarter / Half Moon (about a week after new moon)
4. Waxing Gibbous (within the next week)
5. Full Moon (about two weeks after new moon)
6. Waning Gibbous
7. Last Quarter / Half Moon
8. Waning Crescent
9. New Moon

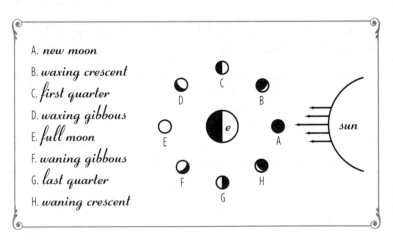

A. *new moon*
B. *waxing crescent*
C. *first quarter*
D. *waxing gibbous*
E. *full moon*
F. *waning gibbous*
G. *last quarter*
H. *waning crescent*

sun

MOUNTAIN LIFE CYCLE

Even mountains are born, age, and die.

1. Great cracks or faults develop in the earth's crust.
2. Huge blocks of rock slip up along these fractures. This is the youth stage.
3. Erosion, stresses, and other natural forces develop the mountain's maturity stage.
4. Rocks eventually drop down, creating the old-age stage.

MOUNTAIN

1. The slipping and sliding of the earth's tectonic plates can cause mountain formation. This can happen when plates crash into each other or when plates slip under neighboring continental plates and lift the lighter land up into mountains.
2. When one plate is forced (subducted) below another, it crumples up the crustal rocks.
3. As the layers of sand (representing crustal rocks) are squeezed horizontally, they become progressively more folded.
4. Simple folds may become completely overturned folds (nappes).
5. By repeated folding, eventually fold mountains are formed.
6. When blocks of rock are raised high between two faults or when the land surrounding the faults sinks—tall, flat-topped, block mountains are often formed.
7. Other mountains can form when two crustal plates tear apart, compressing the margins of the plates. This cracks and lifts up the crust to form mountains.

Mountains can also form under the sea where an ocean plate has cracked open. Magma wells up and cools into fresh rocks which rise to form mountains. Volcanoes can also create mountains.

MRI SCANNER

Magnetic Resonance Imaging uses magnets and radio waves to produce detailed sections of body organs.

1. Inside the tunnel-like MRI scanner, a person is exposed to a powerful magnetic field that lines up the particles inside the body's atoms.
2. Pulses of radio waves then knock the particles out of alignment.
3. As the particles realign, they produce radio signals that are analyzed by computer.
4. The computer creates an image that provides structural and biochemical information about tissue.

MUMMIFICATION

1. In the most expensive method of mummifying, the brain was extracted through the nostrils and the contents of the trunk (except for the heart) were removed through an incision made in the side with a flint knife.
2. In the less expensive method, the internal organs were not removed but cedar oil injected into the body before drying. In the cheapest method, the body was just dried.
3. The body was dried out, which took about 40 days, by being covered with dry natron, a naturally occurring salt compound.
4. The removed internal organs were also dried in natron before being soured in four sealed vases, the canopic jars, near the body.
5. The body was anointed with oil.
6. The body was adorned.
7. The body was bandaged and the bandages impregnated with beeswax and glued with gelatin.
8. The body underwent religious rites.
9. The wrapped mummy was given a face and chest mask made of cartonage (linen and plaster). It might be gilded.

10. The mummy was sometimes placed in a wooden case shaped to the body.
11. The mummy was then put in a rectangular wooden coffin.
12. The wooden coffin was then put in an outer coffin or sarcophagus.
13. The sarcophagus was decorated.

MUSHROOM LIFE CYCLE

This process can happen overnight.

1. Spores germinate when they land in a suitable location.
2. They develop into hyphae, tiny threadlike cells which are loosely woven into a mat (mycelium) which grows underground and gradually expands as the hyphae absorb nutrients.
3. The hyphae pack tightly together to make fruiting bodies, such as mushrooms.
4. This pops up as the small round "button."
5. Soon the outer covering ruptures.
6. The stem elongates and the cap enlarges to its full size.
7. Pores under the cap are exposed to air.
8. The cap grows and pores shed spores.
9. Most mushrooms then wither away within a few days. At other times, the mycelium persists, sometimes living for decades.

NATURAL ARCH FORMATION

1. Movements of the earth's crust produce deep fractures in thick sandstone formations.
2. Running water and weathering enlarge the fractures—leaving widely spaced, upright fins of rock.

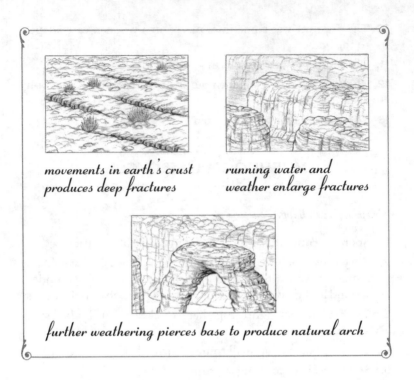

movements in earth's crust produces deep fractures

running water and weather enlarge fractures

further weathering pierces base to produce natural arch

3. Further weathering then eats through or pierces the bases of the fins to produce monumental natural arches.

NATURAL GAS FORMATION

1. In the sea, tiny prehistoric plants sank and a layer of dead plants built up on the sea bed.
2. The sea plants were buried in mud.
3. On land, mud covers dead plants and trees.
4. Slowly, the mud hardens into rock.

5. More layers of rock form above and press down on the plants, burying them deeper and heating them up.

6. The pressure and heat slowly change the sea plants into oil and then into gas.

7. Land plants first turn to coal before becoming oil and gas.

8. A layer of rock now traps the gas in a deep deposit.

9. Earth movements may have raised the rocks containing the gas above sea level, so that the gas now lies under the land.

10. Gas flows up the well to a production platform and a pipeline takes it to a terminal on land. Gas from inland wells flows straight to the terminal.

11. At the terminal, raw gas has to be cleaned and dried before it can be used.

NATURAL GAS REFINEMENT

1. Natural gas collects in pockets (pores and fractures) within the earth's crust. It is obtained by drilling.

2. In gas reservoirs, however, methane is typically found in mixtures with heavier hydrocarbons—such as ethane, propane, butane and pentanes—as well as water vapor, hydrogen sulphide (H2S), which is found in sour gas, carbon dioxide, nitrogen, and other gases.

3. At the refinery, the gases go through a slug catcher.

4. The gas is then sent to an extraction plant.

5. Some of the gas is frozen and then sent liquefied on a natural gas tanker.

6. The rest goes to a fractionation plant, which separates the gas into ethane, propane, butane, and natural gasoline. Each gas has a different boiling point and fractionation relies on changes in temperature and pressure.

7. The natural gas purchased by consumers consists almost entirely of methane, the simplest hydrocarbon.

NEON LAMP

1. Inside the glass tube there is neon, argon, or krypton gas at low pressure.
2. At both ends of the tube are metal electrodes.
3. When a high voltage of electricity is applied to the electrodes, the neon gas ionizes, and electrons flow through the gas.
4. These electrons excite the neon atoms and cause them to emit visible light.
5. Neon emits red light when energized in this way; other gases emit other colors.

NERVE REGENERATION

Injured nerve fibers that are peripheral may slowly regenerate if the cell body and the segments of myelin sheath remain continuous. However, in the brain or spinal cord, injured nerve fibers are wrapped in scar tissue and deactivated.

1. When a nerve fiber just beyond an injury and farthest from the cell body no longer receives vital proteins and enzymes, it begins to degenerate and the myelin sheath becomes hollow.
2. An undamaged neuron cell body stimulates the growth of several nerve sprouts in the remaining portion of the fiber. One of these sprouts may find its way through the empty but intact myelin sheath.
3. The new nerve fiber grows about 1.5mm per day and eventually reaches its previous connection.
4. Function and sensation are slowly restored and unused nerve sprouts degenerate.

NEURON

1. Each neuron can receive different chemical signals from hundreds or thousands of other neurons. Each signal can either excite or inhibit the receiving cell.

2. If the net sum of all incoming messages tells the neuron to fire, it undergoes a chemical change that lets positive ions flow in from the outside and build up an internal electrical charge.

3. The positive electrical spike propagates down the neuron's long axon until it comes to a synapse, a gap leading to another neuron.

4. At the synapse, the electrical signal provokes small vesicles to move toward the gap and disgorge their load of chemicals.

5. Vesicles of one neuron release one or more neurotransmitters across the synapse.

6. They bind to receptors of the receiving neuron, activating an electrical signal there.

7. The synapse is cleared of neurotransmitters after each event; some just float away, some are reabsorbed by the sending cell, and some are destroyed by enzymes.

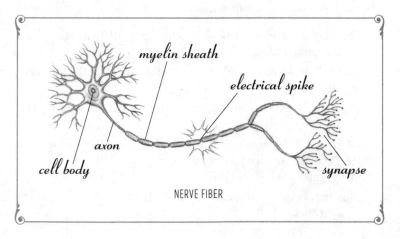

myelin sheath

electrical spike

axon

cell body

synapse

NERVE FIBER

NUCLEAR FISSION

The kind of nuclear reaction that happens inside a nuclear reactor is called nuclear fission.

1. Nuclear fission occurs in a nuclear reactor.

2. The fuel is uranium or plutonium, two very heavy elements with many protons and neutrons in their nuclei.

3. Fission starts when a fast-moving free neutron in the fuel strikes a nucleus.

4. The nucleus cannot take on the extra neutron and the whole nucleus breaks apart into two smaller nuclei (fission fragments).

5. Several neutrons are released and they go on to break apart more nuclei—and so on in a chain reaction.

6. As each fission occurs, gamma rays are released, resulting in a harmful form of radiation.

7. This process can multiply rapidly and produce great heat in a fraction of a second.

NUCLEAR FUSION

Nuclear fusion powers the Sun and also occurs in thermonuclear weapons.

1. The gaseous fuel has two different forms of hydrogen—deuterium and tritium.

2. The fuel is heated to millions of degrees, causing the atoms to hit each other with great force.

3. Pairs of nuclei meet and their protons and neutrons fuse and become a single nucleus.

4. When the deuterium and tritium fuse, they first make a nucleus containing two protons and three neutrons—an unstable form of helium.

5. This breaks apart to create regular helium and an extra neutron escapes.

216

6. The fused nuclei and spare neutrons move off at high speed, producing great heat.

7. Though radiation is not emitted, the neutrons are harmful to people.

NUCLEAR MELTDOWN

A nuclear meltdown occurs when the core of a nuclear reactor melts.

1. In pressurized water reactors, boiling water reactors, and breeder reactors, this can occur after a loss of coolant accident in which emergency cooling systems fail.

2. Although the emergency systems are designed to reinsert the control rods and stop the fission reaction in the event of an emergency, radioactive decay from the reaction products will continue to generate heat in the absence of coolant and fission reactions.

3. This heat will cause the reactor core to melt within an hour after coolant is stopped.

4. The worst case scenario would be if the molten reactor core penetrates the containment vessel and hits groundwater.

5. The combination of molten radioactive material and water may cause a chemical explosion which would spread radioactive material over a large area.

6. The best case scenario would be if the containment vessels held the molten material.

NUTRIENT CYCLE

The nutrient cycle is also known as the circle of life.

1. Producers (green plants) use the sun's energy to manufacture their own food from abiotic (non-living) elements in a process called photosynthesis.

217

2. These green plants provide food and oxygen for other living things (consumers).

3. Some consumers (herbivores) eat producers, while others (carnivores) eat other consumers.

4. Decomposers break down dead plant and animal materials into abiotic (non-living) elements.

5. The abiotic elements return to the soil, water, and air for use again.

OSTEOARTHRITIS

This is the process by which cartilage begins to break down.

1. When cartilage cells (articular chondrocytes) die, surface cracks appear.

2. The cracks allow synovial fluid to leak in, causing more cartilage degeneration.

3. Pieces of the weakened cartilage break off and inflame the synovial membrane.

4. Eventually, a gap in the cartilage reaches the underlying bone.

5. Blood vessels begin to grow and a plug made of fibrocartilage fills the gap.

6. The fibrocartilage plug wears away and exposes the bone surface.

7. If surface cracks deepen, synovial fluid can leak into the narrow space and may form a cyst surrounded by weakened bone.

8. Small outgrowths of osteophytes may further deform the bone surface.

9. Bone surfaces rubbing directly against one another can cause severe discomfort.

OSTEOPOROSIS

This is the process by which bones begin to break down.

1. Bones are continually being broken down and then rebuilt in order to facilitate growth and repair. In the young, the rate of bone formation exceeds the rate at which cells are reabsorbed.

2. In early adulthood, the rate of reabsorption becomes greater than formation.

3. Bones gradually become weaker and lighter.

4. After middle age, bones become distinctly thinner and more porous.

5. Both the collagen framework and deposited minerals are broken down much faster than they are formed.

6. The canals that connect the osteocytes (bone cells) become wider and new spaces appear in the collagen matrix. These changes weaken the bone.

7. Loss of the female hormone estrogen around and during menopause leads to more severe osteoporosis.

OZONE HOLE FORMATION

Complex chemical reactions involving traces of man-made chlorofluorocarbons, halons, and fluorocarbons have created temporary holes in the ozone layer, particularly over Antarctica, during polar spring. See also **Global Warming.**

1. Every time a spray can is used, a tiny bit of propellant is released into the air.

2. The fluorocarbon drifts hundreds of miles into the earth's upper atmosphere.

3. There it changes some ozone into oxygen and creates a "hole" that lets more ultraviolet light through to the earth's surface.

4. This creates health problems for humans and disturbs delicate ecosystems.

PAPER

1. After felling, trees are turned into wood chips.

2. The wood chips are fed into huge digesters.

3. In the digesters, the wood chips are mixed with chemicals like sodium sulphate and subjected to high temperatures and pressures. This separates out the fibers and makes pulp.

4. Impurities, such as resin and pitch, are removed.

5. Wastepaper is added to the pulping machine to make recycled paper.

6. The pulp is bleached.

7. The pulp is mixed with chemicals to give it the right color or make it whiter.

8. The mixture then flows from a large tank with a narrow slit onto a moving screen with tiny holes.

9. The moving screen allows water to drain but retains most of the fibers.

10. The sheet is pressed through rollers to remove more water.

11. The sheet is dried by passing through a series of steam-heated cylinders.

12. The paper may be coated with pigments to improve its surface.

13. The finished paper is wound onto large rolls.

PARALLEL PARKING

1. Know how long your car is and add two feet.
2. Pull into position next to the car in front of the space desired, leaving about 2–3 feet between the cars.
3. Align the edge of your front door with their back wheel.
4. Turn the wheel twice in the direction of the curb you want to end up next to. Cut it all the way.
5. Shift into reverse and glide the car backward into the spot.
6. Keep going until your front bumper is closer to you than their back bumper. Your car should be about halfway into the spot.
7. Apply the brakes as you turn your wheel one-and-a-half times in the opposite direction and continue to glide backward.
8. Come to a stop.
9. Shift out of reverse and move forward and parallel into the spot.

PARASITE

1. In warm, wet soil, parasite eggs are living in feces.
2. The eggs are hatched, and the infective, threadlike larvae may penetrate human skin, usually that of the foot, by way of the sweat glands and hair follicles.
3. They then invade the lymph and blood vessels.
4. The larvae travel through the veins to the lungs.
5. The larvae travel up the respiratory tree through the trachea to the back of the mouth.
6. They are swallowed and travel down the esophagus to the stomach.
7. They are sent to the small intestine where they mature and start a new reproductive cycle.
8. The adult worm attaches itself to the mucosal tissue lining the small intestine, where the female may produce several thousand eggs a day, which are passed in the feces.

There are drawbacks to medicine that either has to be swallowed or administered by injection. Swallowed drugs may not cross the lining of the intestines and enter the bloodstream or they may be broken down too quickly to have an effect. Injections are expensive and difficult to administer correctly. Drug-impregnated skin patches bypass the digestive system and let medication be drawn into the skin via a tiny electrical current.

1. A birth control patch is a small, square, thin, beige-colored patch that's applied directly to the skin of the buttocks, abdomen, upper torso, or upper outer arm. The stop-smoking patch is worn on the upper body.

NICOTINE PATCH

2. A stop-smoking patch releases nicotine through the skin and into the bloodstream. A birth-control patch continuously delivers two synthetic hormones, progestin (norelgestromin) and estrogen (ethinyl estradiol), which are similar to hormones naturally produced by the body.

3. The nicotine patch lessens withdrawal symptoms that smokers feel when they quit. It dispenses nicotine in decreasing doses.

4. The amount of nicotine in the patch is sufficient to help overcome the withdrawal symptoms but is lower than the amount of nicotine which you get from smoking. Therefore, overcoming a reliance on the nicotine in the patch is much easier than overcoming a dependence on the nicotine from cigarettes.

BIRTH CONTROL PATCH

5. The birth control patch impedes pregnancy by preventing a woman's ovaries from releasing eggs (ovulation). If eggs aren't released, sperm can't fertilize them and pregnancy can't occur. The patch also thickens the cervical mucus, making it difficult for sperm to reach the eggs.

6. Use of the birth control patch is timed to a woman's monthly menstrual cycle. On the day after a period ends, she applies the patch to her skin, and it remains in place for one week. On the same day of the following week, she removes the old patch and

applies a new one. The new patch can be placed on a different area of the body. During the fourth week, no patch is applied and her menstrual period occurs. The following week she repeats this sequence.

PEARL

There is an industry that cultivates pearls by having oysters' shells carefully opened and small bits of shell inserted as "seeds" in order to stimulate the production of marketable pearls in 3–6 years.

1. Pearl oysters live on the sandy bottom of tropical seas.
2. They filter the water to extract food.
3. Any foreign matter (sand, parasites) that gets into their bodies can cause irritation.
4. As a defense mechanism, oysters will coat a grain of sand with nacre (mother-of-pearl), a silvery calcium carbonate substance that oysters exude to line their shells.
5. After several years of coating, pearls are formed.
6. Depending on the pigment of the nacre, the pearls can be white, pink, blue, yellow, or black.

PEAT BOG

There is a distinct order to the different groups of plants that grow over time and each stage is adapted to the increasingly dry conditions. A bog can take up to 5,000 years to form.

1. Lake sediment collects around plants on the edge of the lake.
2. Plants like sphagnum moss and cotton grass typically dominate the area.
3. Lake margins begin to fill in and can support larger plants such as willow trees.
4. Plant material slowly decomposes to form peat.
5. Peat bogs grow and thrive in cool, damp environments.

PENCIL

1. At a mill, jets of compressed air containing graphite particles are blasted at one another and as the particles collide, they break up.
2. The fine graphite particles are mixed with pure china clay and water, making a putty-like paste.
3. The mix is fed into a cylinder and forced through a hole at one end, creating a continuous length the diameter of pencil lead.
4. The lengths are cut into pencil-sized sticks.
5. The sticks are dried in an oven.
6. The sticks are fired in a kiln.
7. The sticks are treated with wax to ensure smooth writing.
8. The sticks are sealed to prevent them from slipping out of the wooden casing.
9. Wood is sawed into slats that are the length of a pencil, seven pencils wide and half a pencil thick.
10. Grooves are cut into the slats.
11. The lead is inserted.
12. Another grooved slat is glued on top.
13. This sandwich is fed through machines that cut individual pencils of hexagonal or circular cross-section.
14. The pencils are painted with non-toxic lacquer, which makes them appear to be seamless.

PENDULUM

1. A pendulum swings at a constant rate which depends only on the pendulum's length.

2. In a pendulum clock, the swinging of the pendulum controls the rotation of the escape wheel which drives the clock's hands.

3. As the pendulum swings left, it disengages the first pallet.

4. The constant swing of the pendulum allows the escape wheel to turn a precise amount before the second pallet engages.

5. As the pendulum swings right, the second pallet disengages and the wheel is released until the first pallet re-engages.

PHOTO BOOTH

1. The subject sits in the booth.

2. An electronic flash lights up the subject as the shutter opens.

3. A prism reverses the image formed by the lens onto the paper, so the picture is right.

4. The paper strip moves down after each exposure.

5. A cutter slices the paper strip after four exposures.

6. The exposed paper travels through nine or more chemical tanks. First it makes a negative.

7. The dark silver in the negative is dissolved.

8. The unexposed emulsion that remains is treated and develops to form silver, giving the paper a positive image.

9. The paper strip is washed.

10. The developed photos are dried by a fan.

11. Within five minutes after being taken, the pictures emerge from a slot on the side of the booth.

PHOTOCOPIER

1. The original document is placed on the copier's glass window.

2. The copy button is pressed.

3. A fluorescent or halogen light shines on the original document.

4. The document is scanned by a mirror moving back and forth underneath it, projecting the image onto an electrically charged rotating drum. The drum is coated with photoconductive material (that which conducts electricity when light shines on it).

5. The drum is charged with static electricity in the dark while it is rotating past a high-voltage sensitizer.

6. The black parts of the image on the drum do not reflect light, so the positive charge remains. Light reflected from the white areas of the document destroys the charge where it hits the drum.

7. Toner projected onto the drum is attracted to the charged areas, which correspond to the original document's black parts.

8. Charged copy paper is pressed against the drum.

9. The copy paper attracts the toner.

10. The toner is fused to the copy paper by a heated roller.

11. If the document is in color or has shades of gray, the colored or gray areas reflect light in proportion to how dark they are.

PHOTOGRAPH

1. When a picture is taken, light coming through the lens briefly strikes the film.

2. Each grain of silver struck by light is subtly changed and the photograph is recorded in an invisible pattern of changed grains.

3. The film is immersed in a bath of chemicals (developer).

4. The developer makes the silver salt grains that were struck by light change into silver metal.

5. After a quick rinse with water, the film is placed in a bath of fixer—a chemical solution that dissolves away the unexposed silver salt grains.

6. After fixing, the black silver image is left permanently on the film.

7. Once the film is fixed, it is washed thoroughly in running water to remove all traces of chemicals.

8. The film is then hung up to dry. The pictures are negative, which means the light and dark areas are reversed.

9. To see the picture properly, the negative is printed.

10. It is rephotographed on white paper in a lightproof darkroom using an enlarger.

11. The enlarger lens magnifies the negative by projecting a big version of the picture onto the print paper. The print paper is coated with light-sensitive emulsion.

12. When the enlarger is turned on, silver salts in the emulsion record the magnified picture in the same way as the film.

13. A timer connected to the enlarger ensures that the photographic paper is illuminated for the correct amount of time.

PHOTOSYNTHESIS

Photosynthesis is a light-energized oxidation-reduction process; oxidation refers to the removal of electrons from a molecule; reduction refers to the gain of electrons by a molecule. It is a complicated series of chemical reactions, simplified here.

1. In plant photosynthesis, the energy of light is absorbed by the green pigment chlorophyll in the chloroplasts and used to drive the oxidation of water. Carbon dioxide is taken in through the plant's exposed green parts, and water and minerals (containing nitrogen and sulfur) are taken in through the roots.

2. The plants make their food in the palisade (long, narrow) cells of their leaves.

3. This produces oxygen gas (O_2), hydrogen ions (H+), and electrons. Oxygen escapes from the leaf's cells into the air.

4. Most of the removed electrons and hydrogen ions ultimately are transferred to carbon dioxide (CO_2).

5. The carbon dioxide is reduced to organic products.

6. Other electrons and hydrogen ions are used to reduce nitrate

and sulfate to amino and sulfhydryl groups in amino acids, which are the building blocks of proteins.

7. The simple sugar glucose is formed and stored in the plant's cells as sugars and starch.

8. Sugars and starch are broken down when required.

9. Energy is released for life processes.

10. Carbon dioxide is produced as a by-product of the energy release and returns to the air.

PINEAPPLE RINGS, CANNED

1. A machine called a Ginaca cuts off the shell at the top and bottom and punches out the core.

2. The machine removes the horny outer shell.

3. A device called an eradicator scrapes off surplus flesh adhering to the shell and makes crushed pineapple or pineapple juice.

4. The Ginaca then cuts a cylinder of the pineapple's juicy flesh.

5. The cylinders of pineapple flesh are inspected on a conveyor belt by trimmers, who remove any remaining fragments of shell and any blemishes.

6. The cylinders of pineapple flesh are then put through a slicing machine for perfectly cut rings.

7. The rings are inspected again and put into cans. Discarded pieces are used for crushed pineapple.

8. Each can of rings is filled with either syrup or pineapple juice.

9. The cans are lidded and sealed under vacuum.

10. The cans are cooked in pressure cookers called retorts.

11. The sterilized cans of fruit are cooled in water or by air, then labeled and packed.

PLACENTAL DEVELOPMENT

A placenta is an organ in most female mammals that forms in the lining of the uterus and provides nourishment to a fetus (unborn vertebrate).

1. Specialized cells of the embedded trophoblast (the outer layer of the blastocyst, the mass of cells that implants in the lining of the uterus after fertilization) extend into nearby uterine blood vessels.

2. Blood from the mother flows from these blood vessels into spaces within the trophoblast.

3. Other trophoblast cells extend fingerlike projections (chorionic villi) into the endometrium. These are surrounded by the spaces filled with maternal blood.

4. Fetal blood vessels grow into the fingerlike chorionic villi.

5. Maternal and fetal blood are separated in the placenta by a barrier of cells.

6. Oxygen, nutrients, and antibodies cross the barrier to the fetus.

7. Waste products pass back through the placenta.

8. The placenta continues to develop as the fetus grows so that by the end of the pregnancy it is about 8 inches wide and 1 inch thick. It is attached to the center of the baby's abdomen by the umbilical cord.

PLANT CLIMBING

1. During the course of a day, leaves bend to face the sun and petals open and close.

2. Climbing plants (like gourd plants) send out touch-sensitive tendrils that grope blindly for other plants.

3. When a tendril touches a branch or stem, it begins to loop around it to establish a firm grip, giving the climber extra support.

4. After about 14 hours, the tendril has curled around the stem and starts to coil up.

5. After 24 hours, the tendril has coiled tightly, pulling the plant toward the stem.

6. After 48 hours, more tendrils have made contact and the climber has pulled close to the stem.

PLANT STAYING UP

Plants do not have the woody tissue found in trees, so they rely on turgor pressure—or water pressure with cells—to stiffen their cell walls.

1. Cells take in water by osmosis into the vacuoles until they become so swollen by water pressure that they resist further input.

2. This expands the vacuoles and generates a hydrostatic pressure, called turgor, that presses the cell membranes against the cell walls.

3. Turgor is the cause of rigidity in living plant tissue.

4. Loss of turgor pressure causes plants to wilt.

PLAY DEVELOPMENT

Rising action occurs when the conflict/action of the story unfolds. When there is no shift in a play's energy, the story advances by static action. After the climax, falling action may resolve details of the plot or provide a brief aftermath.

1. A stage play starts at a time and place called an action point. This may not necessarily be the actual beginning of the story; much may have happened between the characters before the play's beginning.

2. The action point serves to move the protagonist and the story forward.

3. The traditional play advances its story via the interplay of conflict (disturbance resulting from the collision of two emotional or social forces) and action (activity in response to conflict).

4. The pattern recurs and grows, building tension to the climax that results in the protagonist's transformation.

POLYESTER

Manmade fabric such as polyester is easier to mass-produce than either cotton or wool. Manmade fiber fabrics can recreate most properties that natural fibers possess. Manmade fibers can also be combined with natural ones.

1. Polymers (plastics) in a liquid form are blown through very thin nozzles (spinnerets).

2. The fine jet solidifies almost immediately and forms a fiber about a quarter of the thickness of human hair.

3. The fibers are stretched, which aligns the long molecules along the length of the fiber. This also contributes to the fiber's stretchiness and shine.

4. These strong threads are then made into cloth.

POPCORN

Popcorn, a kind of flint corn, has harder kernels than other types of corn. Its outer shell surrounds a small amount (11–14 percent) of moist, starchy material.

1. When the kernels are heated, the moisture inside them turns to steam.

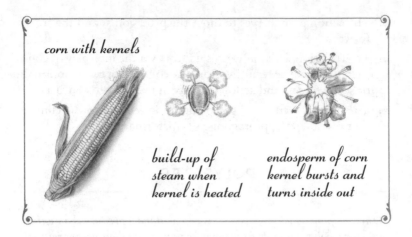

corn with kernels

build-up of steam when kernel is heated

endosperm of corn kernel bursts and turns inside out

2. The kernels have a tough, elastic layer called the endosperm which resists the buildup of steam pressure within the heated kernels.

3. When the temperature reaches around 400 degrees Fahrenheit, steam builds up enough pressure and inflates the starch granules to 35 times the kernel's original size.

4. The endosperm of the kernels then burst and are turned inside out into light fluffy masses.

POSTAL SERVICE

1. Mail is collected at the local post office.

2. The local post office sends the mail to a sorting center.

3. Parcels and large items are separated.

4. Letters are fed into a machine that scans to detect postage, then cancels it and faces the pieces of mail in the same direction.

5. The scan sorts the letters into those with bar codes, those that are machine-readable, and those that are hand-addressed.

6. If a letter is hand-addressed, it is given an ID bar code. A digital image of the address is stored in a database.

7. Technicians take the digital images and type in the address data.

8. This information is sent along with the item's ID bar code to the sorting station, where it will be waiting for the letters when they re-enter the stream.

9. The mail with bar codes goes directly to the final sorter.

10. The mail that is machine-readable (with typewritten or machine-printed addresses) is read with an optical character reader (OCR).

11. The OCR scans the address block, compares the information with its database of ZIP codes, and applies the proper bar code.

12. The hand-addressed mail is put through the OCR in some cases.

13. The rest of the hand-addressed mail moves out of the stream for a short period.

14. Then the hand-addressed mail is matched to the database.

15. Finally, all letters have bar codes and a final scan reads them and sorts the mail according to destinations.

PRESSURE COOKER

All pressure cookers have a lock-on lid and a vent or pressure relief valve.

1. Water boils at 212 degrees Fahrenheit and no matter how long it boils, the water and its steam do not get hotter than that. The only way to make steam hotter is to put it under pressure.

2. Steam has six times the heat potential when it condenses on a cool food product. This increased heat transfer potential is why steam is such an effective cooking medium.

3. Water and food are put in the pressure cooker.

4. When the tightly sealed cooker is set over high heat, steam pressure builds and the internal temperature rises. The steam will remain trapped and pressure will build, which raises the temperature at which the liquid will boil. So at 15 pounds per square inch pressure, the food is cooking at about 250 degrees instead of 212 degrees. This reduces the time needed to cook the food. This high temperature is made possible by raising the pressure to a point greater than atmospheric pressure.

5. Under high pressure, the fiber in food is tenderized and flavors mingle in record time. Also, fewer nutrients are lost because cooking is so speedy and because nutrient-rich steam condenses in the pot instead of being lost in the air.

PRODUCT LIFE CYCLE

This is a marketing theory in which products or brands follow a sequence of stages.

1. Research and development
2. Introduction / launch
3. Market development
4. Growth
5. Exploitation
6. Maturity / maturation
7. Saturation
8. Decline / sales decline
9. End

A second version pertaining to a product's creation and use is:

1. Acquisition of raw materials
2. Production
3. Packaging
4. Distribution
5. Use
6. Recycling
7. Disposal

A third version describes the complete history of a product:

1. Concept

2. Definition
3. Production
4. Operation
5. Obsolescence
6. Disposal

PSYCHOLOGICAL DEVELOPMENT

According to Sigmund Freud, for children:

1. ORAL: the infant understands the world through lips and mouth.
2. ANAL-SADISTIC: the child is fascinated by feces and anus.
3. PHALLIC/GENITAL: the child discovers the genital area as the center of sexual sensation.

PUBERTY

1. In early adolescence, boys' underarm and pubic hair begins to grow, they may perspire more and pimples may appear. For girls, the same things happen and nipples start to enlarge.
2. In mid-adolescence, the boy's facial hair may start to grow and the penis, testes, and scrotum start to enlarge. The menstrual period starts for girls.
3. In late adolescence, boys' voice box enlarges, making the voice deeper. Pubic hair becomes thick and curly and chest and shoulders broaden. Legs become hairy and penis and testes reach adult size. For girls, breasts first become rounder and then reach their full size. The hips widen and pubic hair becomes thick and curly.

PUPIL

1. Pupil size is constantly adjusted by the iris under the control of the autonomic nervous system in order to change the amount of light entering the eyes.

2. Pupil narrowing occurs when the iris's concentrically arranged smooth muscle fibers are stimulated by parasympathetic nerve fibers.

3. Pupil widening occurs when radial smooth muscle fibers (arranged like the spokes of a wheel) are stimulated by sympathetic nerve fibers.

QUARTZ TIMEPIECE

1. A small electrical charge is applied to a low-frequency bar or tuning-fork-shaped quartz crystal.

2. The crystal begins to vibrate and give off pulses (oscillations) of current in a precise, predictable manner. This is known as a piezoelectric reaction and these vibrations make a timepiece much more accurate than a mechanical one.

3. The pulses of current from the oscillating quartz are combined with a microchip that reduces their frequency to one pulse per second.

4. The microchip divides the crystal's frequency down and then translates it into the proper format for the display.

5. The dividers and display drivers control the motor turning the clock's hands, and advance the numerals displayed by the liquid crystals in a digital display.

RABBIT OUT OF HAT

1. As a volunteer steps onto the stage, the magician grasps the brim of the top hat with his right hand. With his left hand, he feels through a gap in the tablecloth and grabs a black felt bag (containing the rabbit) hanging by a drawstring from a headless nail at the edge of the table behind and below the top hat.

2. The magician brings the bag up behind the hat, making sure it is not in the sight line of the volunteer or the audience.

3. When the volunteer has examined the hat, the magician turns it with his right hand so that the the top of it faces the audience. At the same time, he rapidly swings the bag in his left hand into the mouth of the hat.

4. As soon as the bag is inside the hat, the magician grasps the brim and the top of the bag with his left hand and lets go with his right.

5. With the top of the hat still facing the audience, he waves at the hat with his right hand, pointing out that there is nothing concealed around the sides or the brim.

6. During all of this, the magician looks directly at the volunteer and keeps talking animatedly to them, keeping the volunteer's attention away from the hat.

7. Raising the hat above eye-level with both hands, the magician asks the volunteer to hold the brim on opposite sides and lets go, saying, "Now the hat is growing heavier!"

8. When the volunteer has full charge of the hat, the magician suddenly reaches in with both hands, opens the drawstring and takes on the rabbit with his right hand. With the left hand, he makes sure the bag stays safely out of sight in the top hat.

9. The magician then takes the hat and shows the rabbit to the astonished audience.

See illustration on next page

rabbit concealed in bag and hung from edge of table

after empty hat is shown, hat is turned and rabbit bag is swung into hat

volunteer holds hat while magician secretly opens bag

rabbit is revealed

RADIO

See also Tuning In a Radio Station.

1. Sound waves are created by speech or music. These are pressure waves of varying frequency and amplitude.

2. Sound waves are converted into electric signals by microphones.

3. An amplifier boosts the tiny electric signal produced by the microphone. Sound information is represented by the varying voltage of this signal.

4. An oscillator generates a highly regular, radio-frequency electric carrier wave.

5. The sound information is superimposed onto the radio carrier wave. The transmission works by generating this electric carrier wave at the same frequency as the required radio signal.

6. FM signals are generated by altering the frequency of the carrier wave to vary with the voltage of the electric sound signal. AM signals are generated by altering the amplitude of the carrier wave to vary with the voltage of the electric sound signal.

7. The transmitter feeds the modulated signal to a mast (a pole or tower).

8. Electrons in the mast oscillate at the same frequencies as the carrier signal and emit radio waves of those frequencies. The fluctuating current generates a radio signal that reflects the shape of the modulated carrier wave.

9. A tuning circuit selectively filters the oscillations of electrons in the antenna to allow only frequencies within a certain bandwidth to be received.

10. The small oscillating current is a replica of the modulated carrier wave.

11. The signal is then amplified, rectified (half of the voltage swing of the electric signal is removed), and demodulated (the carrier-wave frequency is removed from the signal)—recreating the original electric signal.

12. A loudspeaker then converts the electric signal back into sound waves.

RADIO-CONTROLLED CAR

1. The handheld transmitter has synchronization pulses and a burst sequence. The burst sequence contains information that tells the toy what to do—forward, reverse, left, right, and combinations of these.
2. The transmitter sends bursts of radio waves that oscillate at a specific frequency.
3. The toy is constantly monitoring the assigned frequency for a signal.
4. The pulse sequence is sent to an integrated circuit in the toy's receiver.
5. The toy's receiver decodes the sequence and starts the appropriate motor.
6. A transistor switch looks at the way the user is manipulating the transmitter's controls and gates the oscillations to the amplifier.
7. If the user pushes the "forward" button, the integrated circuit gates the pulses for the synchronization pulses and the burst sequence to the amplifier.
8. The amplifier's transistors amplify the signal and it is sent to the transmitter's antenna.

RAIN CLOUD

1. Moist air that is forced to rise above the dew point forms clouds.
2. They form where warm air rises over cool air at a front (frontal rain). The rain falls along the front.

3. They form where air rises by convection over warm ground, producing a local area of low pressure into which air converges and rises (convergence rain).
4. They form where air rises over mountains (orographic rain) and it cools on the windward slope. Airflow continues on the side of the mountain, sheltered from the wind (lee). The leeward slope receives little rain.

RAINDROP FALLING

1. A drop smaller than two millimeters in diameter remains spherical by surface-tension forces as it falls.
2. As the diameter surpasses two millimeters, the drop becomes increasingly flattened by aerodynamic forces.
3. The sides bulge out because the air pressure there is lower.
4. When the diameter reaches six millimeters, the undersurface of the drop becomes concave because of the airstream and the surface of the drop is sheared off to form a rapidly expanding bubble or bag containing the bulk of the water.
5. Eventually the bag bursts into a spray of fine droplets and the ring breaks up into a circlet of millimeter-sized drops.

RAISIN

Four to five pounds of grapes yield one pound of raisins.

1. Thompson seedless grapes are picked from their vines and placed on paper trays to sun-dry. It takes about 2–3 weeks in the sun before the raisin reaches the correct degree of moisture (15 percent; grapes have 78 percent water). (Muscat seeded grapes are also used for raisins, but must undergo the additional step of being puffed with steam and passed between rollers that force the seeds out.)

2. The grapes are cured with sulfur dioxide to preserve their color and then dried in ovens.

3. All raisins are washed in tanks of hot water, which open up the wrinkles and ensure that they are clean.

RECYCLING

1. The recyclable materials are collected. They are collected in four main ways: curbside, drop-off centers, buy-back centers, and deposit/refund programs.

2. They are sent to a facility where they are sorted.

3. The materials are then prepared in marketable quantities for manufacturers. They are bought and sold like a commodity.

4. The manufacturer who buys the recyclables cleans and separates the materials.

5. New materials are produced by the manufacturer.

6. Recycled products are purchased, completing the recycling loop.

REFRIGERATION

1. A refrigerator has two connected pipes through which the refrigerant is pumped.

2. An electric motor sucks the cold gas from the pipes in the cabinet, compresses it so that it heats up, and delivers it to the pipes on the outside of the refrigerator at the back.

3. Liquid refrigerant at high pressure is passed from the condenser, the first pipe, through a tiny hole (capillary tube) to the evaporator, the second pipe.

4. The pressure of the refrigerant falls, causing it to evaporate and absorb heat from the food compartment. The refrigerant boils under relatively high pressure and at a temperature lower than water's freezing point, so it draws heat from its surroundings.

5. The refrigerant vapor is then pumped at high pressure into the condenser at the back of the refrigerator.

6. The high pressure causes the refrigerator vapor/gas to condense into a liquid, giving out heat at the back of the refrigerator as it liquefies.

REMOTE CONTROLLING

1. Pushing a button on a remote control unit transmits a beam of invisible infrared rays to the television, stereo, or other unit.

2. The handheld transmitter unit contains components like a computer keyboard.

3. Pushing a key routes a signal to the encoder chip.

4. The encoder chip sends a series of electrical pulses to the LED.

5. The pulses form a signal in binary code and the LED flashes on and off to send the signal to the receiver.

6. Some electrons leave the semiconductor atoms and create holes that are then filled by arriving electrons. This combining action produces light or infrared rays.

7. The receiver contains a photodiode, a diode sensitive to light or infrared rays. A microchip connected to the photodiode receives a series of electrical pulses in binary code.

8. When rays strike the diode, they free some electrons, increasing the current to produce a signal that goes to the decoder.

9. The decoded signal is fed to an electronic switch that tells the unit to change the channel or volume, on/off, etc.

REPTILE HATCHING

The example below for a snake is similar for all reptiles.

1. The female snake lays soft-shelled eggs in material such as leaf litter.

2. The leaf litter releases heat as it decays.

3. Inside the egg, the developing embryo snake absorbs nutrients from a sac containing the yolk.

4. Weeks after being laid, depending on the external temperature, the young snake hatches.

5. It uses a temporary "egg tooth" on its upper jaw to break through the eggshell.

6. It "tastes" the air.

7. The snake emerges from the shell and leaves it rapidly to avoid discovery by predators.

RIVER FORMATION

1. A river is a large stream.

2. Streams originate in high ground, from glaciers and lakes or released underground water.

3. When the ground becomes saturated, the water gathers on the surface.

4. The force of gravity channels it through the terrain in a stream.

5. Depending on the hardness and density of the land, the stream develops quickly or slowly.

6. Rivers are fed by smaller streams. The river goes from many short, steep, first-order streams to a single, long, gently sloping, highest-order stream.

7. They barrel through the terrain, ultimately carrying water and sediment to the ocean.

8. The force of this running water erodes and cuts through the earth.

9. Gravity forces everything down to the lowest point, so rivers continue until they reach the ocean, the lowest level of land—sea level.

10. At first, a young river's course from head to mouth is very uneven, with lots of waterfalls and rapids.

11. In time, the river erodes material here and deposits it there, to make the slope much smoother or more graded.

12. If the sea level drops, the river starts cutting back (knickpoints) until the course is smooth again.

ROOTS GROWING DOWN / GEOTROPISM

1. Plants respond to the earth's gravity.

2. Plants can sense which way is up and which way is down. This is controlled by certain plant hormones.

3. When a seed begins to germinate, it does not matter which way it is lying. The root will always grow down and the stem will grow up.

4. The root has to grow down into the soil to obtain water.

5. The stem and leaves must be in the sunlight to undergo photosynthesis.

RUBBER BALL

1. As a rubber ball falls against the ground, it becomes squashed and stores energy.

2. Rubber is made from long-chain polymer molecules. When the ball is still, these long molecules are tangled together like a ball of molecular spaghetti. During a collision, these molecules stretch—but only for a moment.

3. When a ball is dropped, gravity pulls it toward the floor. The ball gains energy of motion, known as kinetic energy.

4. As the ball touches the ground, the bottom comes to rest while the top keeps moving down.

5. The ball is deformed from its original spherical shape. When the ball hits the floor and stops, that energy has to go somewhere. The energy goes into deforming the ball—from its original round shape to a squashed shape.

6. When the ball deforms, its molecules are stretched apart in some places and squeezed together in others. As they are pushed about, the molecules in the ball collide with and rub across each other.

7. The ball comes to a sudden halt.

8. The energy is released as the elastic material springs back into the original spherical shape. Atomic motions within the rubber molecules then return them toward their original, tangled shape.

9. The ball is pushed up into the air again, by the floor. As Newton pointed out: for every action there is an equal and opposite reaction. Much of the energy of the ball's downward motion becomes upward motion as the ball returns to its original shape and bounces into the air.

RUST

1. Corrosion is defined as the involuntary destruction of substances such as metals and mineral material by surrounding media, which are usually liquid (i.e. corrosive agents).

2. During corrosion, metal changes into metallic ions.

3. When iron is in contact with air, it actually burns very slowly to make iron oxide (rust).

4. Rusting of the iron is due to the electrochemical reaction that requires the presence of both air (i.e. the oxygen) and water.

5. Salt or acid, heat or humidity, and contact with a less reactive metal (e.g. copper) will also accelerate rusting.

6. In the initial stage of rusting, some iron atoms lose electrons to become Fe_2+ ions.

7. The electrons are accepted by the dissolved oxygen and water to form OH− ion.

8. The Fe_2+ and OH− ions in the water film react to form iron hydroxide.

9. The precipitate is rapidly oxidized by dissolved oxygen to form iron hydroxide.

10. On standing, this changes to rust, a reddish brown solid. Rust is in fact hydrated iron oxide with variable composition ($Fe_2O_3 \cdot nH_2O$).

11. The reaction with oxygen can occur only at the surface of the iron.

12. The rust eventually crumbles away and makes more new surface.

SALT DESTROYING ROAD

1. Salty water seeps into pavement's cracks.

2. If it freezes again, the salty water expands and cracks the pavement more.

3. When the water reaches the steel reinforcing rods in the concrete paving, it causes them to begin to rust.

4. Rust is a different molecular form of steel that takes up more room than the original steel. The rust pushes against the surrounding concrete and cracks it.

5. The pounding of traffic enlarges the cracks.

6. The weakened pavement eventually breaks apart.

7. Structures like bridges may become weakened and cracked.

SALT MELTING ICE

1. Salt in water breaks into positively charged sodium and negatively charged chloride ions. Ice usually has a very thin layer of water on top of it.

2. Rock salt is thrown onto the icy road.

3. Water is electrically neutral and has a positive and negative end. The hydrogen ends, which are positive, are attracted to the negative chloride ions.

4. The oxygen ends of water molecules are attracted to the positive sodium ions.

5. The attraction of water molecules helps spread the sodium and chloride through the water, thereby dissolving the salt.

6. Since the water molecules are more strongly attracted to the sodium and chloride, they do not lock together into ice crystals.

7. The already-formed ice crystals also break up. When the salt goes from its solid state into solution, a little heat is released, which melts another thin layer of ice and allows more salt to dissolve and create more salt water.

8. This process continues by layers, slowly melting the ice.

9. Salt keeps the road from refreezing. Salt water has a lower freezing point than fresh water.

SAP GOING UP A TREE

Maple sap is xylem sap, containing some sugar in late winter. Phloem, or sieve-tube sap is the fluid carrying sugar from leaves to other parts of the plant in the summer.

1. Minerals and water used by trees come from the roots.

2. Since the soil contains more minerals than the plant, the osmotic pressure (*see* Osmosis) causes the minerals to enter the plant.

3. The dissolved minerals remain in the plant cells.

4. The water evaporates from the leaves through transpiration.

5. The movement of the sap up the tree is a combination of transpiration and the cohesion of water, i.e. the attraction of one water particle for another. Transpiration provides the upward

pull. Cohesion holds the water particles together as they move up the tree.

6. As water evaporates from the cells of the leaves it creates a vacuum in the cells directly below the surface.

7. These cells draw on the cells below them for a new supply of sap.

8. This continues down to the roots of the tree.

9. Water from the soil continuously moves upward through the tree.

SATELLITE LAUNCH

1. Liquid-propellant engines and two solid rocket boosters (SRBs) are used to launch the rocket.

2. A second pair of SRBs is engaged about one minute later.

3. Both pairs of SRBs use up their fuel during the first two minutes of flight.

4. Less than one minute later, the booster package is jettisoned by releasing pneumatic (air-operated) latches.

5. The sustainer engine continues to fire, providing forward thrust.

6. After 3.5 minutes, spring-operated latches open to jettison the protective payload fairing.

7. Once clear of the Earth's atmosphere, a rocket stage is jettisoned.

8. The next rocket stage uses its twin engines to propel itself into the correct orbit.

9. After establishing the correct orbit, this rocket stage releases the satellite from a vertical position.

10. Once the satellite is in orbit, the rocket stage propels itself toward the Earth, where it burns up upon reentry into the atmosphere.

11. The satellite uses photovoltaic cells on extended solar panels to generate electrical power for its operating systems.

12. Gas thrusters and gyroscopes are used to maintain the satellite's orientation and keep its antennae pointed toward Earth.

SATELLITE ORBIT

1. When a rocket launches a satellite, it must give the satellite sufficient horizontal velocity so that its falling trajectory will always miss the Earth.

2. Mission Control chooses a suitable combination of upward and horizontal thrust to put the satellite into an orbit of any size and shape. The greater the thrust, the larger the orbit. The greater the horizontal thrust, the more elliptical the orbit.

3. To send a satellite into an elliptical orbit, it is boosted fast enough from Earth to counteract the Earth's downward pull. The satellite moves away from the curvature of the Earth.

4. Earth's gravity continues to pull on the satellite and eventually it slows down and begins to fall back to Earth.

5. The sideways momentum of the satellite means that it will miss the Earth.

6. As the satellite falls, it speeds up again and by the time it has completed an orbit, the satellite is traveling fast enough again to pull away from the Earth and begin a second elliptical orbit.

7. If a satellite's orbit brings it within a few hundred miles of the Earth's surface, the atmosphere causes friction or drag on the satellite.

8. Eventually this drag slows the satellite and it falls into the atmosphere and burns up.

SATELLITE PHOTOGRAPHY

Cameras are fixed to satellites. These cameras can be as big as a bus and take up half the area of a satellite.

1. Satellites orbiting the Earth can record changing meteorologic features or broadcast the video images to ground stations

where they may be recorded on magnetic tape or converted to hard-copy pictures by suitable printers.

2. The cameras scan electronically the view taken in by a lens and beam the scanning signals back to Earth, where they are recorded and reconverted to visible images.

3. The signals are usually processed electronically to enhance image information and detail. Such enhancement often brings out more information than can be recorded by conventional photography. Similar techniques are used by military satellites monitoring ground features from high orbits above the Earth.

4. Radio waves are used to beam the photographs down to Earth.

SCALE

1. A person steps on a scale.

2. A system of third-class levers pivoting on a case beneath the scale's platform transmits the force of the body on the platform to the calibrating plate.

3. The calibrating plate is attached to a powerful main spring.

4. The levers force the plate down, extending the spring by an amount in exact proportion to the person's weight.

5. The crank (also a lever) turns, pulled by another spring attached to the dial mechanism.

6. The rack and pinion gear of the dial mechanism turns the dial.

7. The person's weight appears in the window on the platform.

SCANNER

1. A picture is placed face-down on the window of the scanner.

2. As the picture is scanned, a bright light under the window moves

along the picture and lights up successive narrow strips of the picture.

3. A mirror moves with the light source, reflecting each strip of the picture as it passes to a second mirror.

4. The second mirror, which is fixed, reflects each passing strip of the picture to a lens.

5. The lens projects an image of each passing strip on a charge-coupled device (CCD).

6. The CCD contains three rows of hundreds of tiny light detectors with red, green, and blue filters.

7. As the image passes, each detector produces an analog electrical signal of varying voltage, depending on the brightness of the light falling on it. Each group of three red, green, and blue detectors creates one pixel.

8. Three lines carry the varying voltage from the CCD to the analog-digital converter.

9. The analog-digital converter changes the three voltage levels for each pixel into 8-bit numbers.

10. The resulting sequence of 24-bit numbers goes to the computer for processing and storage.

11. The set of sequences is processed to display the image on a computer screen.

SCIENTIFIC PROCESS

1. Identify the question.
2. Formulate a theory.
3. Test the theory.
4. Analyze the results.
5. Publish the findings.

SCISSORS

1. Each blade acts like a lever. The fulcrum (pivot about which the lever turns) is placed between the effort and the load.
2. The more the length of the handle or the fulcrum of the scissors, the less force of cutting will be required.
3. The sharpened edges of the blades form two wedges that cut with great force into a material from opposite directions.
4. As the blades come together, they grip the material.
5. When the blades of scissors close, its sharp edges grind against each other and any material which comes between the blades of scissors will get cut. As the blades meet, they divide or tear the material to each side.

SCRATCH-AND-SNIFF CARD

1. The essence of a fragrance is distilled into a perfume that is insoluble in water.
2. Millions of tiny bubbles of essence are suspended in liquid.
3. The bubbles are incorporated into a plastic medium which can be used like ink.
4. The plastic medium is printed onto a stiff card.
5. When the plastic medium dries, the bubbles are trapped inside.
6. When the card is scratched, the bubbles break open and the fragrance is released.

SEAFLOOR SPREAD

The spreading of the seafloor creates a successively younger ocean floor, and the flow of material is thought to bring about the migration, or drifting apart, of the continents.

1. When two oceanic plates pull apart, the central block of the seafloor sinks and a mid-ocean ridge forms.
2. Hot molten magma from the asthenosphere continually wells up through the long median valley that runs down the ridge.
3. The magma emerges and solidifies as lava into the new seafloor.
4. This is then pushed apart by magma rising beneath.
5. As the magma cools, it is pushed away from the flanks of the ridge.
6. The ocean widens as the process continues.
7. Transform faults may form along the ridge. As new crustal blocks subside, fresh cracks in the seafloor appear.

SEASHELL FORMATION

Seashells are usually made up of several layers of distinct microstructures that have differing mechanical properties.

1. The shell is composed largely of calcium carbonate, which is formed from substances secreted by the mantle, a skinlike tissue in the mollusk's body wall.
2. The shell layers are secreted by different parts of the mantle, although actual incremental growth can take place only at the shell margin.
3. Glands in the mantle are able to take the calcium carbonate from the water.
4. The blood of a mollusk is rich in a liquid form of calcium.
5. A soft, outer organ called the mantle concentrates the calcium in areas where it can separate out from the blood, forming calcium carbonate crystals.
6. The mantle deposits sheets of the crystal in varying thick-

nesses. The individual crystals in each layer vary in shape and orientation.

7. The outside is a thin layer of hornlike material that contains no calcium carbonate. This is called conchiolin.

8. Under this is a layer of carbonate of lime called calcite.

9. The inside layer of some gastropods and bivalves and in those of the cephalopods Nautilus and Spirula is the "mother-of-pearl" or nacre, very thin alternate layers of carbonate or lime and a horny substance. For others, it is simply a smooth inner layer of calcium carbonate.

SEA LEVEL CHANGE

1. A global change in sea level is an increase or decrease in the extent of the world's ice sheets and glaciers.

2. When temperatures rise, glacial ice melts and flows into the sea and seawater expands, raising sea levels.

3. The rise is partially offset by depression of oceanic crust by the seawater and, sometimes, by the rise of the continental crust following glacial rebound.

4. When temperatures fall, water is locked into ice sheets and the continental crust is depressed through loading with ice.

5. The overall drop in sea level is relative to the land and sometimes the oceanic crust rises, due to the unloading of seawater.

6. A regional change can occur when a specific area of land rises or falls relative to the general sea level—due to tectonic uplifting or glacial rebound.

7. A rise in sea level can occur when new crust is produced at a fast-spreading ridge.

8. The new crust swells, as it is relatively hot and buoyant, causing the ocean basin to change and pushing the ocean water upward.

SEASONS

The seasons result from the Earth's axis being tilted in relation to the Earth's orbit around the Sun.

1. SPRING: Around March 20–23 is the vernal equinox (Latin for "equal night"), when day and night are of about equal length.
2. SUMMER: Around June 20–23 is the summer solstice, the longest day in the Northern Hemisphere. The North Pole is leaning toward the Sun. The Southern Hemisphere is experiencing winter.
3. AUTUMN: Around September 20–23 is the autumnal equinox, with day and night of about equal length.
4. WINTER: Around December 20–23 is the winter solstice, the shortest day in the Northern Hemisphere. The North Pole leans away from the Sun. The Southern Hemisphere is enjoying summer.

SEDIMENTARY ROCKS

Sedimentary rocks are formed by or from deposits of sediment.

1. Rocks are weathered and eroded on land to create sediments.
2. The sediments are transported to sea by water, wind, and ice.
3. Further transport may occur before deposition, burial, and lithification.
4. Lithification turns loose sediment into hard sedimentary rock.
5. Sedimentary rocks are the lithified equivalents of sediments. They typically are produced by cementing, compacting, and otherwise solidifying preexisting unconsolidated sediments.

SEED GROWING / GERMINATION

This example is for the castor bean.

1. Before sprouting, seeds must absorb water.
2. Water softens the seed coat and it swells.
3. This enables the plant embryo inside to push out. The seed germinates.
4. The stem begins growing up and lifts the bean.
5. This activates enzymes so that the growth process resumes.
6. The fleshy seed leaves (cotyledons) unfold.
7. True leaves develop. The leaves make food for the plant, using water, sunlight, and carbon dioxide.
8. The seed leaves shrivel up.
9. Root hairs develop. The branching roots take in nitrates, minerals, and water that the plant needs.
10. Inside the plant, xylem tubes carry water from the roots up to the leaves. Phloem tubes carry food from the leaves to other parts of the plant.

SEPTIC TANK

A septic tank system consists of a tank, some type of distribution system, and a drain / leach / absorption field. Some systems may include a pump after the septic tank and before the drain field.

1. The wastewater from the home flows from toilets, showers, tub drains, kitchen sinks, dishwashers, and clothes washers to the tank. A septic tank is a one- or two-chamber vault made of concrete, fiberglass, or steel.
2. Sewage enters the inlet baffle (plate that controls or directs the flow of fluid) at the top portion of the septic tank, where it is directed downward.

257

3. The water flows slowly through the tank (which may hold 1,000 gallons of water), allowing solids that are heavier than water to drop down to the sludge level of the septic tank. It is in this liquid environment that bacteria and chemicals like nitrogen and phosphorous break down the organic material in the wastewater and produce a liquid called effluent.

4. Material that is lighter than water floats up to the scum layer.

5. An outlet baffle directs the clarified water to the drain field or to a pump where it is sent to a treatment device.

6. Effluent exits the tank and enters the leaching system where it percolates (seeps) back into the ground.

SHAMPOO

1. When soap is added to water and hair, it forms a film.

2. The soap makes water wetter and acts (like detergent does on clothes) to penetrate the hair fibers. (*See* **Detergents** on page 90.)

3. The soap film wraps itself around the dirt and grease, lifts it away from the hair fibers, and deposits it in the water.

SIGHT

1. Light rays enter the pupils, pass through the cornea and lens to converge on the retina, creating an upside-down image.

2. The cornea does most of the work, but it cannot change shape, so fine adjustments are carried out by the lens.

3. These images are converted into electrical impulses and the medial (inner) and lateral (outer) parts of each retina transmit the signals through the optic nerve of each eye.

4. With faraway objects, the ring of ciliary muscles relaxes, allowing ligaments to pull on the lens, making it slimmer and flatter.

5. With nearby objects, the ciliary muscles contract, the ligaments stop pulling, and the elastic lens returns to its natural rounder shape. These changes are called accommodation and are controlled by the brain.

6. The signals from the medial part of each retina intersect at the optic chiasm at the base of the brain and cross to the opposite side of the brain.

7. The impulses are interpreted by the occipital lobe.

8. Each eye sees a slightly different image but the visual field of one eye partially overlaps the visual field of the other one.

9. The left primary visual cortex processes signals from the left side of both eyes. The right primary visual cortex processes signals from the right side of both eyes.

10. A three-dimensional image is perceived by the brain.

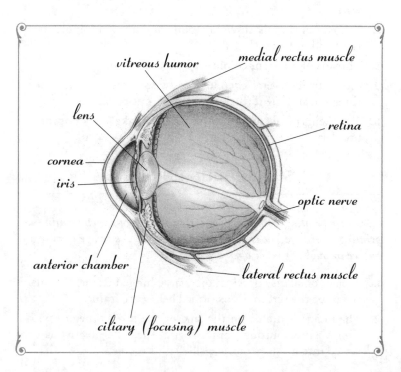

SILK-MAKING

This is the traditional, not automatic, method.

1. Mulberry trees are cultivated as low bushes so their leaves are easily harvested and fed to silkworms.
2. Silkworms are raised in the spring.
3. The eggs, stored in a cool place from the previous season, are incubated as soon as the mulberry bushes come into leaf. They hatch and silkworms emerge, eat the leaves, and spin cocoons.
4. The cocoons are removed before the worm turns into a moth. By preventing the cocoon from being damaged, an unbroken thread can be recovered.
5. Cocoons are sorted and damaged cocoons are removed.
6. The cocoons are washed and then heated by soaking in warm water.
7. The end of the silk thread is found and the long single strand is wound onto a reel.
8. Threads of different colors are boiled until white.
9. Fibers from several cocoons are twisted together to make a thread of sufficient thickness and are put on skeins.
10. The skeins of silk are dyed and used to make fabrics or for embroidery.

SILKSCREEN PRINTING

Silkscreen printing, popular on T-shirts, is a form of stencil printing, i.e., printing where the ink is applied to the back of the image carrier and pushed through porous or open areas.

1. A piece of silk is stretched on a large hinged frame. The material to be the screen is positioned below the frame.
2. The image is drawn on the silk, or the process begins with a film positive output from a digital file. The positive is converted into a woven fabric ("silk") photoscreen.

3. The "silk" photoscreen is lowered onto the stock.

4. The silkscreen paint, or ink, is squeegeed through the open image areas of the photoscreen. The nonprinting areas on the silk screen are blocked out. The ink is pushed through the porous areas corresponding to the design.

5. The product is then placed on special racks to dry.

SILVER TARNISHING

Enemies of silver include table salt, olives, salad dressing, eggs, vinegar, and fruit juices. The acids produced by flowers and fruit as they decay can etch silver.

1. Silver is soft, white, and conducts electricity and heat better than any other metal.

2. Silver reacts very strongly to sulfur and many sulfur compounds.

3. With sulfur and hydrogen sulphide, it forms black silver sulphide, which appears as tarnishing or blackening of silver objects.

4. The sulfur may come from certain foods or from the tiny amounts of sulfurated hydrogen in the air.

SKUNK ODOR

1. A skunk has two anal glands under its tail, filled with musk.

2. When threatened, the skunk raises its tail and stomps its front paws, trying to warn the predator.

3. If the intruder pays no heed, the skunk then stands stiff and struts around.

4. It then stands on its front paws and waves its rear end in the air.

5. After that, the skunk squeezes its anal glands together and musk comes out of an anal opening. It can eject a fine spray of this odiferous yellow liquid as far as 12 feet.

6. The odor of musk arises from the decomposition of certain organic sulfur-containing compounds in the liquid.

SLEEPING

Approximately 25 percent of total accumulated adult sleep is spent in rapid eye movement (REM) sleep and 75 percent in nonrapid eye movement (NREM) sleep.

1. When a person first goes to sleep, they are in NREM sleep Stage 1. There are alpha waves in the brain. The body is relaxed, but the person wakes immediately if disturbed.

2. In NREM sleep Stage 2, the brain wave pattern becomes more irregular and it is more difficult to wake the sleeper. The sleeper often moves about but his or her brain activity drops to a low level.

3. In NREM sleep Stage 3, delta waves appear in the brain. Vital signs like breathing, heart rate, and body temperature decrease.

4. In NREM sleep Stage 4, there is deep sleep and delta waves dominate the brain's activity. Vital signs are at their lowest and arousal is difficult.

5. The usual temporal progression of NREM sleep in the adult human is a period of approximately 70–90 minutes (the stages being ordered 1–2–3–4–3–2).

6. The first period of REM sleep follows, during which alpha waves reappear. The body becomes immobile as the skeletal muscles are inhibited, however vital signs increase, the eyes dart around, and dreaming occurs. This lasts approximately 5–15 minutes.

7. NREM-REM cycles recur throughout the night, with the REM portion lengthening somewhat, and the NREM portion correspondingly shrinking as sleep continues.

SMELLING

1. Odor molecules enter the nose.

2. Olfactory receptor cells are located high in the nasal cavity within a specialized area of mucous membrane called the olfactory epithelium.

3. Fibers of these cells extend up into the olfactory bulb, which links to olfactory areas of the brain.

4. Odor molecules dissolve in the nasal mucus and stimulate the hairlike endings (cilia) of the receptor cells, generating a nerve impulse.

5. The nerve impulse travels along the fibers of the receptor cells.

6. These impulses pass through holes in the cribriform plate of the ethmoid bone into the olfactory bulb.

7. The impulses synapse with fibers of the olfactory nerves.

SMILING

1. Facial muscles have their attachments to moving parts within the skin, which means that even a slight degree of muscle contraction can produce movement of the facial skin.

2. The levator labii superioris lifts the upper lip.

3. The zygomaticus major, the zygomaticus minor, and the risorius muscles pull the angle of the mouth and the corners of the lips upward as well as sideways.

4. The eye muscles involved in smiling, the lower lateral orbicularis oculi pars palpabraeus, crinkle up the lower eyelids and produce "crow's feet."

SMOKE DISSIPATING

1. Smoke is made up of ash, particles that have not burned, plus water droplets formed by the material that did burn.
2. Both types of particles must be light enough to get carried upward in the draft of hot air rising from a fire. You see smoke only when there are a lot of these particles together.
3. As the smoke rises, it mixes with the air around it.
4. The water droplets evaporate as they become water vapor.
5. The ash particles do not disappear but just get farther apart as they mix into the air.
6. When the ash particles spread far enough apart, they become part of the dust in the air, and seem to have dissipated.

SNAIL EMERGING FROM SHELL

1. The snail hides in its shell for protection. It has withdrawn its tentacles and disappeared.
2. When danger has passed, the snail uses its muscular foot to emerge.
3. This motion flips over the shell if it was upside-down.
4. The tentacles extend to check for danger.
5. The snail then moves off, using its muscular foot.

SNAKE DIGESTION

1. An egg-eating snake can swallow eggs up to twice its size.
2. The snake has hinged jaws which it can disengage, thereby expanding its mouth enormously.
3. Once the egg is in the snake's mouth, the jaws, lined with small

backward-pointing teeth, "walk" the egg. This is moving it from side to side into the gullet.

4. The snake breathes by pushing its windpipe in and out of its mouth while swallowing.

5. With the egg in the gullet, strong neck muscles contract and sharp spines on the neck vertebrae push down and pierce the eggshell, spilling its contents into the gut for digestion.

6. The eggshell is regurgitated.

7. The jaws return to their normal position.

SNAKE HEARING

Snakes can feel low-frequency vibrations from the ground. Snakes "hear" vibrations by means of bone conduction.

1. Snakes also pick up some aerial sound waves through their skin and muscles.

2. The vibrations pass through the skin and muscles of the snake to a bone connected to its inner ear.

3. In snakes the stapes is attached to the quadrate bone on which the lower jaw swings.

4. Sound waves travel more rapidly and strongly in solids than in the air and are probably transmitted first to the inner ear of snakes through the lower jaw, which is normally touching the ground, thence to the quadrate bone, and finally to the stapes.

5. From this bone, the vibrations pass to the inner ear, which "hears" them.

SNEEZING

1. A sneeze is a reflex action.

2. It is started by tickling or irritation of the membranes lining the inside of the nose.

3. The sneezing reflex blows out the irritating substance.

4. The reflex response involves many muscles including your stomach, diaphragm, abdomen, chest, and throat; this includes a temporary diversion of respiration from its usual biochemically ordered function, in order to expel the irritant.

5. Since sneezing puts a lot of pressure on your head and respiratory system, your eyes close to protect themselves.

SNOW

1. Cold air masses grow where air is descending from high altitudes.

2. Descending air is compressed, which warms it.

3. The ground loses infrared energy faster than the air.

4. The frigid air chills the air by conduction.

5. As the air cools, it becomes denser, heavier, and spreads out to form a dome of cold air.

6. As the ground continues to lose heat, the air next to it gets colder.

7. The air's moisture turns into ice crystals that make light snow, which dries out the air.

SNOWFLAKES

1. Water vapor condenses into a water droplet.

2. The water droplet grows as water vapor condenses onto it.

3. When sufficiently cooled, it freezes into an ice crystal.

4. If the temperature is around 5 degrees Fahrenheit and there is plenty of water vapor, the crystal grows six branches with arms.

5. The crystal grows heavier as more water vapor condenses onto it.

6. Supercooled drops of water also hit and freeze (riming).

7. The crystal begins falling.

8. Riming continues, changing the crystal's shape.

9. If a cloud was thick enough, the crystal would continue gathering rime, forming a lump of graupel (granular snow pellets or soft hail).

10. When the crystal falls out of the cloud, it continues growing for awhile as water molecules turn from vapor directly into ice, without going through the liquid stage (sublimation).

11. Crystals falling into warmer air begin melting.

12. Water in the crystals acts like glue, holding crystals together in large flakes.

SOAP BUBBLES

1. The molecules in water pull at each other with a strong force.

2. If the surface of the water is stretched—as when one blows up a bubble from below—it becomes larger in area, and more molecules are dragged from within the liquid to become part of this increased area. This "stretchy skin" effect is called surface tension. The surface tension usually pulls the water back and the bubble recedes.

3. If the water is soapy, the surface tension decreases. The film of soapy water stays around the air. The bubble breaks the surface of the water and may be released into the air.

SOIL FORMATION / PEDOGENESIS

Soil takes thousands of years to develop.

1. Moss and lichen form on top of rock fragments which lie on top of bedrock, the parent rock.

2. This solid rock is weathered to form regolith, mantle rock.

3. A layer of organic material, like grasses and small shrubs, begins to form.

4. Immature or skeletal soil forms from weathered rock fragments and the decaying remains of living organisms.

5. Rotting animal and vegetable matter form humus.

6. Worms improve the soil texture.

7. Tiny pores in the soil are filled with air, water, bacteria, algae, and fungi—which alter the soil's chemistry and speed up the decay of organic matter.

8. Over the D horizon or parent rock lies the C horizon of rock fragments. The D horizon is unweathered parent rock. The C horizon consists of unfertile weathered rock. Above this is the B horizon or subsoil, which is rich in minerals washed down from above. The A horizon or topsoil is on top of that and it is rich in both minerals and humus. The O horizon (or H horizon) or humus is on the very top. It is a thin layer of rotting organic matter that covers the soil.

9. Residual soils are made from weathered parent rock; transported soils such as loess are made from fragments carried by rivers, wind, and ice.

10. A fully mature soil develops after 10,000 years or more.

SOLAR ECLIPSE

The Moon orbits the Earth at an angle of approximately five degrees relative to the Earth-Sun plane, and the Moon crosses the Earth's orbital plane only twice a year. These are called the eclipse seasons.

1. It must be a new moon during the eclipse season.
2. The Moon passes in a direct line between the Earth and the Sun.
3. The Moon's shadow travels over the Earth's surface and blocks out the Sun's light.
4. There are three types of solar eclipse to see, depending on which part of the shadow passes over a particular area: total, partial, or annular.

SOLID TO LIQUID TO GAS

1. In a solid, molecules vibrate about mean positions, having molecular potential energy and vibrational kinetic energy. A solid molecule's average internal energy is much less than that needed by it to break free from others.
2. Adding energy breaks down the regular pattern and molecules can move around and thus have translational and rotational kinetic energy as well. A liquid molecule's average energy is just about that needed for it to break free from neighboring molecules, only to be captured by the next one.
3. Adding energy creates molecules with a very large separation and they can move virtually independently of each other. A gas molecule's average internal energy is much greater than that needed by it to break free from others.

SONAR

Sonar makes use of an echo. When an animal or machine makes a noise, it sends sound waves into the environment around it. Those waves bounce off nearby objects, and some of them reflect back to the object that made the noise.

1. A ship emits ultrasonic waves by a device below the ship.

269

2. Waves are reflected back by a submarine below the ship.

3. Echoes are picked up by sensing equipment below the ship.

4. The echoes are converted to electrical pulses which form an image of the submarine on a screen in the ship.

SONIC BOOM

1. An airplane travels forward and creates longitudinal waves in the air, i.e. areas of high and low pressure.

2. Wavefronts are lines or sections taken through an advancing wave which joins all points which are in the same position in their oscillations. Wavefronts can "get away" from an airplane and begin to disperse.

3. The listener will hear these waves as sound—a whoosh of air and a separate sound of engines.

4. A supersonic airplane overtakes its wavefronts while creating more, so they overlap.

5. This causes a large buildup of pressure (shock wave) which is pushed in front of the airplane and unable to "get away."

6. The listener will hear this wave as a sudden loud sonic boom.

SOUNDING A FLUTE

1. When a musician blows air over the mouthpiece of a flute, the air column in the instrument vibrates, producing a note.

2. To create a new note, the flutist covers and uncovers tone holes along the length of the tube. For example, fingertips on fewer holes creates high notes.

SOUNDING A TRUMPET

1. Pressing and releasing a piston on a trumpet causes a valve to open and close an extra section of tubing.
2. In the "up" position, the valve shuts off the loop attached to it and the air goes straight through.
3. In the "down" position, the valve opens the loop and diverts the air through the extra section.
4. Using different combinations of the three pistons, a musician blowing with pursed/tensed lips can create up to eight different notes.

SPAWNING

Adult Pacific salmon die soon after spawning, but many Atlantic salmon return to the sea and after one or two years in open waters may spawn again, some up to three or four times. The salmon may have an internal "compass" that uses very small electrical voltages generated by ocean currents as they travel through the earth's magnetic field. Some scientists believe the salmon may detect varying salinities of the water or specific smells to make these repeat journeys back to their native streams.

1. Pacific salmon live most of their life in the ocean, but as adults they return to the stream where they hatched in order to spawn.
2. The female digs a pit in the stream gravel into which she and a male spawn simultaneously, and she then covers up the eggs with gravel.
3. Most salmon spawning takes place in late summer or fall, and the eggs usually hatch in late winter.
4. Incubation rates depend on temperature, taking from 60–200 days.
5. After hatching, the salmon fry consume the yolk in the attached sac before wriggling up through the gravel to seek food.

6. Young pink salmon descend almost immediately to the sea, while chum salmon leave in a few weeks. Coho salmon remain an entire year in the streams, while young king and Atlantic salmon may remain feeding in streams for one to three or more years. Young sockeye salmon dwell for one to five years in lakes before migrating seaward.

7. The spawning grounds may be close to the sea, but the king and chum salmon swim more than 2,000 miles up the Yukon River to spawn in its headwaters.

8. The migrating salmon, impelled by instinct, fight rapids and leap high falls until they reach their spawning grounds. Even landlocked salmon, which mature in deep lakes, ascend tributary streams to spawn.

SPEAKING

Pronouncing words or making sounds requiring movements of speech organs is a process known as articulation.

1. The vocal cords are drawn together and air is expelled from the lungs.

2. As the air pushes between the vocal cords, they vibrate, creating sounds.

3. Muscles create a configuration of the vocal tract (the larynx and the pharyngeal, oral, and nasal cavities), resulting from the positioning of the mobile organs of the vocal tract (e.g., tongue, cheeks, and lips) relative to other parts of the vocal tract that may be rigid (e.g., hard palate).

4. This configuration modifies an airstream to produce and shape the basic sounds arriving from the throat into recognizable vowels and consonants.

5. Primary articulation refers to either the place and manner in which the stricture is made for a consonant, or the tongue contour, lip shape, and height of the larynx used to produce a vowel.

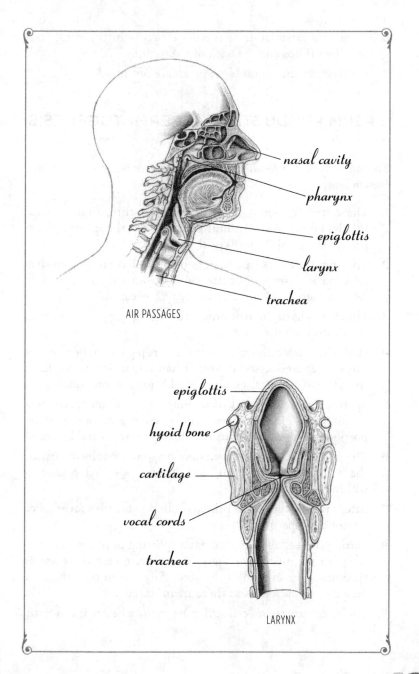

nasal cavity

pharynx

epiglottis

larynx

trachea

AIR PASSAGES

epiglottis

hyoid bone

cartilage

vocal cords

trachea

LARYNX

6. Secondary articulation is further stricture in the vocal tract done by the lips and the back of the tongue.

7. Subtle and varied sounds of speech are produced.

SPERM PRODUCTION / SPERMATOGENESIS

The role of sperm is to fertilize female eggs (ova) in order to produce new human beings.

1. The testes are composed of numerous thin, tightly coiled tubules known as the seminiferous tubules; the sperm cells are produced within the walls of the tubules.

2. The immature cells (spermatogonia) are all derived from stem cells in the outer wall of the seminiferous tubules. The stem cells are composed almost entirely of nuclear material.

3. The stem cells begin their process by multiplying in the process of mitosis (*see* Mitosis).

4. Half of the new cells from this initial crop go on to become the future sperm cells, and the other half remain as stem cells so that there is a constant source of additional germ cells.

5. Spermatogonia destined to develop into mature sperm cells are known as primary sperm cells. These move from the outer portion of the seminiferous tubule to a more central location.

6. The primary sperm cells then develop somewhat by increasing the amount of cytoplasm, and structures called organelles within the cytoplasm.

7. After a resting phase, the primary cells divide into a form called a secondary sperm cell.

8. During this cell division there is a splitting of the nuclear material. In the nucleus of the primary sperm cells there are 46 chromosomes; in each of the secondary sperm cells there are only 23 chromosomes, as there are in the egg.

9. The secondary sperm cell still must mature before it can fertil-

ize an egg; maturation entails certain changes in the shape and form of the sperm cell.

10. The nuclear material becomes more condensed and oval in shape; this area develops as the head of the sperm. The tail is derived from the secondary sperm cell's cytoplasm.

11. The Sertoli cells (elongated cells that support and nourish spermatids) support and nourish the immature sperm cells by giving them nutrients and blood products.

12. As the young germ cells grow, the Sertoli cells help to transport them from the outer surface of the seminiferous tubule to the central channel of the tubule.

13. Once the sperm has matured, it is transported through the long seminiferous tubules and stored in the epididymis of the testes until it is ready to leave the male body.

SPIDER WEB

1. From a horizontal bridge-line, the orb spider drops down on a vertical thread until it reaches a fixed object.

2. It then builds a framework, linking the radials at the hub.

3. A wide spiral of dry silk is laid down on the radials, working from the center outwards.

4. The spider attaches a spiral of sticky silk, starting from the outside.

STAGES OF GRIEF

Identified by Elisabeth Kübler-Ross.

1. Denial (this is not happening to me)

2. Anger (why is this happening to me?)

3. Bargaining (I promise I will be a better person if . . .)

4. Depression (I do not care anymore)
5. Acceptance (I am ready for whatever comes)

STARFISH ARM REGROWTH

Most starfish have five arms and rows of tiny suckerlike feet underneath. If a starfish loses an arm, it gradually regenerates. As long as the central disc is undamaged, some starfish can recover even after losing four out of their five arms.

1. Starfish often lose arms when the movement of the sea rolls rock on top of them. Some species also shed arms if they are attacked, as a way of escaping from the predator.
2. The arm seals itself off at the break.
3. Cells inside the stump start to divide quickly.
4. Within a few weeks, the arm has grown quite a bit. The other arms are used for feeding and moving.

STAR FORMATION AND DEATH / STAR LIFE CYCLE

1. Stars form from the gas and dust of the interstellar medium.
2. A massive cloud will accumulate sufficient matter for its own gravitational attraction to draw it still further together. A natal cocoon is formed; it is a shell of gas and dust blown away by radiation from a protostar.
3. As the core of the cloud begins pulling itself together, its internal temperature and density rise until the protostar within reaches incandescence with a faint red glow.
4. As the internal temperature rises to a few million kelvins, deuterium (heavy hydrogen) is first destroyed.
5. Then lithium, beryllium, and boron are broken down into he-

lium as their nuclei are bombarded by protons moving at increasingly high speeds.

6. As the central temperature and density continue to rise, the proton-proton and carbon cycles become active, and the development of the (now genuine) star is stabilized.

7. The star then reaches the main sequence where it remains for most of its active life.

8. A star shines by turning its hydrogen into helium. This gives out heat and keeps the star hot.

9. When its hydrogen fuel starts to run out, the star begins to die. The production of energy at the star's core is no longer sufficient to prevent further gravitational contraction.

10. The star collapses and its temperature rises enough for elements such as carbon to be "cooked" by fusion reactions.

11. The main-sequence star blows its surface outward like a red-

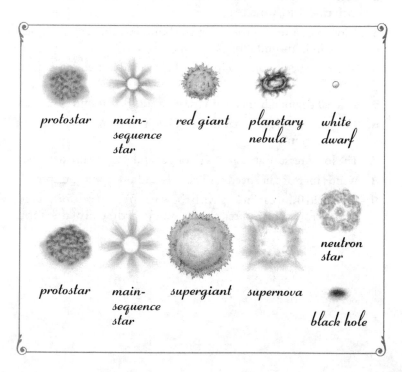

protostar   main-sequence star   red giant   planetary nebula   white dwarf

protostar   main-sequence star   supergiant   supernova   neutron star   black hole

hot cloud and becomes a red giant or red supergiant, depending on its mass.

12. A red giant develops into a planetary nebula and eventually a cold white dwarf.

13. A red supergiant undergoes rapid collapse and causes a huge explosion, called a supernova.

14. The remnants of a supernova may include a neutron star or a black hole.

STORM FORMING

1. Storms form in zones where warm and cold air are close together, sometimes along fronts.

2. Both the warm and cold masses of air are high-pressure areas with clockwise winds.

3. A low-pressure area forms on the boundary and counterclockwise winds around it begin moving the air.

4. Warm air begins advancing on the east side—creating a warm front.

5. Cold air begins advancing on the west side—creating a cold front.

6. The fronts and low-pressure area begin stirring up clouds and precipitation.

7. The low-pressure area grows stronger and its pressure decreases.

8. Winds increase in speed and clouds and precipitation spread.

9. If the cold front catches up with the warm front, it can form an occluded front. This is often the beginning of the end of the storm.

STRIPED TOOTHPASTE

1. The standard toothpaste mixture is white. The fluoride or mouth-wash is often a clear colored gel. They are prepared separately.

2. The two pastes contain colors and consistencies that will not mix so the pastes do not flow into each other.

3. Empty tubes (blanks) are filled from the wide end.

4. The ends are then crimped and sealed.

5. The white and colored stripes emerge from the tube when squeezed.

STUFFED OLIVES

High-quality or fancy stuffed olives may be stoned with a handheld scoop and then filled by hand.

1. The pimiento (red pepper) filling is made and mixed with a gelling agent into a paste.

2. The olives are lined up in rows on a perforated conveyor belt.

3. The olives are stoned (the stones removed) by automated machine heads, somewhat like a dentist's drill.

4. A nozzle then pumps the pimiento paste into the drilled hole in the olives.

5. Double-stuffing olives are stoned and then stuffed with one filling by one machine and then the other filling with a second machine.

6. The stones are later ground and used for animal feed or to make low-grade olive oil.

SUBMARINE MOVEMENT

1. Special chambers called ballast tanks on a submarine are filled with either air or water. The submarine with the ballast tanks full of air creates a balance between its weight and the upthrust of the water, so it floats.
2. To dive, water is let into and floods the ballast tanks, making the submarine heavier. Its weight is now greater than the upthrust, so it sinks.
3. In order to surface or rise, compressed air is blown into the ballast tanks to force out the water, making the submarine lighter again.

SUCCESSION TO THE U.S. PRESIDENT

1. Vice President
2. Speaker of the House of Representatives
3. President Pro Tempore of the Senate
4. Secretary of State
5. Secretary of Defense
6. Attorney General
7. Secretary of the Interior
8. Secretary of Agriculture
9. Secretary of Commerce
10. Secretary of Labor
11. Secretary of Health and Human Services
12. Secretary of Housing and Urban Development
13. Secretary of Transportation
14. Secretary of Energy
15. Secretary of Education
16. Secretary of Veteran Affairs

SUN-LIGHTENED HAIR

1. The hair color comes from pigments (melanin) added to the hair follicle as each hair is created.

2. Most pigments are slowly destroyed or bleached by being exposed to sun.

3. If the hair does not have much pigment (is already light-colored) then the bleaching of some of its pigment will be noticeable and it will become lighter in color.

SUNBURN

The visible manifestations of sunburn usually begin within 6–12 hours after the first ultraviolet exposure and peak within 24–28 hours, followed by a gradual easing of symptoms and light tanning or "peeling" (the sloughing off of the skin), depending on the severity of the burn.

1. The initial blush of the skin is due primarily to heat. Blood is going through the skin in an attempt to push the heat outside of the body and reduce its core temperature.

2. Sunburn begins within 15 minutes after exposure to UV rays, triggering inflammation (erythema, or redness).

3. Real sunburn, though, does not reach its peak until 15–24 hours after exposure.

4. Prostaglandins, fatty acid compounds, are released and can somewhat delay the sunburn.

5. To repair the damaged cells, one or more chemicals, such as kinins, setotonins, and histamines are released.

6. The blood vessels widen in order to rush blood to the skin's surface (vasodilation).

7. Capillaries break down and slowly leak blood.

8. To limit epidermal damage, the pigment melanin is produced by epidermal cells called melanocytes.

9. Melanin darkens through oxidation.

10. Melanocytes increase in both size and number within two to three days, producing more melanin.

11. In mild cases of sunburn, a protective tan is formed within days.

SUN SALUTATION IN YOGA

1. Stand in Mountain Pose.

2. Inhale and raise your arms above your head into Volcano Pose.

3. Exhale and swan-dive forward into Standing Forward Bend.

4. Inhale and lift into Extended Standing Forward Bend.

5. Exhale and bend your knees, then reach your right leg back into Lunge. Inhale.

6. Exhale and move into Plank Pose (or Push-up Pose) and then Stick.

7. Inhale and arch up into Upward-Facing Dog.

8. Exhale and let the legs pull you backward into Downward-Facing Dog. Breathe.

9. Exhale and reach your right foot forward into Lunge. Inhale.

10. Exhale and step your left foot forward into Extended Standing Forward Bend. Inhale.

11. Exhale and release into Standing Forward Bend.

12. Inhale and rise up into Volcano Pose.

13. Exhale and release your arms into Mountain Pose.

14. Repeat the entire series on your left side, using your left foot to reach back into Lunge and your left foot to reach forward to return to Lunge.

Mountain Pose   Volcano Pose   Standing Forward Bend

Stick

Lunge

Downward-Facing Dog

Plank Pose

Upward-Facing Dog

SUNTAN

1. When skin is exposed to sunlight, the pigment melanin is produced by epidermal cells called melanocytes.
2. Melanin overproduction occurs in response to ultraviolet light and protects the skin against sunburn and the carcinogenic actions of ultraviolet rays.
3. Melanocytes deep in the skin produce new melanin granules.
4. These new granules are transferred to the upper cell layers of the skin.
5. Over the next five to seven days, the pigment builds up.
6. This provides a more protective barrier against the sun.
7. The result is darker skin.
8. If untanned skin is exposed a little and then a little more, it can tan.
9. In mild cases of sunburn, a protective tan is formed within days.

SWALLOWING

See illustration on page 273.

1. Swallowing begins as a voluntary process when food passes from the mouth to the pharynx.
2. To initiate swallowing, the tongue rises and pushes food to the back of the mouth.
3. The soft palate then closes onto the back of the tongue.
4. At the same time, the floor of the mouth rises and the bolus is pushed into the pharynx.
5. Automatic reflexes take over to control the subsequent stages of swallowing.
6. During swallowing, the flap of the cartilage (epiglottis) tilts and the larynx rises up.
7. The vocal cords are pressed together, closing the glottis and sealing off the entrance to the larynx.

8. The muscles of the pharynx contract, moving food along, and then squeeze the food so that it moves into the top of the esophagus.

9. When the food has entered the esophagus, the glottis reopens.

SWEATING / PERSPIRATION

Sweat glands, although found in the majority of mammals, constitute the primary means of heat dissipation only in certain hoofed animals and in primates, including humans.

1. When body temperature gets too high, tiny blood vessels in the skin increase in size and fill with blood.

2. Heat travels from the blood vessels through the skin to the outside air.

3. When the body temperature rises even more, the sympathetic nervous system stimulates the eccrine sweat glands to secrete water to the skin surface, where it cools the body by evaporation.

4. Human eccrine sweat is essentially a diluted sodium chloride solution with trace amounts of other plasma electrolytes.

5. The apocrine sweat glands, associated with the presence of hair in human beings (as on the scalp, the armpit, and the genital region), continuously secrete a concentrated fatty sweat into the gland tube.

6. Emotional stress stimulates contraction of the apocrine sweat gland, expelling its contents.

7. Skin bacteria break down the fats into unsaturated fatty acids that possess a pungent odor.

8. When the water of sweat evaporates, it uses up a great deal of heat (latent heat of evaporation). This heat is taken from the body through this evaporation.

TADPOLE TO FROG

1. The male frog clasps the female in a tight mating embrace (amplexus). This can last for days.

2. After fertilization, the single egg cell divides into two, then four, then eight, etc.

3. Gradually, the developing embryo grows longer and takes on a comma shape, still enclosed in its protective jelly.

4. About six days after fertilization, the embryo becomes a tadpole.

5. On hatching, the tadpole feeds on the remaining yolk in its gut.

6. Its tail, mouth, and external gills are poorly developed so it attaches itself to weeds, using two adhesive organs behind its mouth and above its belly.

7. At 7–10 days, it feeds on algae and begins to swim actively.

8. At four weeks, the external gills become covered by the body skin, thereby gradually disappearing. They are replaced by internal gills.

9. The tadpole feeds by using rows of tiny teeth, making a "soup" of plant or algae particles.

10. The oxygenated, food-laden water enters the mouth. The long coiled gut extracts the nourishment.

11. After processing, waste leaves by the spiracle.

12. The tadpoles are active and social and may school like fish.

13. Between 6 and 9 weeks, the hind legs appear as short buds.

14. The body becomes longer and head more distinct.

15. The diet expands to include dead insects and dead tadpoles.

16. After nine weeks, the tadpole now looks like a miniature frog with a long tail.

17. The front legs appear about 12 weeks after hatching. The eyes are more prominent and the mouth gets wider.

18. The tail is gradually absorbed around 16 weeks.

19. They can breathe air because their lungs are now developed.

20. The froglets leave the water and hang out around the edges of the pond.

embryo develops
inside egg

10 DAYS
hatched tadpole
with weak tail

9 WEEKS
lungs form and
back legs appear

12 WEEKS
front legs appear,
mouth is wider

16 WEEKS
tail is absorbed
from tiny frog

frog

TASTING

1. Taste receptor cells (taste buds) are located mainly within protuberances called papillae on the surface of the tongue.

2. Some buds are also on the palate, throat, and epiglottis.

3. Taste buds on different parts of the tongue respond more strongly to one or another of four basic tastes—sweet (tip), bitter (rear), sour (sides), and salty (tip).

4. Other more subtle taste sensations are made possible by the combination of these tastes with other stimuli such as odors.

5. Projecting from the top of a receptor cell are tiny taste hairs, which are exposed to saliva.

6. A substance taken into the mouth and dissolved in saliva interacts with receptor sites on the taste hairs.

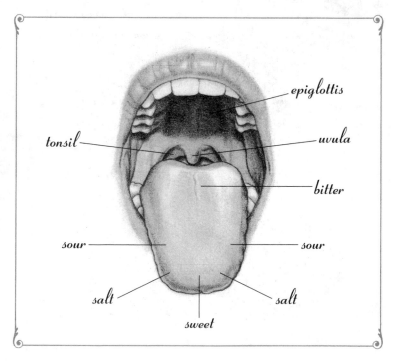

7. Taste signals from the different parts of the tongue are picked up by nerve fibers from one of the four cranial nerves—vagus nerve, glossopharyngeal nerve, lingual branch of the mandibular nerve, or chorda tympani branch of facial nerve.

8. The nerve impulses then travel to the brain.

9. The brain interprets these signals at the same time as smell signals and perceives the result as a flavor.

10. The tongue also has receptors for temperature and pain sensors that respond to things like the chemical in hot chili peppers.

TATTOOING

1. The tattoo artist shaves and cleans the area to be tattooed with antiseptic soap and water.

2. The tattoo artist draws an outline or uses a stencil for the design on the area.

3. The tattoo artist uses a tool with a fine needle. The tool moves the needle up and down at a rate of several hundred vibrations per minute. It only penetrates the skin about one millimeter.

4. Ink in the needle is pushed into the dermis, the outer layer of the skin.

5. The artist works from the bottom of the design to the top, and uses a single-tipped needle to put on the outline in black ink.

6. The area is cleaned with antiseptic soap and water.

7. The tattoo artist thickens the outline and adds shading by using a combination of needles.

8. The area is cleaned again.

9. The tattoo artist applies color and ensures that the tattoo has solid, even colors and lines.

10. The tattoo artist sprays the tattoo with antiseptic and cleans the area.

11. The artist applies pressure with a disposable towel and removes any blood and plasma excreted during the process.

TELEVISION TRANSMISSION

1. Video and audio signals are transmitted by the production company.

2. The video signals are modulated (combined with a radio wave) at the transmitting station.

3. The audio signals are sent at the same time from another transmitter.

4. The composite TV signal is broadcast to a house for any available channel. The composite video signal is amplitude-modulated into the appropriate frequency, and then the sound is frequency-modulated as a separate signal. The signals from the aerial are very weak and have to be amplified. Then they have to be demodulated (separated from the radio carrier wave) and fed into the television.

5. Turning on the television automatically tunes the receiver to the right frequency for reception.

6. The broadcast signals are picked out of the air by the antenna or satellite dish—or sent through a cable.

TEMPERATURE CHANGE

1. The Earth is warmed by the Sun, but it is not warmed evenly. The poles get the least sunshine and the equator gets the most sunshine.

2. Air rises where it is hot and settles where it is cool. There are winds in between these areas.

3. Oceans and other bodies of water, as well as land and landforms change what the winds do. All of these components work to change the temperature of the air.

THREAD SPINNING

1. A mat of cotton fibers (lap) travels through pressure rollers and then through teasing wires in a carding machine.
2. This creates loose bundles of fibers called slivers.
3. The slivers are teased and pulled out by rollers at different rates and wound onto reels or bobbins.
4. The slivers are then thinned even more.
5. They are spun into cotton yarn that is wound around another bobbin, ready for weaving or knitting into cotton cloth.

THUNDER

We hear claps and rumbles of thunder because some of the tremendous energy of lightning flashes is turned into heat and then into sound waves.

1. Lightning heats air to more than 43,000 degrees Fahrenheit, causing air to expand.
2. Expanding air cools, then contracts.
3. The quick expansion and contraction of air around lightning starts air molecules moving back and forth, creating sound waves.
4. Sound travels about a mile in five seconds which is why lightning precedes thunder. The sound of thunder takes a few more seconds to become audible.

THUNDERSTORM

1. Warm, humid air rises from the ground in large swift updrafts to cooler regions of the atmosphere.

2. As the air cools to its dew point, the moisture contained in the updraft condenses to form towering cumulonimbus clouds, and eventually, precipitation. This is the towering cumulus stage.

3. When ice crystals or water droplets grow big enough to overcome the updrafts, they begin falling, dragging down the air. This is the mature stage.

4. In summer, ice melts on the way down.

5. Columns of cooled air then sink earthward, striking the ground with strong downdrafts and horizontal winds. The falling precipitation and air being dragged down form downdrafts.

6. Updrafts continue feeding warm, humid air into the storm. The existence of both updrafts and downdrafts make this the storm's most violent stage.

7. At the same time, electrical charges accumulate on cloud particles (water droplets and ice). Lightning discharges occur when the accumulated electric charge becomes sufficiently large. Lightning heats the air it passes through so intensely and quickly that shock waves are produced; these shock waves are heard as claps and rolls of thunder.

8. Downdrafts grow, choking off updrafts.

9. With its supply of humid air cut off, the storm begins dying and rain tapers off. This is the dissipating stage.

TIDE

Tides are the periodic variations in sea level on the Earth that correspond to changes in the relative positions of the Moon and the Sun and their gravitational pulls. Tides are quite successfully predicted on the basis of accumulated observations of the tides at the place concerned.

1. At the surface of the Earth, the gravitational force of the Moon is about 2.2 times greater than that of the Sun. The tide-producing action of the Moon arises from the variations in its gravitational field over the surface of the Earth as compared with its strength at the Earth's center.

2. The effect is that the water tends to accumulate on the parts of the Earth's surface directly toward and directly opposite the Moon and is depleted elsewhere.

3. The regions of accumulation move over the surface as the position of the Moon varies relative to the Earth, mainly because of the Earth's rotation but also because of the Moon's orbital motion around the Earth. There are approximately two high and two low tides per day at any given place, but they occur at times that change from day to day; the average interval between consecutive high tides is 12 hours 25 minutes.

4. When the tides rise (flood tides), water extends farther inshore.

5. When the tides fall (ebb tides), the shore is uncovered.

6. So, the timing of flood and ebb tides on shorelines is influenced by the relative location of the Moon and Sun and by the Coriolis effect.

7. The effect of the Sun is similar and additive to that of the Moon. Consequently, the tides of largest range or amplitude (spring tides) occur at New Moon, when the Moon and the Sun are in the same direction, and at Full Moon, when they are in opposite directions; the tides of smallest range (neap tides) occur at intermediate phases of the Moon.

8. The inertia of the water, the existence of continents, and effects associated with the water depth create even more complicated behavior. In the oceans, there are amphidromic points at which the tidal rise and fall is zero and patterns of high and low tides rotate around these points, either clockwise or counterclockwise.

9. The details of tidal motions in coastal waters, particularly in channels, gulfs, and estuaries, depend on the details of coastal geometry and water-depth variation.

10. Tidal amplitudes, the contrast between spring and neap tides, and the variation of times of high and low tide all vary widely from place to place.

TIRE CHANGING

Change a flat tire on a flat road and one that is open with clear sightlines. One should be in a place with not too much traffic, and hopefully in daylight or under a streetlamp.

1. Do not slam on the brakes when the tire blows. Slow down gradually and look for a good spot, but don't try to go far or you will wreck the tire rim, too.
2. Turn on the hazard lights.
3. For an automatic, put the car in Park; for manual, put the car in first or second gear.
4. Turn off the ignition.
5. Put on the emergency brake.
6. Assemble the spare tire, a jack, and a lug wrench for the wheel's lug nuts.
7. Check the owner's manual and figure out where to place the jack.
8. Remove the hubcap, using a flathead screwdriver if you have one.
9. Loosen the lug nuts.
10. Reinforce the opposite wheel by putting a rock or piece of wood behind it.
11. Jack the car up slightly.
12. Remove the lug nuts in alternating order and put them in the hubcap.
13. Slide or wiggle the wheel off and set it aside.
14. Jack the car up a bit more, just enough to put on the fully inflated spare tire.

15. Put on the spare tire, aligning the whole in the wheel with the threaded shafts.

16. Screw the lug nuts back on in alternating order.

17. Lower the jack.

18. Tighten the lug nuts in alternating order.

19. Put everything back in the car trunk.

20. Drive slowly, never higher than 55 mph. The spare tire is only meant to be used for a day or two.

21. Have the tire replaced.

TOASTER

1. Insert bread into the pop-up toaster and push down a lever that lowers the spring-loaded rack on which the bread sits.

2. Pushing down the lever activates a timer that will keep the toast inside for the amount of time connected to a particular toast setting.

3. Power starts flowing to the heating elements which create infrared radiation that toasts the bread.

4. A bimetallic strip warms up due to the heat around it or electricity passing through it—and one metal strip of the two expands and lengthens faster with heat than the other.

5. The expanding metal strip arches into a curve and eventually touches a contact to activate an electromagnet.

6. The electromagnet attracts a catch that releases the spring-loaded rack, which pops up the toast and switches off the heating elements.

TOILET

1. The handle is pushed down and the lifting disk pulls water up the siphon tube.
2. The water reaches the bend in the siphon tube and then goes around it.
3. As the water falls, the water in the tank goes down.
4. When the water level in the tank falls below the bottom of the float ball, air enters the ball and the siphon is cut off.
5. In the meantime, the float ball has descended enough to open the valve, and water under pressure enters to refill the tank.
6. The rising float gradually shuts the valve, cutting off the water supply.

TOOTH DECAY

1. Before eating, the natural pH in the mouth is about 6.2 to 7.0, which is slightly more acidic than water.
2. When sugary, carbohydrate-rich foods are consumed, bacteria in the mouth reacts to the carbohydrates and produces acid.
3. The acid begins to dissolve the enamel that makes up the outer coating of the teeth.
4. As the decay process continues, the acid penetrates the dentin, a softer substance located below the tooth enamel that contains nerve endings. This forms a cavity.

TOOTH DEVELOPMENT

1. Teeth are formed deep in the bone of your jaws.
2. As teeth grow and get bigger, they force themselves into position.

3. The first set of teeth, known as primary or deciduous or baby teeth, erupts through the gums in a set pattern from about eight months into the third year.

4. Permanent teeth are already formed and growing several years before baby teeth fall out.

5. As permanent teeth grow, they push out against the roots of the baby teeth, beginning at around age six.

6. The roots of the baby teeth become smaller and the baby teeth get loose.

7. They finally come out and the permanent tooth starts to push through the gum.

8. The set of 32 permanent teeth is complete when the third molars (wisdom teeth) appear in the late teens or early twenties.

TORNADO

Although the full details of how tornadoes form are not well known, they generally form in a huge, rotating thunderstorm called a supercell. Supercell thunderstorms form where cold dry polar air meets warm moist tropical air.

1. A warm updraft punches through the overlying, stable layer of air and continues upward into a zone of cool, dry air. The resulting instabilities produce powerful vortex motions.

2. Most tornadoes are formed when a strong updraft such as those described above acts to concentrate atmospheric rotation, or spin, into a swirling column of air. Spin is a natural occurrence in air because horizontal winds almost always experience both an increase in speed and a veering in direction with increasing height above the surface. The increase of wind speed with height (called vertical speed shear) produces "crosswise spin," that is, rotation about a horizontal axis crosswise to the direction of wind flow. When air containing crosswise spin flows into an updraft, the spin is drawn upward, producing rotation about a vertical axis. The veering of wind direction with

height (vertical direction shear) is another source of horizontal spin, this time oriented in the same direction as the wind flow and known as "streamwise spin." When air containing streamwise spin is drawn into an updraft, it too is tilted upward and rotates about a vertical axis.

3. At first, the tilting of crosswise spin into the vertical appears to be the principal mechanism of rotation; subsequently, as updraft rotation intensifies, the tilting of streamwise spin becomes more important. The resulting swirling column of rising air, perhaps 6–12 miles in diameter and only weakly rotating, is called a mesocyclone.

4. Tornadoes generally form in the mesocyclone. A mesocyclone draws energy into the storm, helping the storm to last for hours.

5. The mesocyclone's rotating action begins to reorganize airflow in the updraft. The local pressure field and the strongly curved wind field move toward a dynamic equilibrium called cyclostrophic balance. When cyclostrophic balance is achieved, air readily flows in a circular path around the mesocyclone's axis, while flow toward or away from its center is strongly suppressed. This is known as the dynamic pipe effect.

6. The extension of a concentrated swirling core to the surface can occur once the mesocyclone is established.

7. A condensation funnel forms because at lower atmospheric pressure air flowing upward in the core cools more quickly with increasing height than air rising at higher pressure just outside the core. Because pressure is lowest at the axis of the vortex, air rising along this center line reaches its dew point nearer the ground than air spiraling up just a short distance outward. This process gives rise to the characteristic conical or funnel shape of the condensation cloud.

TRAFFIC LIGHT SENSOR

1. A loop of wire in the road surface is connected to the box that controls the traffic lights.

2. A current passes through the loop.

3. As a vehicle moves over it, the vehicle's metal parts interfere with a weak magnetic field set up in the loop.

4. This produces a signal in the loop.

5. The signal goes to the control box to register the vehicle's arrival.

6. Other traffic lights use radar detectors to sense vehicles and older traffic lights run on a preset timed cycle.

TSUNAMI

Tsunami (Japanese tsu 'harbor' and nami 'wave') are huge waves that start when an earthquake or volcanic eruption shakes the ocean floor. Many tsunamis occur in the Pacific Ocean.

1. An earthquake, volcanic eruption, or landslide occurs beneath the ocean (submarine). A tsunami could also be caused if an asteroid struck the earth.

2. Great ocean waves are started and roll along the ocean floor as fast as a jet plane. In the open ocean, tsunamis may have wavelengths of up to several hundred miles and travel at speeds up to 450 mi per hr (720 km per hr), yet have wave heights of less than three feet (one meter), which pass unnoticed beneath ships at sea.

3. The period between crests of tsunami waves varies from five minutes to about one hour.

4. When these great ocean waves reach shallow coastal waters, they are slowed, causing their length to shorten and their height to form waves about 100 feet (30 meters) high.

5. The first indication is often a sharp swell, followed by a sudden outrush of water that often exposes offshore areas as the first wave trough reaches the coast.

6. After several minutes, the first huge wave crest strikes and rushes inland to flood the coast. Generally, the third to eighth wave crests are the largest.

7. When they break, they often destroy piers, buildings, and beaches and take human life. The wave height as they crash upon a shore depends almost always upon the submarine topography offshore.

TUNING IN A RADIO STATION

A radio's tuning circuit picks a station and tunes out all the others by permitting current to oscillate at a single frequency.

1. The two conducting plates of a capacitor (or condenser) store energy as electricity, while a coil to which they are linked stores energy as a magnetic field.

2. The magnetic field collapses and sends an electric current to recharge the capacitor, which discharges again through the coil, instigating an oscillating current of one frequency.

3. The capacitor blocks the flow of direct current while allowing alternating and pulsating currents to pass.

TWELVE LINKS OF DEPENDENT ORIGINATION

The Buddha said that all conditioned things and events come into being only as a result of causes and conditions. Each link in the following is dependent upon the one preceding it.

1. Ignorance, a willful blindness that leads to

2. Karmic formations or all our volitional actions, thoughts, and words, which generate

3. Consciousness, which requires

4. Mental and physical existence, a vehicle or body to carry consciousness through the world, which has

5. Six sense organs, the windows and doors that stimuli cause to experience

6. Contact or sense impressions, which generate
7. Feelings (pleasant, unpleasant, or neutral), which cause
8. Craving or desire, an intoxicant that leads to
9. Clinging or attachment, that triggers
10. Becoming/being, which leads to
11. Birth/rebirth, which produces
12. Death.

ULTRASOUND SCANNER

The principles of sonar are used in an ultrasound scanner, which is used to produce an image of an unborn child inside the mother's body.

1. A probe is rolled over the abdomen, over the womb.
2. Pulses of sound are emitted by the probe.
3. These pulses bounce off the features of the interior of the abdomen.
4. Echoes return from the womb.
5. A computer receives electrical signals from the probe as the echoes return.
6. The computer plots points of light from the various echoes' wavelength depths.
7. As it scans across, the points build up a cross-section image of the mother and baby.

URINE

1. The two kidneys process blood to produce urine. Water and other substances are reabsorbed from the filtrate as it passes along the coiled renal tubules of the kidneys.
2. Surplus acids and potassium are secreted.

3. The kidneys can vary the amount of a substance that is reabsorbed and secreted, which changes the volume and composition of urine.

4. Urine travels along the ureters, narrow tubes that carry it to the urinary bladder.

5. An internal sphincter (ring of smooth muscle) at the junction of the bladder and urethra contracts to hold urine inside the filling bladder.

6. A lower, external sphincter is provided by pelvic floor muscles contracting around the urethra.

7. As the urinary bladder fills, stretch receptors in its wall send nerve impulses to the spinal cord.

8. In a reflex action, this returns signals telling the internal sphincter to relax and the bladder wall muscles to contract.

9. At the same time, messages sent to the brain make a person feel the need to urinate.

10. The person can then voluntarily relax the external sphincter and the bladder wall contractions push urine out through the urethra.

VACUUM

1. The vacuum cleaner is plugged in and turned on, starting a motor that drives a fan.

2. Most vacuum cleaners have a rotating brush that loosens the dust and dirt out of the carpet or off the floor before being sucked into the machine.

3. The fan pumps the air toward the exhaust port.

4. The air pressure decreases on one side of the fan and increases on the other. The side with the pressure decrease creates suction inside the vacuum cleaner.

5. The ambient air pushes into the vacuum cleaner through the intake port as the air pressure inside the vacuum cleaner is lower than the air pressure outside. The dust and dirt are pulled in.

6. The dusty and dirty air then passes through a dust bag, which is made of porous material that acts like an air filter. It holds on to the dust and dirt and passes air out the back of the vacuum cleaner.

VIDEO RECORDER

Video signals are recorded as a series of tracks. Sound signals are recorded on one lengthwise edge of the tape.

1. The videotape is magnetic. Each recording head in a video recorder is an electromagnet.
2. When the record switch is pressed, the erase head cancels any existing pattern recorded on the tape.
3. The electromagnets in the recording heads draw metal particles on the tape into a pattern set by the television signals.
4. As the tape is drawn past the recording heads, each head in turn records on the tape the signals it is fed by the current.

VINEGAR

Vinegar is made from wine in wine countries, but it may also be made from apples, malted barley, rice, or sugar.

1. The alcoholic liquid is pumped into a vessel capable of holding up to 12,000 gallons, but the vessel is only filled halfway.
2. In the middle of the vessel is a stage on which layers of birch twigs are placed.
3. Below this, air holes are bored in the stage.
4. The liquid is then pumped over the birch twigs through a sparge, which is a device that is similar to a sprinkler. A large amount of the liquid is exposed to the air.
5. The vinegar is kept in large storage vessels for the amount of time it takes for the right flavor to be produced, up to 2–3 months.

VIRUS DEVELOPING

1. A virus is inactive until it touches a living cell.
2. Before a virus invades a host cell, its surface proteins must attach to specific receptor sites on the surface.
3. After attaching itself, part or all of the virus penetrates the host cell and sheds its protein coat to release its nucleic acid. Other viruses, like bacteriophage, just inject their genetic material through the cell wall.
4. The nucleic acid makes copies of the virus's genetic material and protein coating, using the host cell's raw materials and sometimes its enzymes.
5. Replicated nucleic acid makes new virus particles.
6. The cell swells with new virus particles.
7. It bursts and the virus particles escape, thereby infecting other cells. Some viruses, however, do not do this (such as herpes viruses) but instead take away a part of the host cell's membrane.

VOICE CHANGING IN PUBERTY

The vocal cords can be made tense or slack. If the vocal cords are slack, the result is long sound waves or deep tones. See page 273 for location of vocal cords.

1. A child has short vocal cords, producing short sound waves and high tones.
2. As a child grows, the vocal cords become longer. In boys, this growth often takes place very quickly in puberty.
3. The voice changes in pitch because of the enlargement of the larynx and lengthening of the vocal cords, initiated by action of the male hormone testosterone.
4. The whole larynx changes so quickly that the child can't con-

trol it perfectly and the change may first be noticed as the "breaking" voice.

VOLCANO

Under the earth's crust there are pockets of intensely hot molten rock called magma. Magma is heated by pressure, friction, natural radioactivity, and the intense heat of the earth's core.

1. The magma is lighter than the surrounding rock, causing it to rise.
2. If the magma finds a weak spot in the earth's crust, it collects in a bubble called a magma chamber.
3. Gases from the earth collect under the magma chamber.

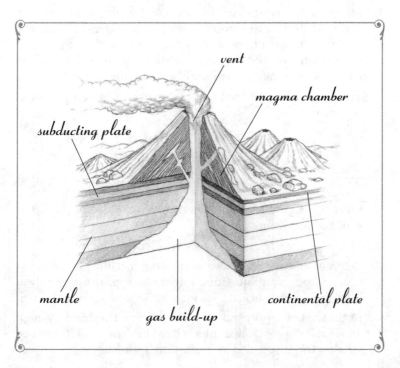

vent

magma chamber

subducting plate

mantle

gas build-up

continental plate

Magma itself contains water vapor, carbon dioxide, sulfur dioxide, and hydrogen sulfide.

4. If enough pressure builds up in the chamber, the magma bursts out through the ground as a volcano.

5. If the magma forces itself to the surface, the pressure of it mixed with the gases makes it explode.

6. The volcano then erupts with gas, ash, rock, and lava.

WARM MILK INDUCING SLEEP

Some researchers feel it is simply the act of taking time to warm the milk and relax as you drink it, while others feel it could be staving off hunger that might wake you during the middle of the night. Others believe it makes a person sleepy because it contains a sleep-inducing chemical.

1. Milk contains tryptophan, an amino acid, which is the precursor of a brain transmitter, serotonin, which is known to have sedative qualities. The warmth of the milk does not change the amount of tryptophan, but cold milk is more shocking to the human system, so warm milk seems to work better in this instance.

2. Tryptophan is converted to a sleep-enhancing compound in the brain.

WASHING MACHINE

1. Clothes are put into the washer and soap added to the detergent compartment.

2. The settings on the machine are selected by the user.

3. Before the hose releases water into the machine, it sends the water through an anti-siphon device that prevents the wash water from being sucked back into the house water supply lines.

4. At the start of a wash cycle, water pours into the drum through an electrically controlled inlet valve. The drum is stabilized by weights and suspended by heavy-duty springs.

5. Once the water reaches a certain level in the drum, a sensor turns off the inlet valve.

6. The soap is released into the drum from the detergent compartment.

7. The pressure of the water in the inlet pipe helps shut the valve firmly.

8. The water is then heated (if not a cold wash) by the machine's heating element.

9. Once the pre-set temperature is reached, a thermostat switches off the heating element.

10. The motor-driven agitator in the washer moves the clothes back and forth in a tub filled with soapy water. The motor that drives the pump and the drive mechanism/gearbox spins one way when running a wash cycle and recirculating the water; it spins the other way during the spin cycle and when draining the water.

11. When the wash cycle ends, a timer directs the motor to free the agitator and spin the inner basket.

12. Water is pumped out of the machine and into a drain between cycles.

13. Centrifugal force spins water through the holes into the outer tub and presses the clothes against the sides of the basket. During a spin cycle, everything spins at the same speed as the motor.

14. After the water drains, valves open and refill the tub for the rinse cycle.

15. Another spin damp-dries the laundry.

WASP NEST

This example is for the potter wasp.

1. The female potter wasp uses mud to sculpt a nest. If the mud is too wet, she will wait for it to dry. If it is too dry, she will regurgitate water to soften it and then knead it with her jaws and legs.

2. When the consistency is just right, she takes a small pellet and flies with it to her nest—which might be on a leaf, under a piece of bark, or in undergrowth.

3. Molding the pellet into a long strip, she lays it into a ring.

4. Returning to the mud patch for another pellet, she continues building the next layer on the hardening rim of the first.

5. She sculpts a shaped vase (pot) with bulbous base and slender neck.

6. Then she catches a caterpillar or spider and puts it into the mud nest.

7. She lays a single egg in the pot/nest.

8. She then seals the neck with mud.

9. When the grub hatches a few days later, it eats the imprisoned insect.

10. The grub pupates.

11. The new adult potter wasp breaks out of the pot/nest.

WASTE TREATMENT

1. A network of sewers, usually underground, carries the waste by gravity or by pumping it from homes and other buildings.

2. The waste goes to the city's sewage works.

3. At the sewage works, the sewage flows through screens which filter out large objects.

4. The large objects are either torn into small pieces by machines and fed back into the treatment process, or taken for burning or burial elsewhere.

5. The sewage is pumped through grit removal channels. Sand and stones sink to the bottom.

6. The detritus is dredged out and washed. It may be used for future construction.

7. The remaining sewage passes into preliminary sedimentation tanks, where the solid material (crude sludge) again settles to the bottom.

8. The sludge and liquid are usually separated and follow different routes.

9. The liquid may go to secondary treatment plants where microbes feed on and destroy the waste matter.

10. The liquid then passes through final sedimentation, where the microbes themselves are separated out and re-used.

11. Chlorine is added to the water at various stages to purify it.

12. The water that is left is clean enough to go into a river.

13. The crude sludge is pumped to digestion tanks.

14. It spends weeks in the tanks, where microbes convert part of it into gas containing methane.

15. The methane is piped off and is used to create power to run the sewage works.

16. The rest of the sludge has more water removed.

17. It is then sold as fertilizer.

WATERFALL

Within a river's time scale, a waterfall is a temporary feature that is eventually worn away.

1. Rivers tend to smooth out irregularities in their flow by processes of erosion and deposition. In time, the long profile of a river takes the form of a smooth curve, steepest toward the source, gentlest toward the mouth.

2. If a river passes from a resistant rock bed to a softer one, it is likely to erode the soft rock more quickly and steepen its gradient at the junction between the rock types. This situation can occur as a river cuts and digs out a junction between different rock beds.

3. A related cause of waterfalls is the presence of bars of hard rock in the riverbed. A series of cataracts can be created where the

river has worn its bed sufficiently to uncover the hard crystalline basement rock.

4. Other waterfalls are caused by the structure or shape of the land. Uplifted plateau basalts, for example, may provide a resistant platform at the edge of which rivers produce waterfalls.

5. Tectonic movement along a fault may bring hard and soft rocks together and encourage the establishment of a waterfall. A drop in sea level promotes increased down-cutting and the retreat upstream of a knickpoint (or sharp change of gradient indicating the change of a river's baselevel). Depending on the change of sea level, river flow, geology, etc., falls or rapids may develop at the knickpoint.

6. Many waterfalls have been created by glaciation where valleys have been over-deepened by ice and tributary valleys have been left high up on steep valley sides.

WATER FILTER

Commercial water filters in the form of pitchers or attachments for faucets or supply lines, remove contaminants with charcoal, ion exchange resins, and/or actual particle filters.

1. Activated charcoal removes chlorine and other odoriferous gases and a variety of chemicals such as herbicides and pesticides.

2. Ion exchange resins remove metal ions such as lead, copper, mercury, zinc, and cadmium.

3. They exchange the metals' positive ions for harmless positive ions—sodium or hydrogen.

4. The metals' ions get trapped in the resin, which eventually becomes loaded and must be replaced.

5. If the water is hard, the ion exchange resin will also remove calcium and magnesium ions.

6. Most domestic water filters contain both activated charcoal and an ion exchange resin, usually in a single cartridge.

WATER FREEZING

1. Water is made up of fast-moving molecules. The speed of the molecules' movement depends on the temperature of the water.
2. As the temperature falls, the molecules slow down.
3. At the freezing point (32 degrees Fahrenheit), the movement of the molecules is so slow that each molecule begins to exert a pulling force on the molecules around it.
4. The molecules start to line up in rows.
5. Though the molecules do not stop moving completely, each now vibrates in one position instead of moving freely.
6. As the molecules line up in position, the water changes from a liquid to a solid (ice).
7. In its solid form, ice, water is less dense than when it is liquid, which is an unusual property.

WATER FROM FAUCET

Compression faucets have washers or seals that close against a valve seat to restrict water flow through the faucet body when you turn the handle off. The other types don't use washers for the off-and-on action, though they do have O-rings and neoprene seals to prevent leaking.

1. As the handle of the faucet is turned, the screw mechanism inside lifts up, which presses a rubber washer onto the water pipe.
2. The pressure of the water trying to push through the pipe pushes the washer upward and the water flows through.
3. Water does not leak around the spindle because the spindle fits snugly inside the water-sealing nut.

WATER HEATER

1. A water heater consisting of a heavy inner tank, insulation, and steel outer tank has a burner under it.

2. A thermostat controls the temperature of the water in the tank.

3. A pressure relief valve keeps the tank from exploding and an anode rod keeps the tank from corroding.

4. Either a burner under the tank heats the water (gas) or heating elements inside the tank heat the water (electric).

5. You can use hot water from the tank while the tank heats incoming water. The water heater uses the "heat rises" principle to separate the hot water from the cold water in the tank.

6. Cold water is fed and then released into the bottom of the tank by a dip tube/pipe at the top of the tank. Cold water, which is more dense than hot water, stays at the bottom until it is heated.

7. The heated water rises to the top of the tank, ready to be used through the outlet pipe.

WATER POLLUTION

Water pollution is the process by which a lake or any other body of water changes from a clean, clear condition—with a relatively low concentration of dissolved nutrients and a balanced aquatic community—to a nutrient-rich, algae-filled body and then to an oxygen-deficient, waste-filled condition. These are the ways in which water can become polluted.

1. Pollution may begin as water moves through the air, if the air is polluted.

2. Soil erosion adds silt as a pollutant.

3. The use of chemical fertilizers, pesticides, or other materials on

watershed lands is an additional factor contributing to water pollution.

4. The runoff from septic tanks and the outflow of manure from livestock feedlots along the watershed are sources of organic pollutants.

5. Industries located along waterways downstream contribute a number of chemical pollutants, some of which are toxic if present in any concentration.

6. Cities and towns contribute their loads of sewage and other urban wastes.

7. These combine to exceed the biologic capacities of aquatic systems, causing waters to become choked with an excess of organic substances and organisms to be poisoned by toxic materials. When organic matter exceeds the capacity of those microorganisms in water that break it down and recycle it, the excess of nutrients in such matter encourages rapid growth, or blooms, of algae.

8. When they die, the remains of the dead algae add further to the organic wastes already in the water.

9. The water becomes deficient in oxygen.

10. Anaerobic organisms (not requiring oxygen) then attack the organic wastes, releasing gases such as methane and hydrogen sulfide, which are harmful to the oxygen-requiring (aerobic) forms of life.

11. The result is a foul-smelling, waste-filled body of water.

WATER TO HOUSE

1. Watersheds supply water to the city water system. Other people have wells.

2. Water from the water main flows under great pressure through pipes to the home and into the cold-water tank, which may be in the basement or up in the attic.

3. One pipe runs from this incoming main to the kitchen cold-water faucet, which is why this tap has such a powerful flow.

4. Water from the cold-water tank also flows to the cold taps in the baths/showers, basins, and toilet tanks through a maze of water pipes separate from the central-heating system.

5. The cold-water tank also supplies the hot-water tank.

WAVE FORMATION

1. The most common cause of surface waves is the wind.

2. Waves within the ocean can also be caused by tides, interactions among waves, submarine earthquakes or volcanic activity, or atmospheric disturbances.

3. The wind whips the water's surface into ripples.

4. The ripples build into waves if the wind is strong enough.

5. As the waves travel through water, they cause it to move around in circles (orbital paths).

6. The size of a wave depends on wind speed, wind duration, and the distance over which the wind blows. The longer the distance the wind travels over water, or the harder it blows, the higher the waves.

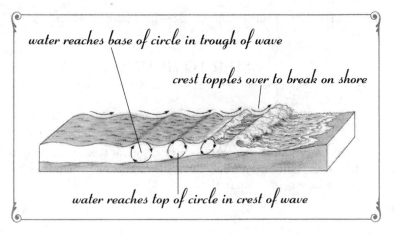

water reaches base of circle in trough of wave

crest topples over to break on shore

water reaches top of circle in crest of wave

7. As the wind blows over water, it tries to drag the surface of the water with it. The surface cannot move as fast as air, so it rises.

8. When it rises, gravity pulls the water back, carrying the falling water's momentum below the surface.

9. Water pressure from below pushes this swell back up again. The tug of war between gravity and water pressure is wave motion.

10. Capillary waves are caused by breezes of less than two knots.

11. At 13 knots, the waves grow taller and faster and their steepness causes them to break, forming whitecaps. Waves grow steeper and get closer together as they approach the shore.

12. Breaking, which happens when the wave reaches the shore, is caused by the change in the orbital path of the water—from circular to elliptical—as the water becomes shallower.

WEATHERING

1. Weathering is the disintegration or alteration of rock in its natural or original position on the Earth's surface through physical, chemical, and biological processes induced or modified by wind, water, and climate. Weathering is different from erosion because in the latter, sediment is usually transported away from the site.

2. Physical weathering causes the disintegration of rock by mechanical processes and force and breaks rocks into smaller pieces. Disintegration involves the breakdown of rock into its constituent minerals or particles with no decay of any rock-forming minerals. The principal sources of physical weathering are thermal expansion and contraction of rock, pressure release upon rock by erosion of overlaying materials, the alternate freezing and thawing of water between cracks and fissures within rock, crystal growth within rock, and the growth of plants and living organisms in rock.

3. Chemical weathering changes, reorganizes, or redistributes the mineral composition of the rock and creates more stable minerals. The rock minerals are exposed to solution, carbonation, hydration, and oxidation. There are also the effects of living organisms and plants as nutrient extraction to alter rock.

4. Physical and chemical weathering interact and thus increase each other's impact.

5. Weathering varies geographically by type and rate depending on climate, rock types, vegetation, and topography.

WEB COOKIES

Data known as cookies provide a Web site with information about the user and tracks the user's visits.

1. The user connects to a Web site via a browser. A message is sent to the browser.

2. The Web server for that Web site responds to the browser and packages its response with header information that helps the browser interpret the page.

3. The server might also send a cookie.

4. Most browsers are configured through their Options or Preferences setting to prompt a user (or not) to decide whether to accept a cookie.

5. If the user accepts, the data from the browser is stored on the user's hard drive in a special cookie file or folder.

6. If the cookie is accepted, on the next visit to the same Web site the browser checks its cookie file or folder and finds that it has a cookie stored for this Web site.

7. The cookie is retrieved and inserted in the text that the browser sends to make the next file request.

8. The server receives the cookie and can store it in a file that tracks visits to the Web site.

9. On a shopping site, the server might retrieve items selected by the user on a previous visit.

10. Some sites use cookies to greet users by name.

WEB PAGE VIEWING

1. To view a Web page, a user connects his or her to the Internet via an Internet Service Provider (ISP).

2. The user then types in a Web page's address in the browser or clicks on a hyperlink found on another Web page or in an e-mail, etc.

3. A copy of the Web page's HTML file is then transferred from the Web server where it resides, to the user's computer (client).

4. Once the HTML file is loaded into the user's computer Web browser, signals are sent to the Web server requesting that other files comprising the Web page be sent.

5. The files stream onto the user's computer.

6. The browser interprets the tags in the HTML file and assembles all of the files into a layout on the computer screen.

7. Files may also be saved to a hard disk area called a cache.

WEB SITE SEARCH

1. When a Web site's address is typed in the browser, the computer asks other computers (servers) for directions.

2. The last part of the Web site's address, such as .com, directs the user to root servers around the world which keep track of the location of every Web site address that ends in .com.

3. Most Web browsers remember which root servers give the quickest responses, so they ask them first.

4. Each night a master list is updated on the root servers.

5. The root server directs the user to another computer server.

6. This server acts like a telephone operator and sends the user to yet another server, a more specific one for the desired Web site.

7. Then the request is sent to that Web site's www server.

8. The requested Web page is displayed.

WETLAND

Freshwater wetlands often occur on peat bogs, which form as lakes are infilled by sediment.

1. Mud collects on an impervious lake bed.

2. Fen peat develops above the lake mud as the partly decomposed remains of plants, such as sedges and rushes, gather under the influence of mineral-rich (alkaline) groundwater.

3. As fen peat fills the lake, the surface is isolated from alkaline groundwater, and slowly becomes more acidic.

4. The acid at the surface encourages the growth of bog mosses, whose remains gather as bog peat.

WIND

Wind is caused by two or more masses of air with different air pressure running into each other.

1. Wind occurs because of horizontal and vertical differences in atmospheric pressure. High pressure areas move toward adjoining low pressure areas.

2. The attempt to equalize the pressure between the different air masses results in wind.

3. Near the Earth's surface, winds generally flow around regions of relatively low and high pressure. They rotate counterclockwise around lows in the Northern Hemisphere and clockwise around

those in the Southern Hemisphere. Similarly, wind systems rotate around the centers of highs in the opposite direction.

4. In the middle and upper troposphere, the pressure systems are organized in a sequence of high-pressure ridges and low-pressure troughs. They have a wavelike motion and interact to form a rather complex series of ridges and troughs.

5. Local winds are associated with specific geographic locations and are influenced by topographic features. The most common of these local wind systems are the sea and land breezes, mountain and valley breezes, foehn winds (also called chinook or Santa Ana winds), and katabatic winds. Local winds exert a pronounced influence on local climate and are themselves affected by local weather conditions.

6. Wind speeds and gustiness are generally strongest by day when the heating of the ground by the Sun causes overturning of the air. By night, the gustiness dies down and winds are generally lighter.

WINE

1. Wine grapes are harvested.

2. The grapes are crushed and pressed.

3. The grape juice (must) is mixed with wine yeast found in the grapes themselves and begins to ferment. The wine yeast changes the sugar in the must to alcohol.

4. The must is exposed to air since the wine yeast thrives on oxygen.

5. The temperature of the fermenting grape juice is controlled.

6. When fermentation stops (depending on the grape), the juice is transferred to large wooden vessels called casks.

7. The wine is matured through common clarifying / stabilization steps: racking (transferred to a clean tank to remove it from lees); centrifugation to use gravity to pull particles from the wine; filtering to clarify and sterilize; cold-stabilization

through chilling to prevent tartrate crystals from forming; and/or putting in additives to clarify and balance the wine.

8. The wine is blended for balance or to augment its complexity or correct faults. This can be done by interplanting different grape varieties and harvesting and crushing them together, or by separately crushing, pressing, fermenting, and aging several different grape varieties and adding them together before bottling.

9. The wine is bottled. Sterilization is present at every stage in the bottling line.

10. The bottles are then aged, anywhere from a few days to several months to decades. Storage conditions at this point are the same as for any cellared wine: dark, vibration-free, with constant cool temperatures ranging from 50 to 68 degrees Fahrenheit.

WINE TASTING

1. See the wine.
2. Smell the wine.
3. Sip or slurp the wine.
4. Swallow or spit the wine.

Variation with five steps.

1. Look at the wine.
2. Swirl it.
3. Smell it.
4. Taste / sip it.
5. Savor it.

WRINKLES

Skin may wrinkle as a result of aging.

1. The living part of the skin is an inner layer of cells. These cells create protein that will become the outer layer.

2. The ability of the skin to take up slack and remain closely adherent to the underlying structures is due to the presence of fibers of the proteins elastin and collagen.

3. The primary age change in the skin is a gradual loss of elasticity. There is a reduction in elastin as one ages. Also, the collagen fibers show an increase in cross-links which greatly restricts the elastic properties of the collagen network.

4. Other factors, such as exposure to the weather and familial traits, also contribute to the development of wrinkles.

Skin may also wrinkle temporarily when exposed to water for too long.

1. Under normal conditions, the skin is water-resistant. The protective barrier is the protein keratin, manufactured in the epidermis to block moisture, bacteria, and other foreign matter.

2. Prolonged exposed immersion in water causes the cells in the epidermal layer to absorb water and swell.

3. The enlarged cells cause the skin to pucker and wrinkle.

4. After drying off, the water in the skin cells evaporates and the cells return to their normal size and shape.

X-RAY

X-rays are similar to light, but have more energy than light, so they can penetrate more materials than light can.

1. When an x-ray image is taken, the x-ray machine sends an x-ray through your body and that image forms on the x-ray film.

2. When the x-rays hit the film, they expose the image just as light would.

3. When x-rays pass through the body, more x-rays are absorbed by the denser parts (such as teeth and bone) than by soft tissues (such as cheeks and gums) before striking the film.

4. This creates an image on the radiograph.

5. Teeth, for example, appear lighter because fewer x-rays penetrate to reach the film; cavities appear darker because of more x-ray penetration.

6. Since bone, fat, muscle, tumors, and other masses all absorb x-rays at different levels, the image on the film reveals different structures inside the body because of the different levels of exposure on the film.

7. The interpretation of these x-rays allows the doctor or dentist to detect hidden abnormalities.

ZIPPER

1. The zipper contains two rows of interlocking plastic or metal teeth (alternating tooth-and-socket plates) which are sewn on strips of tape attached to each side of an opening.

2. The zipper also has a sliding tab/pull with wedges on each side.

3. When you pull on the tab, the wedges force the rows of teeth together, closing the opening. Each tooth fits into the socket of the one in front.

4. Pulling the zipper's tab in the opposite direction allows an upper wedge to force the interlocked teeth apart.

ABOUT THE AUTHOR

Dr. Barbara Ann Kipfer is the author of more than 25 books, including the bestselling *14,000 Things to Be Happy About* and Page-a-Day calendars based on it. Her other books include *The Order of Things*, *4,000 Questions for Getting to Know Anyone and Everyone*, *Roget's 21st Century Thesaurus*, *Encyclopedic Dictionary of Archaeology*, *The Flip Dictionary*, and *Roget's International Thesaurus, Sixth Edition*. Barbara has an MPhil and PhD in Linguistics from University of Exeter, a PhD in Archaeology and MA in Buddhist Studies from Greenwich University, and a BS in Physical Education from Valparaiso University. Dr. Kipfer is the managing editor/senior lexicographer for Dictionary.com, Thesaurus.com, and Reference.com. She is also a Registered Professional Archaeologist.

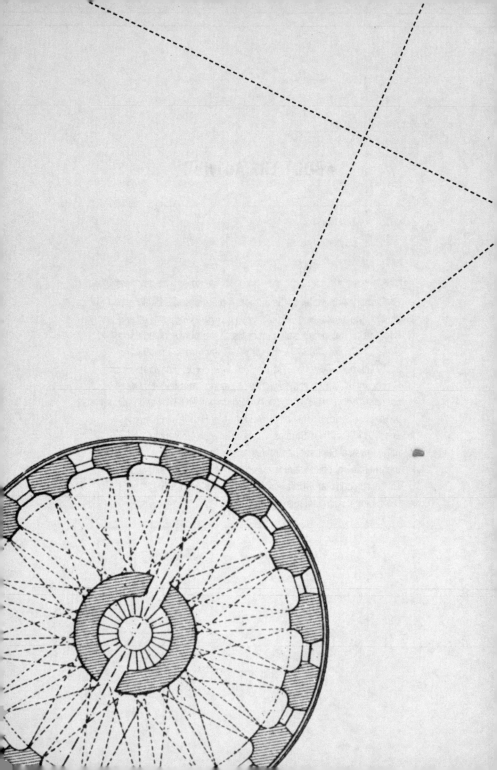